Contentious Europeans

Governance in Europe
Series Editor: Gary Marks

Differential Europe: New Opportunities and Restrictions for Policymaking in the Member States
By Adrienne Héritier, Dieter Kerwer, Christophe Knill, Dirk Lehmkul, Michael Teutsch, and Anne-Cécile Douillet
Transatlantic Governance in the Global Economy
Edited by Mark A. Pollack and Gregory C. Shaffer
The New Political Economy of EMU
Edited by Jeffry Frieden, Daniel Gros, and Erik Jones
Regional Integration and Democracy: Expanding on the European Experience
Edited by Jeffrey J. Anderson
How to Democratize the European Union . . . and Why Bother?
By Philippe Schmitter
Democracy beyond the State? The European Dilemma and the Emerging Global Order
Edited by Michael Th. Greven and Louis W. Pauly
A Wider Europe: The Process and Politics of European Union Enlargement
By Michael J. Baun
Multi-Level Governance and European Integration
By Liesbet Hooghe and Gary Marks
Contentious Europeans: Protest and Politics in an Emerging Polity
Edited by Doug Imig and Sidney Tarrow

Forthcoming

Wiring Europe: Reshaping the European Telecommunications Regime
By Giorgio Natalicchi
Between Global Economy and Local Society: Political Actors and Territorial Governance
Edited by Jeanie Bukowski, Simona Piattoni, and Mark E. Smyrl
Europe and America: Partners and Rivals in International Relations, 3rd Edition
By John Peterson
Policy and Process in the New Europe
By Jessica R. Adolino and Alan N. Katz
Politics as Usual in the European Union
By Mark E. Smyrl
Political Economy of the European Union: Critical Studies of a Neoliberal Hegemonic Project
Edited by Alan W. Cafruny and Magnus Ryner

Contentious Europeans

Protest and Politics in an Emerging Polity

Edited by
Doug Imig
and
Sidney Tarrow

ROWMAN & LITTLEFIELD PUBLISHERS, INC.
Lanham • Boulder • New York • Oxford

ROWMAN & LITTLEFIELD PUBLISHERS, INC.

Published in the United States of America
by Rowman & Littlefield Publishers, Inc.
4720 Boston Way, Lanham, Maryland 20706
www.rowmanlittlefield.com

12 Hid's Copse Road
Cumnor Hill, Oxford OX2 9JJ, England

British Library Cataloguing in Publication Information Available

Library of Congress Cataloging-in-Publication Data

Contentious Europeans : protest and politics in an emerging polity / edited by Doug Imig and Sidney Tarrow.
p. cm. — (Governance in Europe)
ISBN 0-7425-0083-7 (alk. paper)—ISBN 0-7425-0084-5 (pbk. : alk. paper)
1. Political participation—European Union countries. 2. Protest movements—European Union countries. 3. Lobbying—European Union countries. 4. Pressure groups—European Union countries. I. Imig, Douglas R., 1962– II. Tarrow, Sidney G. III. Series.

JN40.C65 2001
322.4'094—dc21 00-054436

Printed in the United States of America

∞™ The paper used in this publication meets the minimum requirements of American National Standard for Information Sciences—Permanence of Paper for Printed Library Materials, ANSI/NISO Z39.48-1992.

Contents

Preface

Every research effort has a beginning, a middle, and an end. This volume represents the completion of one research project—although we fervently hope it marks a beginning for another: the systematic study of European contentious politics in the twenty-first century.

Our collaboration began—as many do—at the junction of two separate and apparently distinct ideas; the first author's interest in using machine-coded online press agency dispatches and computer-assisted coding to analyze large masses of information about protest over time and across space; and the second author's impatience from working on social movements within individual European countries and his growing interest in transnational politics. We thought the method of computer-assisted protest event analysis could solve the knotty methodological problems that scholars have encountered in the study of transnational contention. We decided that Europe—and its increasing degree of integration in the 1990s—would be an ideal field for such an experiment. If there was anywhere in the world where people were mobilizing transnationally, we reasoned, it would be in Western Europe, where economic integration was producing a structure of regulation that was spilling over into national life and forcing social actors to expand their claims to new and supranational targets.

We still think so, but to prove it, scholars will need to overcome a number of obstacles and to design methods fit for such a task. This is an up-by-your-bootstraps process that is still in its infancy. We found little in the literature on European integration that could tell us how to study large-scale processes of contention connected to European policy and institutions. On the one hand, for most of its history, European integration has been an elite enterprise; on the other, most of the extant scholarship either focused on the EU's constitution or took a problem-solving, elite-network approach that left ordinary people and their claims on the sidelines. Only a few scholars—many of them represented in this volume—seemed prepared to question the elitist character of Europeanization and take seriously the proposition that a "field" of contentious politics involving ordinary people might be developing around the expanding process of European governance.[1]

Our progress was spurred by our initial excitement at helping to create a new field of research, but with it came a certain innocence that cost us both time and wasted effort. As we elaborate in chapters 1 and 2, the shape of transnational contention turned out to be far more complicated than we had supposed and the methods needed to study it had to be adjusted accordingly. While we learned much from the employment of computer-assisted protest event analysis, it proved to be no magic bullet; a good deal of human input and a lot of qualitative trial-and-error examination proved necessary. We found much evidence of contention extending beyond national boundaries, but it seldom took the forms we had expected. To put it simply, if European contention was "Europeanizing," most of it was taking place in domestic politics, into which our international press agency data did not penetrate very deeply.

This was our initial motivation for inviting our collaborators to join us. And as we worked with them and learned more about the nature of European contention, we came to regard our aggregate findings more as a road map than a completed picture. Their work both adds topography to our map and provides insights into how social and political actors at Europe's "periphery" access decision-makers at its core.

These issues will be discussed in greater detail in the chapters that follow. But because of the changes in direction required by our initial discoveries, the "middle" of our project took considerably longer than its beginning and end and required us to depend more than most authors and editors do on the support and collaboration of others. We wish to thank them here.

We were helped by generous research support, both together (with a National Science Foundation grant for data collection and analysis) and separately. For his part, Imig is grateful to the Program on Nonviolent Sanctions and Cultural Survival in the Weatherhead Center for International Affairs at Harvard University for generous research support to develop and pursue the methodology of the project. Tarrow is grateful for support from the German Marshall Fund of the United States and from the Robert Schuman Centre of the European University Institute for the interviews in Brussels and for a period of study in San Domenico. We are both grateful to the San Giacomo Foundation of Turin for the financial support for the Cornell workshop at which the theoretical framework and many of the chapters were first developed.

Three home institutions were also supportive of the project. The University of Nevada, Las Vegas, and the University of Memphis provided generous research assistance and Cornell University's Institute for European Studies and its Peace Studies Program provided logistical and financial support for the 1999 workshop.

A number of colleagues attended that workshop and helped to make it a success: Jeff Checkel, Lance Compa, Maria Cook, Matt Evangelista, Liesbet Hooghe, Peter Katzenstein, Nathan Lillie, Gary Marks, Philip McMichael, David S. Meyer, Beate Sissenich, and Lowell Turner. Tammy Gardner and Antonina Gentile helped us to organize it. Geoff Harris and Alberta Sbragia could not attend, but at various stages of the project their help was invaluable.

The data collection phase of our work was particularly arduous and rested on the help of several zealous young people. Before joining our array of authors, Felix Kolb shared the work of interviewing in Brussels. Pete Simi was an indefatigable research assistant at UNLV, as was Michelle Sabathier at the University of Memphis. Marwan Hanania provided much of the human insight that helped reduce the proportion of "false positives" that our initial computer runs produced. Doug Bond deserves special thanks for generously sharing his time and expertise in order to guide us through the theoretical and empirical issues involved in automated data collection and coding.

Finally, we thank the collaborators who contributed the chapters to this book and tolerated seemingly endless rounds of comments and requests for revisions. We are impressed by their efforts and grateful for their patience.

NOTE

1. We should also mention the work of several European scholars, among them Ruud Koopmans and Paul Statham (1998), Uwe Reising (1997 and 1998), and Christilla Roederer (1999).

1

STUDYING A MOVING TARGET: THEORY AND DATA ON EUROPEAN CONTENTION

1

Studying Contention in an Emerging Polity

Doug Imig and Sidney Tarrow

Some books are the products of solutions; others of puzzles. This one started out with a solution but soon revealed two puzzles.

- The "solution" was a method for studying European contention through the computerized analysis of online international press agency dispatches, to analyze contentious interactions of citizens protesting EU policies. This was a method that proved useful in the study of international conflict events in the 1990s and was being currently adapted to the study of domestic protests when we encountered it in the mid-1990s.[1]
- The first puzzle grew out of what we were able to learn about the dynamic of contention at this stage from the use of this new tool: we found that Europeans are increasingly protesting against European Union policies—*but on domestic soil and not directly against the institutions that produce them.*
- The second puzzle came from what our aggregate data-based method *couldn't* tell us—how protesters interact with their national governments and European lobbies and institutions and when—if at all—they become "European" collective actors.

These puzzles led us to bring together a group of scholars who knew more than we did about the processes of contention in different sectors of European policy. Most of this group met in a workshop at Cornell in early 1999 to study European contention and link it to the broader literature on transnational politics. What we learned from this experience and what we have still to learn are offered in this book. We propose it as an incentive to others trying to go beyond elite interaction and to bring the behavior of ordinary people into their models of European integration.

We begin with a brief introduction to the literature on event-based contentious politics that we and several of our collaborators employ. We then turn to our working hypotheses and to a brief review of the literature on European contention. Next we survey four major approaches to European integration. Finally, we lay out the logic of the empirical sections of the volume.

Before we begin, let us briefly state some of our own guiding assumptions:

- While much of the interaction around Europe's central political processes is intra-institutional, elite network-based, and problem-solving (Kohler-Koch and Eising, eds., 1999), we focus here on the effects of these processes on Europe's citizens and on the forms of contentious politics they use in responding to them. By bringing citizen-to-citizen and citizen-to-elite contention into the picture, we hope to balance the excellent work that has been done on European governance with an approach that grows out of recent work on social movements and contentious politics.[2]
- By "contentious politics" we mean *episodic, collective interaction among makers of claims and their objects when (a) at least one government is a claimant, an object of claims, or a party to the claims; and (b) the claims would, if realized, affect the interests of at least one of the claimants*.[3]
- In this sense, ours is neither a neofunctionalist, a neorealist, nor a constructivist perspective but an *interactionist* one: we believe that if a European polity emerges, it will not be as the result of the autonomous formation of European identities or of the diffusion of hegemonic concepts from above, but as a long-term outcome of conflict and cooperation between and among nonstate and public actors.[4]
- We and our collaborators examine different forms of contentious politics, concentrating on those forms that reach upward from the grass roots toward the sources of European decision-making; across the member-states as Europeans forge alliances with one another; and within Europe's institutions as public interest groups and NGOs (nongovernmental organizations) try to influence European policies in the name of population groups they claim to represent.
- In other words, this is not only a book about *social movements*—as the term has come to be understood (e.g., politics in the street)—but of the many forms of episodic contentious interaction that have grown up around the policy-making processes of the European Union.

Let us therefore begin from the tradition of research from which we both come—the systematic study of social movements and contentious politics.

FROM NATIONAL COLLECTIVE ACTION TO EUROPEAN CONTENTION

When we first conceived of this project in the mid-1990s, we were trying to solve a methodological problem that has dogged students of contentious politics since the Tillys began its systematic study in the 1970s (1975): how to fashion an instrument for the analysis of contentious events with both the *reach* to cover several countries and the *grasp* to follow its dynamic over time.

Though they studied three countries—Italy, Germany, and France—the Tillys opted mainly for grasp: studying long rhythms of national contention side by side and turning to comparisons only in their conclusions. By doing so, they launched a new tradition of work that focused in great depth on national histories of contentious politics.

Scholars learned a lot from *The Rebellious Century* and from the work that followed it: about how British, French, Germans, Italians, Americans, or Russians strike, march, petition, build barricades, and make war and in the name of what claims (Tilly 1978); how their struggles occasionally turned into revolutions within longer rhythms of contention (Tilly 1993); how they reacted to the creation of national states (Tilly et al. 1975); and how their struggles changed from violent attacks on immediate enemies to mediated conflicts within national institutions (Tilly 1995). A major tradition of research developed out of this work, using event histories to chart periods of conflict in order to understand the dynamics of contention and its interaction with underlying social processes. But because the preoccupations of these scholars were rooted in the protest histories of individual populations and the sources that archive their behavior, this tradition has taught us less about general trends in Western contention than about its profiles in each country.

Charles Tilly's later efforts and those of his followers—among whom we count ourselves—plumbed national histories of contention even more deeply.[5] Though still interested in the long rhythms of each country's history of contention and concerned with world-historical systems like capitalism, Tilly was historian enough to focus on shorter rhythms within these histories. But the very depth of his attention to these events made it difficult to place contentious histories within more general comparative rhythms. Were French or British patterns of contention artifacts of each country's path to modern democracy, or were they different species of a more general trend of state-building and capitalism? Was the American civil rights movement *sui generis*, or was it the earliest of a wave of "new social movements" in the West (McAdam 1982)? Was the long Italian cycle of the 1960s and 1970s unique, or was it no more than a "sliding May"—like the French one (Salvati 1981)? Was the Russian working class heading toward Western forms of mobilization when 1917 exploded, or was it inherently different from Western models (Bonnell 1983)? The difficulty of answering these questions was rooted in the effort it took to ask the same questions of British, French, German, Italian,

American, or Russian historical contention while using different sources and understanding the contexts in which contention arose.[6]

From National to Comparative Studies of European Contention

It was a testament to the Tillys' lasting influence that only in the mid-1990s did a truly *comparative* study of European contention appear. Hanspeter Kriesi and the team he assembled in Amsterdam built a data set out of fifteen years of newspaper data on contentious politics in four European countries—France, West Germany, the Netherlands, and Switzerland (1995). Their data were as comparable as one could get with the use of a common instrument that tapped different newspapers intended to serve different publics. Beginning from a common "political process" framework and studying a much shorter period than the Tillys had, their book opened a new tradition of the systematic comparison of contentious politics, comparing national histories of contentious politics in Europe.

However, during the period that Kriesi and his collaborators analyzed, something profoundly new was happening in Western Europe: the creation of a European political entity. It was first adumbrated in the form of diffusion in studies of the 1960s movements—all too easily encapsulated in the shorthand of "'68"[7] and then in the "new" social movements of the 1970s (Melucci 1996). Only as that decade ended did scholars begin to ask whether truly "European" movements were unfolding. With a European economic and political entity developing and with international travel and mass communications reducing the significance of internal borders, was it still possible to limit research on European contention to the influence of *national* structures of political opportunity and threat? More specifically: were supranational institutions and international trends creating new opportunities and threats and possibly linking social actors in different European countries to one another in transnational social movements (della Porta, Kriesi, and Rucht, eds., 1999)?

The answer given depended on the nature of the European entity that scholars saw emerging.

- Was it going to be a Europe of States? Some scholars took this as an assumption, while others set out to prove it (Hoffmann 1966, Moravcsik 1998, Wolf 1999). If so, then popular contention targeting Brussels' decisions would be no more than a sideshow and the real action would take place across the conference table.
- Or was the EU shaping up as an elite-constructed supranational state (Haas 1958)? In that case, why look outside the intricate interest group world of Brussels, Strasbourg, and Luxembourg?
- Or would Europe be some version of a multilevel polity, as scholars like Scharpf (1994) or Marks, Hooghe, & Blank (1996) thought; a system of

"network governance" (Kohler-Koch and Eising, eds., 1999); or "corporate governance" (Falkner 1998)? If so, then the place to look would be in the informal but problem-solving relations between national and supranational elite actors—but still not at popular protest.

None of these theoretical approaches explicitly *excluded* popular contention from the emerging Europe—but few of them specified it in their theoretical frameworks. Moreover, in the burgeoning empirical literature on European integration, there was little systematic attention paid to contentious politics and—except for survey-based work on attitudes—little attention to ordinary people at all.[8] Apart from folkloric press accounts—French farmers dumping produce on the city streets, British matrons blocking calves headed for slaughter in continental *abattoirs,* Spanish fishermen sequestering French fishing boats—scholars of European integration focused mainly on elites, got most of their information from them, and studied their interaction with other elites—mostly within the EU's institutions. We know much more about participation in consultative committees in the five square kilometers of Euroland in Brussels than we do about contention over the effects of their decisions among the 375 million people who have to live with their consequences.

Our Three Hypotheses

In the 1980s, under the Delors commission, integration seemed to take off—but it was still seen as an elite-driven process. By the 1990s, scholars and EU officials began to wring their hands over the "democratic deficit"—but few examined this hypothesis from the standpoint of mass politics. We join Beate Kohler-Koch in her call to link discussions of the "democratic deficit" to European policy-making (1999: 16). We think a social movement perspective can help us to understand whether, how, and with what consequences Europeans mobilize to make claims against policies made in their names—even if the results turn out to be different than the national social movements of the past. If Europe is becoming a polity, we hypothesize, sooner or later ordinary citizens will turn their claims and their forms of contentious politics beyond their borders and toward this new level of governance. We think contentious politics is one way they will do this—with profound consequences for the Europe of elites.

To investigate this hypothesis, it seemed important to go beyond an anecdotal approach to European protest. If more and deeper integration was co-occurring with a shift of contentious politics toward European issues, then in at least one respect Europe could be said to be moving toward a mass-based polity. This was our major working hypothesis and the one to which our own empirical work was addressed. The next chapter and part 2 of this volume will focus on whether and in what ways ordinary Europeans are responding to policies of the European Union with contentious forms of collective action. (A cognate issue is whether Euro-directed collective action is more frequent and more intense in those sectors—such as agriculture and the approval of genetically modified foods—in which the EU plays a critical role, than in sectors of European life that are governed by national and subnational authorities.)

To our first working hypothesis, we were soon impelled to add a second. The most sustained studies of national social movements in Western Europe had shown that a rising curve of contention since the 1960s was accompanied by a routinization of the forms of collective action that citizens employ.[9] In most European countries, there has been a shift from the "hard" forms of contention familiar from the 1960s to well-oiled mass demonstrations, media-aimed events mounted by professional movement organizations, and growing cooperation with authorities (Tarrow 2000a). The question is whether this shift in the repertoire of contention is reflected in how Europeans mount claims against the European Union. Some scholars, especially Gary Marks and Doug McAdam (1996, 1999), think so. In part 3 we and our colleagues entertain the hypothesis that Europe's authorities not only tolerate but encourage the expression of claims through lobbying and other routine forms and that this has a containing effect on more contentious forms of collective action.

As we devised the instruments for our study, we were confronted with a third hypothesis from the new literature on transnational politics that was developing mainly outside Western Europe.[10] In the course of the 1990s, a new term entered the dictionary of social scientists—*globalization*. Whatever that term means (and there is reason to suspect that it has come to mean very little), evidence began to accumulate toward the end of the 1990s that social actors were increasingly protesting against the intrusive policies of international agencies; that they were taking their claims against national antagonists into international forums through transnational activist networks; and that they were framing grievances against their own governments as if they were claims against international or foreign actors.

Much of the evidence for these trends came from outside of Europe and was fairly vaguely specified. But if the trends were robust, we reasoned, transnationalization ought to be strongest in the region that has gone furthest in creating international institutions—Western Europe. To the extent that Europe is becoming an integrated polity, European integration might be creating an opportunity structure for the formation of *transnational* social movements. That was our third—and our boldest—hypothesis. In part 4, we examine whether it is giving rise to European political actors.

These three hypotheses could be conjoined; a move from national to supranational institutions might lead social actors to:

- shift their claims from the national to the European level;
- model their repertoires of action around the forms of collective action that work best at that level; and
- lead to the formation of transnational networks and common identities across national boundaries.

If all three hypotheses could be verified, then the creation of European identities and a European level of citizenship might not be far behind, not through the appearance of postnational or supranational identities (Soysal 1994), but through precisely the kind of long-term conflictual processes that created national citizenries from the sixteenth to the nineteenth century in Western Europe (McAdam, Tarrow, and Tilly in preparation). If this is happening in Europe—where international institution building is well advanced—then it may show the way to the rise of nongovernmental forms of governance across borders elsewhere in the world. In his concluding chapter, Sidney Tarrow explores the evidence for this possibility. Those are the broader questions that we hope our book will raise.

TRIANGULATING TRADITIONS

How could we test these hypotheses? This takes us back to the methodological problem of "grasp" and "reach" from which we began. We soon found that the current organization of research in and about Western Europe provided little evidence and few methodological pathways to examine so large a subject as the impact of European integration on contentious politics:

- On the one hand, scholars who focused on interest representation in the European Union started at the summit and seldom ventured far beyond it—giving rise to a vast number of studies on lobbying and interest intermediation[11] but largely ignoring the forms of contentious politics that students of national social movements were examining at the same time.
- On the other hand, scholars of contentious politics had not yet elaborated an instrument that would permit them to look systematically at contentious politics in a number of nation-states and over a sufficiently long period of time to detect the kind of broad changes we have hypothesized (for a recent survey of the field, see Rucht, Koopmans, and Neidhardt, eds., 1998). Moreover, most studies focused on social movements as traditionally defined and excluded key actors—like trade unions, public interest lobbies, volunteer groups—that are central to the European interest group research tradition but that look very little like social movement organizations.

- There was another contrast as well: while knotty methodological problems made it hard for students of popular contention to go beyond single-country studies, the receptivity of European decision-makers to the politics of lobbying and their desire for "transparency" (Kohler-Koch 1999: 18) made them increasingly receptive to scholars who became specialists on interest representation in Brussels. There was a danger of what could be easily seen at the summit blotting out what could only with difficulty be studied at the periphery.

The result of these contrasts was a bifurcation between studies of how citizens at the base of Europe engage in contentious politics and how European-level interest groups operate at the summit. This bifurcation has made it difficult to confront the question of whether—and if so, how—popular contention is being affected by the process of European integration. European lobbying might be completely unconnected to contentious politics; but if the students of European lobbying and scholars of contentious politics continue to focus on different levels with different methodologies, we are unlikely to discern their relationships. Are European lobbies directly representative of citizens in the member-states? Or only of the particular national-level groups that support them? Or are they "virtual representatives": claiming representation on the basis of the policy positions they believe in but with no real relationship to those they claim to represent?

Before we lay out how we approach these questions, let us be careful not to claim to be working in a vacuum. Over the past decade, a number of scholars have examined forms of contentious politics in the European Union. We can identify four main types of work:

- Studies of protest *against* European unification, focusing mainly on the defeat of Norwegian entry and the near-defection of Denmark from the EMU and on the persistent Euro-skepticism found in some countries (e.g., the United Kingdom) and among some population groups (e.g., Liebert 1999). But since opposition to the European Union has been studied mainly through survey research, we found little evidence in this literature about how people interact with authorities and with others in the give-and-take of contention over policies that affect their interests and their values in the emerging European system.
- Studies of particular sectors of activity over time—like the protests of French farmers against the reform of the Common Agricultural Policy, or CAP (Roederer 1999). These go part of the way toward an answer to our questions, but on their own, they do not permit us to assess whether a general shift of claims-making from the national to the supranational level is occurring.

- As conflict intensified in the 1990s, first over CAP reform and then over the stabilization requirements for entry into the EMU (European Monetary Union), studies of episodes of conflict involving the European Union began to multiply.[12] But without placing these events within longer histories of contention and in a comparative framework, it is difficult to know if they are becoming more frequent and what long-term effects they may have on popular contention or on European integration.
- There is also a large and speculative literature on the so-called "democratic deficit." This literature dovetails with our concerns—for in the absence of well-oiled representative institutions, people may well fill the democratic deficit with protest. More is the pity that much of this literature is only hortatory and lives "happily in a state of peaceful non-communication with the well developed literature on policy-making" (Kohler-Koch 1999: 16).

It is to begin to fill these gaps and to link the rich research tradition on contentious politics to the literature on European governance that we offer our study. We began our quest from an analysis of the quantitative data presented in chapter 2 and elsewhere.[13] But before long, we recognized that we would make little headway unless we could triangulate our findings with more detailed and more qualitative accounts of contention in various policy sectors. Those results are presented in parts 2 to 4 of the study. Before we introduce them, however, let us make clear how our work relates to how others have seen the emerging European polity.

FOUR VISIONS OF THE EUROPEAN POLITY

When we turn to the models of European integration that scholars from Europe and the United States have developed to guide them through the European project, we find two main types: two early views that focused on the constitution of a united Europe; two more recent approaches that deal with the day-to-day processes of the Union's operation. Figure 1.1 summarizes these four approaches as the intersection of two main dimensions: whether they focus on the constitution or on the processes within the European system and whether they examine single or multiple levels of interaction.

Two Constitutive Models

Since the publication of Ernst Haas's *The Uniting of Europe* in 1958, some political scientists have seen Europe becoming integrated through a process

Figure 1.1 Four Approaches to European Integration

		Focus of Attention	
		States	***Nonstate Actors***
Levels of Attention	***Single***	Intergovernmental	Supranational
	Multiple	Multilevel Governance	Network Governance

of what Haas called "spillover." As the EEC's competencies expanded, he argued, groups of elites would begin to find one another across national boundaries, exchanging resources and making arrangements for future cooperation. This process would snowball as interpersonal networks and trust-building routines developed. A later generation would have said that the "transaction costs" across borders would lower to the point at which those with something to sell or buy would find their optimal partners regardless of state boundaries. In Fligstein and Mara-Drita's words, ultimately "the interests of states will change by the existence of these groups and [as a result] cooperation will move in new directions" (Fligstein and Mara-Drita 1996: 6).

When we consider the dense tissue of transnational lobbies and trade associations that flourishes in Europe today, Haas's model has proven remarkably prescient (Schmidt 1997: 145). But in focusing so centrally on the process of elite transaction and inferring from it an ultimately supranational outcome, he gave little attention to the deliberate choices of national states or to the actions of ordinary citizens within them. Had his book been written in 1998 instead of in 1958, he would no doubt have had more to say about the interactions of the states responsible for negotiating the treaty bases of European policy-making. He might also have noticed that not all transnational interactions between social actors lead to spillover: many produce spill-*back*—creating costs and competition and leading groups to turn to their national states for protection and to form counterorganizations to protect their interests at the supranational level (Schmitter 1969). "Spillover" has led to both state protection for intrastate interests damaged by integration and to counter-spillover; both could block progress to the kind of integration that Haas foresaw and widen the patterns of conflict and coalition building in the European system.

As convinced as neofunctionalists like Haas were of the inexorable logic of European integration, a second school—intergovernmentalists, like Hoffmann and Moravcsik—was equally convinced of the staying power of the states that make up the European Union. For these scholars, "cooperation among national states can occur only when interests coincide or when states can trade off in a series of agreements." (Fligstein and Mara-Drita 1996: 7). When state interests do not coincide, the integration process stalls—as it did when first France, and then Britain, put on the brakes. Intergovernmentalists do take issue with conceptions of international relations limited to the relations among unitary state actors; but like the neofunctionalists, they focus on a single locus of power—in their case, the national state—and its interactions with other national states (Marks, Hooghe, and Blank 1996: 345).

The typical form of institution-building in the EU—the treaty-making power of the European Council—lends support to the intergovernmentalist view (Keohane and Hoffmann 1991). But their focus on constitutive behavior leaves out much of the day-to-day operation of the European system. For example, it elides the considerable degree to which citizens have gained avenues other than their governments for the representation of their interests (Kohler-Koch 1999: 19); it makes little of the policy networks that have formed at the supranational level among nonstate actors (Fligstein and Mara-Drita 1996, Peterson 1997); it ignores the possibility of "fusion" between state and European elites (Wessels 1997); it leaves out the terrain of transnational relations (Risse-Kappen, ed., 1995); and it asks us to understand the working of a complex multilevel system through the interaction of one level of actors—however powerful they are.

Two Processual Models

The realization that day-to-day decision-making goes beyond state-to-state negotiation produced a set of processual approaches. More institutionally sensitive than the neofunctionalists and more vertically oriented than the intergovernmentalists, "policy domain" theorists like Neil Fligstein and Iona Mara-Drita argue that both schools missed the key elements that link domestic groups to supranational authorities. They write that "neither the neorealist (e.g., intergovernmentalist) nor the neofunctionalist accounts can theorize about how actors find collective solutions in bargaining situations marked by differing and incompatible interests" (1996: 7). These scholars turn deliberately to the negotiation of conflicts within vertical policy domains that include subnational, national, and supranational actors.

They are not alone: building on the policy research of the 1970s and 1980s, a broad group of political scientists have used the related concept of "policy network" to describe and explain variations in the pattern of interest intermediation in the EU. Writing in *West European Politics,* John Peterson argues that "policy network analysis can help us assess both how much has changed in specific policy sectors, as well as the tightness of fit between intergovernmental bargains and EU policy outcomes" (1997: 1).

Shifting the focus to "policy domains" and "policy networks" from the constitutive models of the intergovernmentalists and neofunctionalists helps writers like Fligstein and Peterson avoid the trap of focusing on *either* the national or the supranational levels of power. For them, interest groups in different policy domains operate "both at home and in Brussels" (Fligstein and McNichol 1997: 33). But by focusing so single-mindedly on vertical policy domains, they cannot deal with political contention that either escapes sectoral decision-making or arises out of the intersection between sectors.

Consider environmental governance with Andrea Lenschow: "European environmental policy," she writes, "represents a regulatory and sector-transgressing policy field" (1999: 39). Though the existence of a Directorate-General for the environment would make it tempting to define an "environmental policy domain," analysis of any major environmental issue (for example, the recent dispute over genetic engineering) makes clear that multiple actors and a number of policy-making units across the Union's institutions—as well as national governments–are deeply involved in such decisions (Gottweis 1999).

These examples suggest the need for a more complex, multitiered, and cross-sectoral model of how the European system works. Political scientist Gary Marks and his collaborators responded to this need with a model of "multilevel governance" (Marks, Hooghe, and Blank 1996: 346).

- Like neofunctionalists, they agree that "collective decision-making among states involves a significant loss of control for individual state executives."
- Like intergovernmentalists, they agree that subnational actors contest European policies within national states, but disagree with them in rejecting the view that subnational actors "are nested exclusively within them." Instead, "subnational actors operate in both national and supranational arenas, creating transnational associations in the process."
- And like policy-network scholars, they argue that "decision-making competencies are shared by actors at different levels."

Marks and his collaborators were mainly concerned with *vertical* multilevel governance involving different levels of government; a broader step is taken by Beate Kohler-Koch and her collaborators with their concept of "network governance" (Kohler-Koch and Eising, eds., 1999). Based on two basic variables of the "constitutive logic of the polity" and the "organizing principle of political relations," their "core idea is that politics is about problem-solving and that the setting of policy-making is defined by the existence of highly organized social subsystems." European integration is about "fitting new regulatory mechanisms into an environment which is functioning according to its own regulatory logic" and the formation of collective interests through negotiation and persuasion:

> The Community tends to be a negotiating system, specifically a negotiating system with a variable geometry because, depending on the issue at stake, different actors have to be considered. It is not only member governments who negotiate; various public and private actors are also part of the game. (Kohler-Koch 1999: 25)

Kohler-Koch's idea of negotiation among different regulatory logics, the formation of collective interests through the process of negotiation, and a system with a "variable geometry" puts Marks' and his collaborators' concept of "multilevel governance" into motion. But in its emphasis on "problem-solving," the concept of "network governance" calls attention mainly to *inter-elite* bargaining in the reconciliation of the logics of different regulatory systems to one another. It has little to say about how interests are represented outside these networks and about how they impinge on them—especially among those who refuse to accommodate their interests to collective interests.

In summary, "process-oriented" models of European integration go well beyond the "constitutive models" toward analyzing the mechanisms of decision-making at the European level. But from our point of view, both have the defect of limiting attention to elite transactions within policy networks and leave no space for the examination of the possible role of nonelites in the broader European system. We see a need to work toward the formation of models that will include how citizens can influence or contrast their decisions, both through their own states and within Europe's governance networks. We want to work toward the construction of models of the European polity that move beyond governance to include lines of cleavage and alliance-formation involving sets of actors who are not part of these networks but whose expressed or perceived preferences act as external constraints on their decisions. The concept we will put forward is what we call "a composite polity," by which we mean:

> *A system of political relations in which actors at various levels and in different geographical units within a loosely linked system face both horizontal and vertical interlocutors and find corresponding opportunities for alliance building across both axes.*

We will lay out this construct and illustrate it in the final chapter of this book. But before it can be elaborated, three questions will need to be addressed:

- First, how does European policy-making articulate with patterns of national contention within the EU's nation-states?
- Second, what are the forms of collective action that European integration encourages among social actors?

- Third, what evidence do we have for the formation of European collective actors or for the transformation of individual interests into collective identities through European interaction?

These three questions structure the organization of this book. Let us now briefly survey them before turning to our evidence and to that of our co-authors.

EUROPEAN POLICY-MAKING AND NATIONAL CONTENTION

In a Europe of states, political contention would be neatly segmented: with local issues decided in municipal and provincial arenas, national conflicts fought out in national politics, and national states—representing coalitions of intranational actors—negotiating with their opposite numbers in European arenas. In a fully supranational polity, all important episodes of contention would gravitate to the European level, with functional interests mobilized through European lobbies, territorial representatives organized in the European Parliament, and state interests represented in the European Council.

Whatever the shape of the future European polity, the reality today is far more complex, with conflict and reconciliation occurring at a number of levels and between them. While national governments negotiate with functional groups and European Commission representatives on behalf of state interests, subnational groups and institutions do not meekly await decisions made in their name but leapfrog over their national governments and organize pan-European lobbies. Although MEPs (members of the European Parliament) are chosen to represent territorial constituencies, they are as likely to reflect the claims of their parliamentary groups or of the Eurolobbies they are close to as the claims of the citizens who elected them. European policies are made officially by councils of ministers representing their national governments, but these ministers arrive in Brussels briefed by functional groups in their own states about what they would like to get from Brussels. Europe is a composite polity composed of semisovereign states, quasi-autonomous European institutions, and virtually represented citizens.

This kind of polity fosters ambiguity, perceptions of uncertainty, and shifting alliances—exactly the combination of properties that scholars of social movements have found to be most likely to produce contentious politics. It may not be a federal state in the strict sense intended by constitutional lawyers, but it offers the multiple access points, ambiguities about who is responsible for what, and possibilities of shifting alliances that are typical of such states. The best placed among the groups that come to Brussels to advance their interests—business and professional associations—have learned the routines of European policy-making and focus most of their efforts on the corridors of power. Others—like farmers, organized workers, and environmentalists—have gained footholds in the Directorates-General that regulate their sectors but employ more contentious forms of action as well. Still others—like antinuclear campaigners and marginal social groups—find few entry points into the European Commission and must look for alternative ways to advance their claims.

In a world without important transaction costs or variations in resources, citizens would automatically bring their claims to the agents most directly responsible for their grievances. But when these agents are distant, indirect, and often obscure, claims are more likely to be directed to where people possess dense social networks, organizational resources, and visible political opportunities (Imig and Tarrow 1999). We deduce four ways in which domestic groups can respond contentiously to threats to their interests or values, based on the intersection of two main variables: the reach of their grievances and the targets of their claims.[14]

- *Routine Domestic Protests:* "ordinary" intranational contentious politics. People organize domestically and petition, march, strike, demonstrate, sit-in, obstruct premises, and more rarely commit acts of violence against intranational targets.
- *Cooperative transnationalism:* in which parallel protests make claims on different national targets in cooperative but recognizably separate acts of contentious politics.
- *Collective transnationalism:* in which protest is organized across borders against common European targets.
- The *domestication of conflict:* in which national actors protest at home against policies of the European Union.

We leave a detailed analysis of our aggregate data on the distribution of these types of contention in Europe for the next chapter. The first category is the

Figure 1.2 A Typology of European Protests

		Target of Protest	
		Domestic	***European***
Actors in Protest	***National***	Routine Domestic Protest	Domestication
	Transnational	Cooperative Transnationalism	Collective Transnationalism

stock-in-trade of domestic contention; the two transnational forms are what scholars of "global civil society" or the "world polity" would expect to lie at the end of the road of the process of globalization; and the fourth is how domestic actors respond to external challenges on home ground. Suffice it to say, we find that the vast bulk of European contentious politics still resembles the routine domestic protests familiar from the literature on national social movements and has little or no relation to European policy-making. When it comes to Europe-centered contention, both forms of transnationalism are in the minority but are increasing in number. The major responses to European policy-making are cases of what we call "domestication"—*when domestic groups target national or subnational agents in response to their claims against the European Union.* This finding is perfectly compatible with liberal intergovernmentalism—but not with supernationalism—and it occurs outside of both policy networks and multilevel governance; but unlike the intergovernmentalists, we see it as evidence of *the intrusion of European politics into Europe's national political systems.*

Farmers' protests illustrate the classic form of "domestication." Although "European institutions have become the fulcrum of [farmers'] protest activity in the 1980s and 1990s," concludes Christilla Roederer from her own detailed study of *Le Monde,* French "farmers saw at the *domestic* level a more probable venue for pressure" (1999). In their chapter, Bush and Simi reinforce Roederer's findings from a different database: from Reuters' European press releases, they find that few farm protests are organized crossnationally and those that are tend to target an *external* actor—like the United States—and seldom the European Union. This is not simply because farmers are "locals"; it is primarily, we think, because they follow a strategy of targeting the agents against whom they can exercise maximum leverage, in the hope that this will translate into more robust governmental policies on their behalf in Brussels.

French farmers are not alone. German miners protesting against pit closures; Italian milk producers objecting to EU fines for overproducing; British farmers opposed to EU policies on Bovine Spongiform Encephalopathy (BSE) disease; Spanish tuna fishermen objecting to French and British overfishing: all have tended to protest domestically against European policies. Even migrants—the epitome of non-national actors (Koopmans and Statham 1998)—do the same. In some cases it is not entirely clear who the objects of domestic actors' protests are—since policies made in Brussels are often implemented by national courts and administrators.

Two direct corollaries and an important institutional speculation follow from this process:

- First, as Andrew Martin's and George Ross's chapter 3 shows, well-organized national actors—like national trade union confederations—continue to mobilize supporters domestically even though capital and technology are mobile and despite the fact that they have well-organized representatives in Brussels. In fact, Martin and Ross find that the key level for the creation of European collective bargaining—that of the Industry Federations—is the one in which the least amount of union Europeanization has occurred.

- Second, as Bert Klandermans and his collaborators find in their comparative study of Dutch and Galician farmers in chapter 4, different national settings produce different perceptions of the European Union and thus of the responsibility of the EU or national governments for the same policies; this means that when Galician and Dutch farmers protest, the Galicians will tend to blame Madrid for what ails them, while the Dutch are more likely to target Brussels with their claims.

We do not think these findings vitiate the notion of a European polity in formation: rather, they underscore our view that Europe is a composite polity of variable geometry,[15] more complex in its interactions than a two-level game, multilevel polity, or system of network governance. We will lay out our own speculative view in the final chapter of this book. Whatever the ultimate form of the European polity, most social actors respond to European policies and institutions within the routines and the traditions of their national political systems. And this leads to a challenging institutional implication:

- If citizens—backed by their electoral connections—continue to react to European policies by making claims on national governments, and the latter respond to these protests by acting in European venues as agents for the claims of their citizens, this may lead to a shift in the role of the national state in Europe to that of a broker between contentious citizens using domestic pressure to advance their claims and European forums in which states have to balance their citizens' claims against state interests and their commitments to collective decision-making.

If this is true, then there would be no reason to predict a homogenization of the forms of collective action between the European center and the national peripheries: citizens will continue to use the same forms of contention at home that they have always employed, while depending on their governments and on supranational interest groups to represent them in Brussels. Part 3 of our study turns to this issue.

LOBBYING AND PROTEST: THE RELATION BETWEEN INSTITUTIONAL AND NONINSTITUTIONAL CONTENTION

What we have said previously argues that the strategically logical place for grass-roots groups to operate is in their interactions with those over whom they can have the maximum influence—their local and national representatives. How then do Europeans engage in collective action with respect to European policies when they do so? Two American scholars, Gary Marks and Doug McAdam, reason that when they encounter the institutions of the European Union, Europeans model their behavior around the techniques of interest representation that are accepted by European officials—they lobby them instead of engaging in more contentious behavior (1996, 1999).

If Marks and McAdam are right, then political learning today is considerably more rapid—and less culturally inscribed—than what Tilly found in the European past (1995a).[16] And if they are right, we would expect to find differences in the way Europeans make claims between the European and the national levels. But this is not an easy hypothesis to test: first, because there has been a *general* shift in Western societies away from the more contentious forms of behavior since the 1960s (Dalton 1996; Meyer and Tarrow, eds., 1998); and second, because Europeans have shown a remarkable capacity to make claims in a variety of ways—and this is less a function of European integration than of the diffusion of the resources that used to be monopolized by political parties and formal movement organizations (Tarrow 2000a).

Since we have no direct evidence of lobbying from our own aggregate data, our quantitative analysis in chapter 2 will only take us a short distance toward examining this hypothesis. When we examine the forms of contention they use in European and national venues, however, we find few differences in citizens' repertoires of contention. But since most of the protests we examined take place on domestic ground, a fair test of Marks' and McAdam's hypothesis will have to await studies that find a common metric for studying how the same groups behave at both the supranational and the national levels. This we have not been able to do in a systematic way.

The evidence in parts 2 and 3 gives us a variegated picture of how Europeans make claims against the European Union. The group that appears least often in our protest data—women—has succeeded handsomely in using the European Court of Justice, the European Commission, and, on occasion, the treaty-making process to advance its goals (Hoskyns 1991, Caporaso and Jupille 2000). Barbara Helfferich and Felix Kolb show in chapter 7 that the European Women's Lobby [EWL] aims its activities at a variety of targets, European and national, and uses a variety of means of influence—but seldom uses public protest. Helfferich and Kolb find that with support from national women's affiliates, from some member-state governments, and from sympathetic voices in the Commission, the lobby was able to achieve the insertion of a clause on gender equality in the Amsterdam treaty.

When we turn to the migrants' associations studied by Virginie Guiraudon in chapter 8, we find a greater disarticulation between grass-roots protest and European interest representatives. Brussels-based groups lobby, organize conferences, and carry out expert studies for the Commission, while country-based groups like the French *sans-papiers* were engaging in highly contentious forms of politics in close alliance with religious, civil rights, and antiracist groups. We do not see strong evidence of migrants' lobbying influence in Brussels (indeed, Guiraudon entitles her chapter "Weak Weapons of the Weak"), but this may simply reflect their lack of electoral influence in the member-states.

Other sectors lie somewhere in-between the multilevel strategy of the EWL and the disarticulation of the migrants' groups. The best studied are the European environmental groups, which profit from vigorous ecological movements in the member-states, a Directorate-General dedicated to their claims, and generous subsidies from the Commission. Environmental groups are better connected to their national homologues than migrant groups, but they engage heavily in the politics of expertise and look askance at the grassroots protest activities that many national ecologists engage in at home. Transverse coalition building has helped these groups to gain influence in Brussels, but we are skeptical that—without sustained support from within the member-states—they can exercise effective clout on basic environmental policy-making.

Trade unions reveal a different form of disarticulation: while the ETUC (European Trade Union Confederation) engages deeply in concertation within the European Social Dialogue in Brussels (see Martin and Ross's chapter), national trade unions continue to engage in hard—and at times, contentious—struggle at home. After all, for the foreseeable future, that is where collective bargaining will continue to be carried out. Martin and Ross show that the workers' representatives that could best link center and periphery—the sectoral Industry Federations—are the weakest link in the chain of union representation in Europe. This creates a greater degree of disarticulation than the combination of lobbying and contentious politics that unions practice on the national level.[17]

Why, then, pay attention to the activities of European lobbies on behalf of citizens' interests? The answer is simple: because European decision-makers do so. This has less to do with these groups' representative clout—which is often fragile—than with the need that Commission officials feel for legitimization of their positions and for the expression of public support for them. That, in turn, produces a form of legitimization for Euro-lobbying groups among their constituencies in the member-states. The risk for them is that the differentiation between contentious politics at the periphery and lobbying and expertise at the center will isolate Brussels-based public interest groups from those they claim to serve. Such groups do excellent work on behalf of the interests they claim to represent, but their disarticulation from domestic political struggle is unlikely to advance the formation of European collective actors.

THE FORMATION OF EUROPEAN ACTORS

In the mid-1990s, there was a flurry of interest in the formation of European citizenship. Eurobarometer polls repeatedly took the pulse of European publics to detect whether there was an increase in a sense of support for Europe and a decline of national identity. Students of immigrant politics posited non-national forms of citizenship that would short-circuit national citizenship limits (Soysal 1994). Scholars began to ask "when and how the idea of a European identity emerged" and how "identities and interests are constructed in the intersection between self-images and images of the Other" (Bartolini, Risse, and Strath 1999). The discovery of the democratic deficit added urgency to the desire in Brussels to gain new support for the European idea; in countries that few would have suspected of cosmopolitanism—like Italy—there turned out to be a surprisingly high level of identification with Europe.

But the significance of these concepts and findings is difficult to interpret. For example, what does it mean to discover from surveys that citizens "support" Europe when so few understand its workings and many don't even bother to vote in European elections? What significance can be attributed to European citizenship for immigrants when the EU is shifting the focus of immigration policy from rights and social benefits to the "Third Pillar" of justice and internal affairs? And what can European identity mean when enthusiastic Europe-identifiers include a nation like Italy that is so fed up with its own government that even the far-off EU can seem a port in a storm? Instead of producing a common collective identity, contention over Europe's future may actually be creating or crystallizing diverse identities around the opportunities and costs of the integration process.

Of course, identity is a fluid concept, and the same norms that citizens used to identify with their own political traditions may come to adhere to Europe. Consider the outrage against the inclusion of the far-right, anti-immigrant, and probably anti-Semitic Freedom Party in the Austrian government in 2000. The striking aspect of European governments' condemnation was that such a government transgresses *European* norms. If values that used to be identified largely or wholly with national political traditions come to be seen as "European," we may witness a formation of European identities without a shift in loyalties or normative commitments.[18]

Norms, as Thomas Risse-Kappen has written (1994), do not float freely. We believe that European collective identities may eventually develop but that their formation will depend not on abstract norms floating in transnational space, but on the habitual relations that develop among ordinary people, their governments, the groups that represent them, and significant others in European institutions and in other member-states. Just as national states in the sixteenth to nineteenth centuries created the conditions for the formation of national citizenship by standardizing how their people were treated, imposing on them the same taxes and military obligations, and offering a fulcrum for the negotiation of their conflicts with others, it is the struggle over European policy-making that may, in the long run, create European citizens.

We have already argued that citizens incensed with European policies continue to turn predominantly to their national political systems for political redress. We have claimed that the influence of European lobbies depends less on reciprocal ties with domestic constituent groups than on the resources they enjoy and the legitimization they offer to Commission decision-makers. How can a sense of European identity develop out of these tenuous and indirect ties between citizens and European institutions? We propose four main mechanisms, all of them supported by the contributions to this study:

- First, the brokerage of interests between national groups from different countries by the European Union itself, as it attempts to standardize its relations with member-states and provides an institutional fulcrum for their mutual encounters. Andrew Martin and George Ross's study of the role of the ETUC in negotiation of the European social protocol suggests how such a dynamic can operate.
- Second, the construction by the media and other cultural institutions of European meanings around issues that are not inherently European. Eric Lagneau and Pierre Lefébure provide a telling example in the case of the media coverage of the protests against the closure of the Vilvoorde plant by Renault in 1997.
- Third, the calibration of activities of national groups with collective action in the European Union around issues in which states and the European Union share competence. Vera Kettnaker's study of the campaign against genetically modified foods shows how protest campaigns at the national and European levels can intersect. Helfferich and Kolb's concept of "multilevel lobbying" shows how it can work when it succeeds.
- Fourth, identity shift: the "Europeanization" of values that citizens and elites may already hold but that come to be defined as European.

We cannot prove the working of these mechanisms empirically in the chapters that follow but will return to them in the final chapter to assemble fragments of evidence about whether they are occurring.

Two Historical Analogies

Let us not anticipate a development that seems to be in its early stages; our quantitative data in the next chapter do not reveal a groundswell of either form of transnational contention or the formation of sustained social movements, except in isolated and perhaps very unusual sectors like the campaign against genetic modification. But lest we give in to the undertow of Euro-pessimism that greeted the turn of the century, we should remember that *national* citizenship took generations to be created. Never the result of short-term transactions at the summit of national polities or of the propagation of national images, it developed from the slow, conflictual, and often contradictory weaving together of both common interests and connected conflicts around the formation of national states.

This is not the first time that this has occurred in European history. Consider the integration of Switzerland between 1830 and 1848. For centuries, communal and cantonal identities had formed the stuff of public politics, with national identity rarely providing answers to the question "Who are you?" even when it came to relations with foreign powers. Yet from the Catholic Sonderbund's formation in 1845, divisions between conservative Catholics and a liberal alliance deepened to the point of civil war. That polarization created a new boundary, across which the constitution-makers of 1848 had to negotiate. It did not for a moment erase all differences among constituent actors on either side of the boundary. Its first effect was to polarize the Swiss polity to the point of lethal conflict in 1847. That conflict produced a violent civil war that ended only with the predominance of the liberal alliance in 1848. It was only through a process of negotiation, struggle, and concessions to the local power of parochial cantonal elites that a Swiss identity was forged. Only in the 1970s did that bargain permit the extension of the suffrage to the 50 percent who had been denied it for a century (McAdam, Tarrow, and Tilly in preparation: chap. 11).

Italian unification followed a similarly conflictual and non-normative pattern. Until 1861, the peninsula was divided into a number of more or less petty states, many of them controlled by or allied to Austria; others under the domination of the Vatican; and the Kingdom of the Two Sicilys (note the plural), run by a Bourbon house that was "surrounded by salt water on three sides and by holy water on the fourth"—as a dismissive English historian put it. When it came, unification was not the result of a groundswell of national identity-formation; it combined an expansionist royal conquest from Piedmont, an ideological drive from a Mazzinian minority, a series of more-or-less manipulated plebiscites in the central states, an invasion of Sicily by the guerrilla leader Garibaldi, and his reception there by a partly autonomist and partly integrationist bourgeoisie and a peasant class whose land hunger far outstripped its interest in unification (Riall 1998). The most significant aspect of these events was that the process turned actors (like Cavour) who had shown little interest in unifying the entire peninsula into Italian nationalists (McAdam, Tarrow, and Tilly in preparation: chap. 10).

Swiss confederation and Italian unification took centuries to develop. In our age, mass communications and rapid travel, external threat, and a common currency may accelerate the process at the European level. But the burden of our contributors' findings is that the process is slow, halting, complex, and impeded by the considerable pull of the national networks, resources, and opportunities that surround contending groups. We think it will not be inevitable spillover, intergovernmental agreement, elite policy networks, or vertical governmental bargaining that produce European citizenship but emerging patterns of habitual interaction—conflictual, cooperative, and consolidating—that develop around European institutions. Our contributors' work will help us to examine this hypothesis. We will turn to their work after presenting the findings of our quantitative research on contentious politics in the European Union in the next chapter.

NOTES

We wish to thank Mabel Berezin, Lars-Eric Cederman, Didier Chabanet, Donatella della Porta, Rainer Eising, Virginie Guiraudon, Ron Jepperson, Bert Klandermans, Vera Kettnaker, Beate Kohler-Koch, Andrea Lenschow, Gary Marks, Dieter Rucht, and the members of the European Forum of the European University Institute in 1999–2000 for useful comments on an earlier version of this chapter.

1. See the discussion in appendix A and the sources cited there.

2. We refer particularly to work in what has been called "the political process" approach to contentious politics. For recent work, see, in particular, McAdam, McCarthy, and Zald, eds., 1996; Tilly 1995a; Tarrow 1998b; and della Porta, Kriesi, and Rucht, eds., 1999.

3. See chapter 2 for a more elaborate definition and operationalization of this concept and others that follow from it. Also see McAdam, Tarrow, and Tilly, *Dynamics of Contention,* forthcoming.

4. Though focusing on different parts of the world, our work is closest in spirit and strategy to that of Margaret Keck and Kathryn Sikkink 1998.

5. Using both print and archival sources, Tilly studied how the French contended in five regions over five centuries (1986); then through a more systematic use of print sources, he showed how British claims-makers shifted from a logic of local, parochial, and sponsored protests to national, autonomous, and modular ones (1995a). For a review essay on Tilly's major contributions to the study of contentious politics, see Tarrow 1996).

6. For a collective set of reflections on the achievements and problems of using events data to study contentious politics, see the contributions to Rucht, Koopmans, and Neidhardt eds., 1998. A somewhat different tradition—the "World Handbook" approach to conflict events—stressed broad coverage over context and international trends over comparison. See Taylor and Hudson 1972; and Taylor and Jodice 1983.

7. Mistakenly so, since many of the movements of that year had their roots in earlier episodes of conflict and in many European countries showed strong continuity with the following decade. For an example of these continuities, see Tarrow 1989.

8. But note the forthcoming volume edited by Balme, Chabanet, and Wright (2001) and the empirical work by Reising (1997, 1999) and Roederer (1999).

9. For a survey, see Meyer and Tarrow, eds., 1998, and the data in Dalton 1996 and Gundelach 1995.

10. For major sources, see Risse-Kappen 1995; Smith, Chatfield, and Pagnucco, eds., 1997; Keck and Sikkink 1998; della Porta, Kriesi, and Rucht, eds., 1999; and Risse-Kappen, Ropp, and Sikkink, eds., 1999.

11. We cannot hope to survey this vast literature—much of it focused on specific sectors of activity. For a good general introduction, see Justin Greenwood, *Representing Interests in the European Union* (1997), and its excellent bibliography.

12. For example, on the 1995 "Tuna War" among Spain, France, and Britain (Tarrow 1998a), the Mad Cow" dispute in 1996 (Jasanoff 1997), and the Vilvoorde strike in 1997 (Lagneau and Lefébure 1999).

13. For additional research reports, see Imig and Tarrow 1999, 2000.

14. Didier Chabanet proposes an interesting addition: when social actors from several states combine in protests against the European Union with their national states' policies as the indirect target. He suggests the example of the march of the unemployed in 1997. We are grateful for this insight, which we will examine in the concluding chapter.

15. The origin of this term is obscure, but we first encountered it in Philippe Schmitter's "Imagining the Future of the European Polity with the Help of New Concepts" (1996). Also see his *How to Democratize the European Union and Why Bother?* (2000).

16. In her research, Beate Kohler-Koch reports parallel findings about interest groups: that they adapt their behavior to the rules of the game—e.g., "consensus oriented, presenting expert advice." In contrast, contentious politics is looked down upon. I thank Professor Kohler-Koch for her insights in a personal communication to the authors. We take up some of her arguments in the concluding chapter.

17. We are grateful to Didier Chabanet for this observation.

18. We are grateful to Ron Jepperson for this reflection.

2

Mapping the Europeanization of Contention: Evidence from a Quantitative Data Analysis

Doug Imig and Sidney Tarrow

EUROPE LOSES ITS APPETITE FOR HIGH-TECH FOOD

On February 27th, 2000, Prime Minister Tony Blair published an article in *The Independent on Sunday,* proclaiming his "government's determination to have as informed and balanced a debate as possible on GM (genetically modified) food and crops" (p. 28). "There is no doubt," he continued,

> That there is potential for harm, both in terms of human safety and in the diversity of our environment, from GM foods and crops. It's why the protection of the public and the environment is, and will remain, the Government's overriding priority.

In front-page coverage, the *Independent* gleefully recalled that only one year before, the prime minister had called GM foods safe, said he happily ate them himself, and criticized the press and "the tyranny of pressure groups" for questioning their promotion by his government. "This is a fantastic leap forward," commented Friends of the Earth director Charles Secrett; "For the first time, Mr. Blair seems to be listening to the people on these issues" (p. 1).

What had happened since February 1999, when Blair lambasted the critics of GM foods for "an incredible campaign of distortion"? As a consummate political tactician, Blair was responding primarily to events like these:

- Over the summer of 1999, anti-GM "Eco-Warriors" launched a series of assaults against experimental fields in the United Kingdom. Near Norfolk, they plowed under a field of GM crops in the dead of night. In

Udney and Watlington, groups of protesters wearing white decontamination suits and face masks uprooted fields of GM crops; and near Edinburgh, protesters ripped genetically modified sugar beets from an experimental field (*Aberdeen Evening Express,* 26 July 1999; *The Evening Standard,* 26 July 1999; Press Association Newsfile, 18 July 1999).

- Worried by threats of consumer boycotts, Sainsbury's—Britain's largest supermarket chain—announced it would take GM foods off its shelves, while the Local Government Authority—which represents all the local councils in England and Wales—removed foods containing GM organisms from school menus (*Daily Mail,* 28 July 1999, p. 35).
- Granada Food Services, which operates the cafeteria at Monsanto's UK headquarters, announced a ban on GM foods, to the delight of anti-GM activists (*Chemical Week,* 5 January 2000).
- The Prince of Wales called for more research before GM products were freely used in the United Kingdom—to the irritation of Her Majesty's government, but earning the prince the title "most inspirational figure worldwide" from *Green Futures* magazine (*The Economist,* 19 June 1999: 17; *Reuters,* 25 January 2000).

The agitation against genetically modified foods was not confined to the United Kingdom. Consider these examples:

- In December 1999, activists from Denmark, Norway, Finland, Sweden, France, and Germany blocked deliveries of GM maize to Hamburg and Brest harbors (Greenpeace, 8 December 1999).
- In January 2000, as delegates from 134 nations gathered in Montreal to debate the International Biosafety Protocol, Greenpeace activists gathered at the port of Aarhus in western Denmark to prevent the ship *Legionario* from unloading 45,000 tons of genetically engineered soy pellets from Argentina (*Nordic Business Report,* 25 January 2000).
- In Switzerland, Gerber—an affiliate of GM-producer Novartis—announced that its baby food would henceforth be GM-free; while Nestlé and Unilever—two of Europe's largest food manufacturers—announced lines of GM-free products (*AFX News,* 30 July 1999; *The Economist,* 24 June 1999, p. 25).
- Even the United States—whose officials had scoffed at the campaign—was not immune to anti-GM protests. In August 1999, two California groups—the Lincolnshire Loppers and Croatistas—uprooted acres of GM corn near Lodi, California. A representative for the Loppers explained: "The attack was taken to send a message of solidarity to organic farmers around the world who are resisting the genetic monster" (*The Sunday Times of London,* 2 August 1999).

- In April 2000, a mysterious group in East Lansing, Michigan, torched a Michigan State science building housing research on genetic engineering (*International Herald Tribune,* 10 April 2000).

There was an international institutional response as well:

- only days after the *Legionario* incident, delegates to the Montreal Biosafety talks passed a "precautionary protocol"—allowing countries to reject imports they believed presented a danger to health even in the absence of strong scientific evidence—leading European Environmental Commissioner Margot Wallstrom to declare the anti-GM activists "victorious" (*Reuters,* 31 January 2000; Greenpeace, 31 January 2000).

What explains the outburst of European—and eventually international—protest against high-tech foods and its rapid diffusion in 1999 and 2000? In part, the strong reaction was no doubt due to European resentment that many of the patents on GM crops are held by American multinationals such as Monsanto. Part may be due to distaste for industrially produced foods in general (*New York Times,* 27 June 1999: 3; 30 June 1999); and part may be a response to the Mad Cow catastrophe in Britain (Jasanoff 1997, Tarrow 2000a). The European Union's own vacillation about what to do about GM imports no doubt also contributed to the strong European reaction.

When protests against GM products first broke out in 1995–1996, "EU institutions were discussing several drafts of the 'Novel food' directive which regulates which food products have to be labeled" (Kettnaker, chapter 10). Since the European Parliament, the Commission, and the European Council could not agree on the directive's wording, a conciliatory committee passed a labeling directive that was so draconian and confused that—by May 1998—only a few products had unambiguous labeling rules. In turn, this uncertainty produced an ideal opportunity structure for environmental groups, health safety groups, nationalists, organic and low-tech farmers, and consumers to enter the fray. Western Europe entered the new century in the vanguard of a movement against genetically modified foods.

WHAT'S HAPPENING HERE?

What are the implications of this story, and how far can these implications extend beyond the future of GM production to European contention in general? Some observers have seen in the anti-GM campaign a preview of a future European polity in which not only policy-making, but also contentious politics, will produce—in short order—transnational actors banding together in common protests against centralized targets. In this respect, the anti-GM campaign may be an example of a new and much-trumpeted phenomenon—the transnational social movement—and may represent a popular response to Europe's democratic deficit.

But the anti-GM campaign may have attracted so much attention and had so powerful an effect precisely because it was unusual in a number of dimensions: the issue was unknown and full of potential risks yet potential promise; there was an identifiable villain—vast foreign multinational corporations, apparently hand-in-glove with the world's one remaining superpower; there were heroes, ranging from small farmers unable to fight on their own to frightened consumer groups and skilled transnational campaigners like Greenpeace and Friends of the Earth; and there was an available target—an EU splintered between a technocratic Commission, a divided Council, and a Parliament searching for an identity and a role as democratic tribune. There were also national governments vulnerable to populist pressures and frightened of becoming the victims of another "mad cow" scandal.

It isn't every day that such a combination of issues, villains, heroes, and targets comes together. This makes it hard for us to extrapolate general lessons from this campaign. But at the very least, the anti-GM campaign raises a number of tantalizing questions about the developing realm of European contentious politics—if not as a current reality, then as a long-term potential.

- First, is this type of transnational European mobilization likely to become an increasingly common phenomenon?
- Second, how is the development of transnational movement mobilization linked to the stages and the patterns of European integration?
- Finally, do campaigns such as this suggest a new role for European social movements, as they increasingly will be called to action in a multilevel political context, or will they produce an altogether new form of citizen politics?

There are theoretical and empirical reasons for asking these questions at this time. Over the last decade, a new tradition of "transnational relations" has developed, which turns its attention from that old standby, the multinational corporation, to other kinds of nonstate actors—NGOs, principled issue networks, transnational activists, and professional and business groups. Recently, some authors have begun to posit the development of a whole new spectrum of transnational social movements (Smith, Chatfield, and Pagnucco 1997; Smith 2000); others focus on one particular movement family—like human rights (Risse, Ropp, and Sikkink, eds., 1999), the environment (Young, ed., 1997), or the concerns of indigenous peoples (Brysk 1998; Yashar 1998). Still others focus on emerging transnational activist networks, but have not applied their model to Europe (Keck and Sikkink 1998). While some scholars discern a new level of global civil society or world polity emerging, others are more circumspect, seeing a variety of types of beyond-border activism on the part of actors whose interests continue to be framed by domestic political opportunities and constraints (Imig and Tarrow 1999, 2000; Tarrow 1998a).

In the remainder of this chapter, we address these issues from the perspective of our own efforts to analyze the effects of European integration on contentious politics across the member-states of the European Union. This effort should serve three main purposes: first, we begin to map the actors, prevalence, nature, and forms of contentious political action when European citizens respond to the policies and institutions of the European Union. Second, we use our findings to provide a general background for the more qualitative and process-oriented contributions in the rest of the volume. Third, since European institutions are the most elaborate set of regional institutions in the world today, we reason that our findings are relevant to more general debates about transnational politics (Tarrow 2001).

THE CHANGING WORLD OF EUROPEAN CONTENTION

Why begin our study with a quantitative data set on European contentious politics, despite all the well-known lacunae in this kind of data (see the appendix for a discussion of these problems)? One alternative would be to limit our analysis to single events or sensational campaigns, like that launched against GM products. Doing so, however, would run the risk, first, of selecting only dramatic cases that might turn out to be rare or idiosyncratic. Second, by looking at contention at one point in time, we would have little grasp of whether European contention is growing as the European Union expands its competencies. To avoid these dangers, we set out to develop a source of data that would allow us to track the evolving pattern of collective political action across the member-states of the EU and over the recent history of European integration.

We began by looking for a data source that would both cover a significant period of the EU's development and provide comparable information for the range of member nations. Drawing on the techniques of contentious events analysis, we turned to the record of political events reported in the international news media. The usual source of protest event analysis[1]—national newspapers—would be problematic because of their bias toward coverage of their own national news and because they are written for different audiences. For these reasons, we drew our event reports from the *Reuters* news wire, which has been available in electronic format for the past fifteen years, has an explicitly international perspective, and is consistent in style and coverage.

The data set that we have constructed covers the fourteen full years from January 1, 1984, through December 31, 1997, and is built from an analysis of every political report filed with *Reuters* for the twelve nations that were members of the EU for the majority of this time period. Within this record, we found accounts of some 9,872 discrete contentious political events, launched by a broad range of social actors, including farmers and workers, environmentalists, and peace activists, as well as students, skinheads, immigrants, and many others. Moreover, our data set catalogs a broad and evolving spectrum of routine forms of political engagement, including strikes, marches, sit-ins, and rallies, as well as more violent forms, like rock throwing, hunger strikes, and soccer hooliganism. It also includes a range of more confrontational—but generally peaceful—forms of protest, including obstructions and blockades.

Some Essential Definitions

We set aside a detailed discussion of the data set and the way in which it was constructed for the appendix to this volume.[2] In the following sections we report on our findings concerning the Europeanization of contentious politics. But first we need to put a short set of definitions on the table. We do not consider all protests that take place in Europe as "European"—on the contrary, most of these actions are aimed at purely domestic public or private targets. Only those that in some way involve the European Union fit our definition of:

- *Europrotests* are all incidents of contentious claims-making to which the EU or one of its agencies is in some way either the source, the direct target, or an indirect target of protests and the actors come from at least one member-state. In contrast, *national* and *subnational protests* are those in which domestic actors target other domestic actors or institutions in the name of purely domestic claims.

Within the category of Europrotests, we distinguish between two broad subtypes:

- *Domesticated protests* are examples of contentious claims-making in which the EU or one of its agencies is either the source or an indirect target of a protest by domestic actors, but the direct target of the action is either the state, its components, or other actors present on its territory.
- *Transnational European protests* are instances of contentious claims-making in which the EU is either the source, the direct target, or the indirect target, and in which actors from more than one EU member-state take part.

And within the category of transnational protests, we identify three subcategories:

- *Competitive transnationalism:* in which private actors from one member-state protest against and may target private actors from another state.
- *Cooperative transnationalism:* in which parallel protests make claims on different or the same targets in cooperative but recognizably separate acts of contentious politics.
- *Collective European Protest:* in which groups from different member-states combine and take action against the same national or international target.

Europeanization and the Domestication of Protest

These distinctions may seem hair-splitting, but they are important because—as we will show further on—most grievances sparking protest in Europe, as well as most venues in which protest takes place, continue to be within domestic rather than transnational political space. In fact, by far the largest share of recent European protest (almost 95 percent of our total), is made up of examples of purely domestic protest, in which private actors launch contentious political action against national or subnational targets in response to purely domestic grievances. From the perspective of transnational social movement mobilization, this finding alone is a healthy corrective to the notion that the nation-state is withering rapidly as a focus of citizens' claims and that Western Europe will become a transnational polity in short order. On the other hand, a 5 percent Europeanization of protest should also give pause to Euro-skeptics who find little indication of the importance of integration to most Europeans, either in Eurobarometer findings or in party manifestos.

But what can we say about these Europrotests—in which private citizens are motivated to take action in response to the European Union—and about the ratio of European to domestic contentious events? In order to address this issue, we first needed to be able to isolate the share of our set of 9,872 events that were launched in response to the policies or institutions of the EU. Identifying this subset proved to be a complicated issue because of the composite relationship between national governments and European institutions. While some claimants who are directly affected by EU decisions are likely to frame their grievances in terms of European institutions and policies, others are more likely to continue to frame their grievances in national and domestic terms. This makes it difficult—short of generous and possibly subjective interpretation of the press data—to isolate the subset of European protest.

The dislocations caused by the process of monetary union in the late 1990s illustrate this difficulty. In the spring of 1997, for example, coal miners shut down all eighteen of Germany's coal pits and laid siege to the city of Bonn to protest federal proposals to drastically cut subsidies to the coal industry. While government ministers and the news media were quick to blame European integration—particularly the budgetary qualifications for monetary union—for the subsidy cuts, the miners and their union representatives instead framed their protest in terms of jobs and survival—targeting the Kohl government in their protests, rather than European institutions and policies.[3]

In order to be sure we were dealing with the subset of contentious events in our data that are most clearly examples of Europeanization, we adopted a conservative operationalization of the concept of European contentious events. In the findings reported here, an institution or policy of the EU had to be linked to the protest action in the first sentence of a media report in order for that action to be included in our subset of Europrotests. Working with this set of parameters, our trained coders gleaned 490 contentious events that fit our definition of European protest. These 490 events provide the foundation for our discussion of protests against the EU from 1984 through 1997.

Europrotest: A Small but Growing Phenomenon

Our conservative coding criteria no doubt limited the number of European protest events we found. Even so, 490 protest events over a period of fourteen years of European integration constitutes a mere 5 percent of the population of contentious events contained in our data set. The implication is clear: across Europe, most people, for most issues, continue to protest about domestic issues and against domestic targets. This suggests that Europe is still a continent of independent states where contentious politics is concerned.

But there is also evidence in the data that European conflict patterns are changing. Figure 2.1 plots both the frequency count and the percentage of Western European contentious events generated in response to EU policies and institutions. As the trendlines presented in the figure suggest, although EU-motivated contentious protests continue to account for a small share of the total, they rose rapidly post-Maastricht, as a percentage of all reported contentious political activity. In this respect, Europeans are increasingly likely to take to the streets in protest against the European Union, its agents, and its policies—though still much less often than when they protest against domestic grievances.

The trends reported in the figure also hint at the influence of phases in the development of the European Union on patterns of protest activity. In a recent analysis, Doug McAdam and William Sewell, Jr., stress the importance of crucial junctures in the timing and frequency of contentious politics (in press). Do specific sets of events trigger peaks in European protest, or is there a more incremental and linear development of European contention? In chapter 5, Evelyn Bush and Pete Simi demonstrate that for farm-

Figure 2.1 Frequency and Percentage of Western European Contentious Events Provoked by EU Policies and Institutions, 1984–97

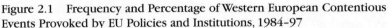

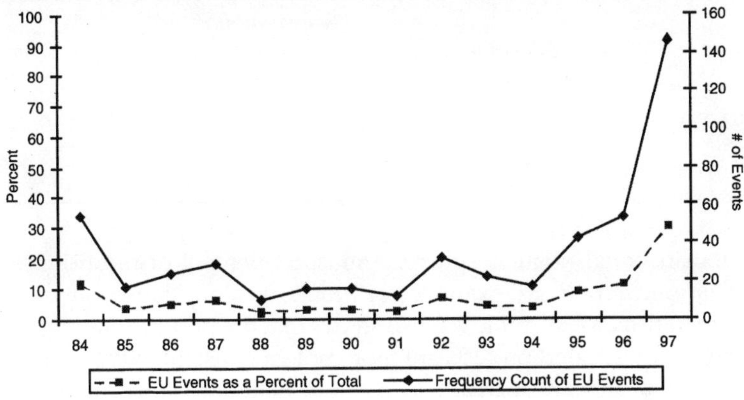

ers, periods of EU deliberation over Common Agricultural Policy accords correspond with peaks in protests against the EU. Periods of national agricultural policy implementation, in contrast, should provoke higher levels of national and domestic, rather than EU-directed, claims-making. Christilla Roederer finds general support for this thesis in her study of French farmers (1999).

The combination of a general upward trend alongside the more erratic inflections in figure 2.1 suggest that both processes may be at work simultaneously. Domestic actors may be learning to engage supranational policy makers incrementally, while at the same time, specific policy disputes selectively heighten the incentives for certain groups to make claims across national borders. Returning to the campaign against genetic modification, we see the confluence of general trends in Europeanization—in the form of implementation of the Maastricht and Amsterdam treaties—alongside specific political junctures like the "mad cow" crisis and debates about approval and labeling of GM products in both Europe and the United States (c.f., Bush and Simi, chapter 5; Kettnaker, chapter 10).

DOMESTICATION AND TRANSNATIONALIZATION

Where does protest against European policies take place and against whom is it aimed? In chapter 1 we suggested that the significant transaction costs of transnational mobilization increase the incentives for domestic actors to seek ways to respond to EU policy initiatives by attacking domestic rather than European targets. Table 2.1 confirms our suspicion that the preponderance of protest against the EU to date has occurred within the domestic rather than

Table 2.1 Domesticated and Transnational Contentious Action against the European Union, 1984–1997

	Domestication *N = 406*	*Transnational Protest* *N = 84*	*Total* *N = 490*
1984–92	84.2%	15.7%	42.8% (210)
1993–97	81.7%	18.2%	57.1% (280)
Total	82.8%	17.1%	100% (490)

in the transnational political sphere. Almost 83 percent of the EU-directed protests in our sample are examples of "domestication," while only 17 percent were transnational. Table 2.1 also shows that the proportions of transnational and domesticated protests are more or less constant, with a slight, but statistically insignificant increase in the transnational category after 1992. People who protest against European institutions and policies do so predominantly on home ground.

Against whom do they protest? Table 2.2 reports on the targets chosen when domestic contentious action is launched against the European Union. By far, the largest share of these events targets national and subnational political institutions, which account for more than 56 percent of all instances of domestication. Other domestic private actors and foreign national government outposts and foreign citizens also bear the brunt of a large share of domesticated EU contention. Domestic private actors were targeted in 17.5 percent of the domesticated events in our sample. On a number of occasions, for example, farmers angered by the imports of foreign produce have responded by tipping over produce carts stocking the offending merchandise. In turn, foreign nationals and foreign government institutions are targeted 17.1 percent of the time. This targeting usually occurs through blockades of foreign embassies or the closing of national borders to foreign imports. Finally, a smaller share of domesticated European contention (8.8 percent) is targeted against a collection of direct objects even more tenuously linked to the EU.[4] The continuing predominance of domesticated, rather than transnational, contentious responses to the EU suggests that if the phenomenon of collective European protest is growing in relation to globalization, liberalization, and the Europeanization of policy-making, it is doing so at a glacial pace.

Table 2.2 Targets of Domesticated European Contention, 1984–1997

Domestic Governments	56.6%
Domestic Private Actors	17.5%
Other Governments and Foreign Nationals	17.1%
Other Targets	8.8%

Types of Transnational Protest

Still, as national groups explore their commonalities with one another and experiment with collective forms of European protest, these protests may become more and more common. Within the 17 percent of the total in which EU protests are organized transnationally, who is protesting and against whom? We identified three principal forms of transnational action: cooperative transnationalism, collective European protest events, and competitive transnationalism.

What we call *cooperative transnationalism* finds actors from various countries joining together in linked and coordinated protest campaigns in different national settings. In April of 1993, for example, workers from across the European Community launched strikes and took to the streets in protest of the failure of their own governments to halt and reverse the steep rise in unemployment. Similarly, from 1996 on, anti-GM campaigners coordinated their efforts against the approval of genetically modified foods. And in 1998 a major campaign of farmers' protests was mounted across the EU by farmers' groups coordinated by their national organizations. And in chapter 7, Barbara Helfferich and Felix Kolb show how women's groups coordinated campaigns to lobby their national governments to support a gender equality plank in the Amsterdam Treaty.

Competitive transnationalism suggests a far different dimension of European integration. In these instances, extremely common among farmers—as Evelyn Bush and Pete Simi demonstrate in their chapter—protesters rally against, rather than join with, their competitors from other nations. Other examples include fishermen seizing fishing vessels from other nations, provoked by arguments over EU fishing regulations. Through the summer of 1994, for example, French and Spanish fishermen clashed off the northern coast of Spain as part of their long-simmering dispute over the use of oversized drift-nets (Tarrow 1998a). And in December of 1997, Scottish farmers turned back twenty truckloads of cheap Irish beef destined for British markets. The Scotsmen were "jubilant over this show of solidarity with their English and Welsh colleagues" (*Reuters,* December 1997).

Collective European protest is the more widely anticipated form of transnational contentious politics. Here, major protest events draw the participation of citizens from across the EU. In April 1992, 30,000 European farmers gathered outside the European Parliament and the U.S. embassy in Strasbourg to demonstrate against proposed EC agricultural reforms. Similarly, in November 1997, thousands of trade unionists from across Europe converged on Luxembourg to demonstrate for jobs as European Union leaders gathered for a two-day summit on joblessness. And in the same year, as Pierre Lefébure and Eric Lagneau show in chapter 9, Renault workers from Belgium, France, and Spain converged on Brussels to demonstrate outside the headquarters of the European Commission against the closure of the firm's plant in Vilvoorde.

These three forms of European transnational protest follow different trajectories, involve different combinations of social actors, and need to be differentiated and separately traced. For example, the implications of "competitive transnationalism" for the formation of European citizenship are very different from those of cooperative or collective European protest. Competitive transnationalism is entirely compatible with a Europe of states and contradicts the goals of those who see a unified European polity developing in short order; while collective European protests—however rare they still appear to be—may presage a Europe in which borders are no obstacle to contentious politics.

WHO PROTESTS AGAINST THE EU?

The transaction costs of transnational collective action may be easier for some groups to surmount, resulting in differential access to supranational institutions. As a result, European integration may encourage certain social and political groups to mount protests against European institutions or policies while others continue to engage in routine national protests.

Some scholars doubt that well-organized occupational groups—such as workers—will easily abandon their well-worn national opportunity structures to organize at the European level (Streeck 1995). Others, like Turner (1996), think that such a change depends on the development of a crossnational mobilizing capacity and an infrastructure for transnational mobilization. Still others, as Andrew Martin and George Ross argue in chapter 3, see a disjunction between the level at which Europeanization is occurring—in the European Trade Union Confederation—and the level at which collective bargaining is centered, in the different industrial sectors. If Martin and Ross are correct, we may see a degree of Europeanization for labor, but at a level that is so far from the point of production that it barely impinges on the consciousness of workers concerned about preserving jobs or raising wages.

On the other hand, *non*occupational groups—such as ecologists—may find the transition to the European level easier. First, they draw on a mobile, educated, professional constituency whose members can talk more easily to Eurocrats or to others like themselves from other member-states. Second, the problems that concern them cross national boundaries—like air and water pollution. This gives nonoccupational groups a leg up on economic groups in turning to Europe with their problems. On the other hand, once they reach Brussels, according to scholars like Marks and McAdam (1996, 1999), such groups are likely to take advantage of the lobbying opportunities that the European Union makes available rather than to take to the streets. Thus we may find them *in* Europe but less likely to engage in contentious politics *against* Europe.

If we compare the propensity of occupational and nonoccupational groups across Europe to protest against the EU, we find that, through 1997, the former initiated a much larger share (82.1 percent) of the total than the latter. It appears that those issues most likely to affect the livelihood of workers are also likely to encourage their contentious political action against the EU. This finding is particularly striking when we compare it with the groups that protest most frequently in Western Europe around *domestic* issues. Across the twelve nations we studied, nonoccupational groups accounted for more than twice as many protests against domestic grievances as do occupationally based groups (c.f., table 2.6). Table 2.3 shows that occupational groups make up a much larger share of the protests triggered by the European Union than nonoccupational groups. This imbalance, however, has declined slightly but significantly since the early 1990s.

What are the occupational groups that are most active in protests against EU policies? Readers may quickly conjecture that the EU-oriented protests by occupational groups probably consist predominantly of farmers—and they would be right. Farmers' long involvement with the Common Agricultural Policy makes them more attuned to European policy than many other groups. We see evidence of this in chapter 4, where Bert Klandermans and his collaborators show that Dutch farmers, who have been involved with European institutions since the outset, are far more likely than Galician ones to see Brussels at the center of their concerns. Table 2.4 compares the distribution of EU protests by farmers with other occupational groups. The table verifies that farmers account for the largest share of protests by economic groups against EU policies—accounting for roughly half of the protests launched by occupational groups across these fourteen years.

Alongside farmers, we find a vigorous range of contentious actions launched by other occupational groups, including fishermen, construction workers, and miners. Not coincidentally, it is these same groups that are confronting the painful realities of integration at first hand: through reductions in agricultural subsidies and production quotas, shifting trade restrictions, limitations on net sizes and fishing territories, and layoffs and closures in the name of fiscal austerity and monetary union. In addition, as West European plants consider relocating to newly acceding countries of East-Central Europe and adopt forms of subcontracting and contracting-out, the efforts of

Table 2.3 Occupational and Nonoccupational Protests against the European Union, 1984–1997

	Occupational *N* = *402*	*Nonoccupational Groups* *N* = *88*	*Total* *N* = *490*
1984–92	88.1%	11.9%	42.9% (210)
1993–97	77.8%	21.2%	57.1% (280)
Total	82.1%	17.9%	100% (490)

Table 2.4 Protests by Farmers and Other Occupational Groups against the European Union, 1984–1997

	Farmers *N = 200*	*Other Occupational Groups* *N = 202*	*Total* *N = 402*
1984–92	47.1%	52.9%	46.0% (185)
1993–97	52.1%	47.9%	54.0% (217)
Total	49.7%	50.3%	100% (402)

EU labor unions to defend the interests of their members are complicated further. Against such moves, domestic protests against national states can have little impact.

The activism of these occupational groups highlights the much more fragile presence of other social actors in contention against European policies and institutions. NGO representatives in the environmental, migrants', and women's sectors interviewed in Brussels concede that their grass-roots memberships are largely indifferent to the growing importance of European decision-making (c.f., the chapters in this volume by Virginie Guiraudon and Barbara Helfferich and Felix Kolb). Without grass-roots support, their lobbying efforts lack the clout of the better-financed business and professional groups they oppose.

In summary, while there are dramatic cases of contentious action on the part of the environmental, student, antinuclear, animal rights, and antiracist movements in Europe—and these are growing as a proportion of total European protests—the largest proportion of contentious responses to the European Union continue to involve farmers and other occupational groups. Europe may be developing at the summit as the "Europe of the Banks," but European contentious politics is emerging as the Europe of those who work.

REPERTOIRES OF EU CONTENTIOUS POLITICS

There is another important issue to consider: the rise in contentious political action that we document from the mid-1980s through the late 1990s may ultimately prove to be epiphenomenal, as the institutional logic of the European Union sublimates the role of contentious protest in European policy formation under the driving force of Brussels' lobbying culture. We have not collected information on lobbying with the same level of density as our protest event data—although many of our collaborators have done so—but we can transpose the question of lobbying versus protest into a narrower one: Do forms of protest become more routine and less contentious as groups approach the European Union?

We take our bearings in asking this question from our colleagues Gary Marks and Doug McAdam, who have argued that contentious political action is poorly suited to the Euro-realm because it is expensive and time-consuming to transport activists to Brussels; because public discourse is deeper at the national level than it is in Europe as a whole; and because the structure of political opportunity in the EU is more open to conventional than to unconventional activity (1999: 103-104). If McAdam and Marks are right, then three corollaries should follow:

- First, European contentious action should prove to be less contentious and more institutionalized than the comparable realm of domestic contentious activity.
- Second, the already small share of domestically based EU contentious activity would be expected to decrease further with time, as claimants respond to the institutional logic of the EU.
- Third, EU claims-making should become more institutional with time, as claimants learn to leverage the institutional opportunities afforded by the EU.

Though our data are not precisely what would be needed to test Marks and McAdam's hypothesis and its corollaries, we will try to employ them to compare the repertoires of domestic and European contentious political action.

A Typology of Contentious Forms

We begin by dividing our data set into five categories of protest: peaceful protests and demonstrations; strikes; confrontational protests; violence against property; and violence against people.

Peaceful protests range from small protests to large demonstrations, marches, and picketing. Here is an example:

> Months of despair among the farming community culminated in thousands of Westcountry farmers and their families making the pilgrimage to London to force the government's hand. They carried banners proclaiming "Keep Britain Farming" and pleaded with Ministers to "Listen to us!" (*Western Morning News*, 1 March 1999)

The second category of nonviolent direct action is made up of occupational *strikes*. By definition, this category implies more sustained, though still legal, protest activity. Here is an example:

> In response to the Kohl government's announced cuts in federal subsidies to the beleaguered coal industry, some 5,000 miners demonstrated in Saarbruecken and a convoy of miners streamed into Bonn, where they waved their shirts in

the air and chanted "do you want the shirts off our backs?" (*Reuters Western European News Service,* 14 March 1997)

Our third category of mass-based protest activity bridges the boundary between nonviolent and violent protest. These *confrontational protests* include blockades, property seizures, sit-ins, and building occupations. These actions are generally illegal, and yet they fall within the traditional and accepted repertoire of contentious collective action. Here is an example:

> Angry pig producers closed a meat-cutting plant owned by Malton Bacon last week for nearly seven hours in protest against imports of live pigs from Ireland. (*Farmers Weekly,* 12 March 1999)[5]

Some contentious events go over the edge from confrontation to violence. Within this last category, we need to differentiate between violence against property and violence against people. The anti-GE campaign is a source of a number of examples of *violence against property,* including the following example:

> They gathered at the edge of a field here late one night, about 20 people wearing dark clothes and gardening gloves. . . . When lookouts in three cars all gave the go-ahead, the shadowy figures illuminated the battery-powered miner's lamps atop their heads, crept from behind the hawthorn hedgerows and began ripping every gene-altered plant from the earth. (*International Herald Tribune,* 26 April 1999)

By comparison, *violence against people* is seen most often in clashes between protesters and their adversaries, including the police, or else in acts of sabotage. An example from May 1997:

> French farmers seized lorries attempting to import Spanish produce into France. Not content to simply destroy their cargoes, farmers held their drivers hostage, and sliced the brake-lines on some vehicles. (*Reuters Western European News Service,* 22 May 1997)

In table 2.5, we present the distribution of European and domestic contentious claims-making across these five categories of contention.

As table 2.5 indicates, in the aggregate there continues to be a great deal of similarity in the repertoires of contention that Europeans employ against the EU and in those with which they advance domestic claims. Peaceful protests comprise the greatest share of activity in both categories—accounting for nearly 32 percent of actions against the EU and almost 27 percent of actions against other adversaries. At the same time, we find two points of divergence between European and domestic contention. First, strikes—while an important part of the repertoire of domestic contention—have much less

Table 2.5 Principal Components of the Repertoires of EU and Non-EU Western European Contentious Action, 1984–1997

	Non-EU Protests (%) N = 9,382	*EU Protests (%) N = 490*
Peaceful Protests	26.8	31.9
Strikes	14.8	7.6
Confrontational Protests	31.4	43.7
Violence against Property	8.3	7.7
Violence against Persons	18.7	9.1

utility in transnational politics. This difference likely reflects the continued rooting of industrial relations in national opportunity structures (Turner 1996; Ross and Martin, chapter 3) and the absence of a parallel realm of routinized forms of contention appropriate for action beyond the state. Given these realities, it is also interesting to note that Europeans *have* employed strikes in their protests against EU policies in a small number of cases (7.6 percent of our total). In these instances, the EU is either blamed for plant closures, or EU policies are seen to pose a significant threat to an industry.

Second, our most striking finding relates to the more contentious forms of collective action. Contrary to some expectations, Europeans have not shied away from confrontational actions—including blockades and occupations—against the EU. In the aggregate, protesters were nearly a third more likely to employ such actions when responding to EU issues as they were in response to non-EU grievances (accounting for 43.7 and 31.4 percent of the totals in each category). These findings suggest that contentious action continues to comprise a substantial share of the repertoire Europeans employ in making claims against the EU and may be of particular importance in gaining attention from a set of institutions that are distant from domestic politics, with its logic of electoral representation. On the other hand, the picture is more mixed when it comes to violent contentious action. While the rates of violence against property are roughly equivalent between the two subsets of data, EU-linked actions are *less than half* as likely to devolve into violent clashes and riots.

But is it the same or different groups of actors that are protesting in domestic and European politics? Moreover, when groups move from protest against domestic to supranational issues, do they employ the same or different repertoires of action? Table 2.6 offers some preliminary insights into this question by comparing the domestic and European repertoires of action for both occupational and nonoccupational groups.

The table indicates a number of striking differences in the repertoires employed by these groups in domestic and European protests. For occupational

Table 2.6 The Domestic and European Repertoires of Contentious Action for Occupational and Nonoccupational Groups, 1984–1997

	Peaceful Protests	*Strikes*	*Confrontational Protests*	*Violence against Property*	*Violence against Persons*
Occupational Groups N = 3,439					
Europrotests N = 402	27.6%	9.3%	45.3%	8.6%	9.1%
Domestic Protests N = 3,037	18.0%	45.7%	27.8%	3.3%	5.2%
Nonoccupational Groups N = 6,433					
Europrotests N = 88	50.0%	0.0%	36.2%	3.7%	10.0%
Domestic Protests N = 6,345	30.9%	0.0%	33.2%	10.7%	25.2%*

*In these results, a large share of the domestic contentious political action of nonoccupational groups is cataloged as violence against persons. The largest share of this violent protest (38.8 percent of the total) was the product of intensive media coverage of nationalist groups, primarily associated with the Basque, Catalan, and Irish Nationalist movements. The second largest share of this category (33.2 percent of the total) is made up of events that escalated from more peaceful protests, demonstrations, and strikes to the point where there were major violent confrontations either with the police or with special police riot units. If we were to re-classify these two categories of protest, violence against people would account for 9.1 percent of the contentious political action of nonoccupational groups in domestic politics.

groups, the most notable differences follow from the presence or absence of routinized opportunities for political expression. This is most evident in terms of occupational strikes, which comprise a much larger share of the repertoire of occupational groups in domestic politics than in European events (accounting for 45.7 percent and 9.3 percent of the totals for each category). Conversely, occupational groups are much more likely to engage in confrontational protests over *European* issues than they are against domestic ones (accounting for 45.3 percent and 27.8 percent of each category). This difference also likely reflects the absence of a routinized and accepted repertoire of claims-making at the European level. The difference in available opportunities is also likely to account for the slightly higher propensity of occupational groups to undertake more violent contentious action at the European level.

In comparison, nonoccupational groups are more likely than their occupational counterparts to undertake peaceful actions against European issues (accounting for 50 percent of nonoccupational EU events, and 27.6 percent of occupational EU events). They are also more likely to engage in violent contentious action in domestic politics. As catalogued, fully 25.2 percent of the contentious political activity of nonoccupational groups involves violence against persons.[6] In sum, our analysis suggests that occupational groups have been more likely to engage in peaceful and routinized forms of protest at the domestic level and in more confrontational protests at the European level, while for nonoccupational groups, just the opposite is true.

In chapter 10, Vera Kettnaker undertakes a more detailed analysis of these same questions concerning domestic and European repertoires of action for one particular campaign—the effort to ban GM products from Europe. Her findings suggest that the relationship between domestic and transnational repertoires is likely to vary by groups of claimants and the resources they command. Kettnaker evaluates the intensity of collective action employed by anti-GM protesters against national and supranational government targets as well as against industry outposts. Her analysis indicates that—within this sector at least—the repertoires that activists employ when they protest against supranational, national, and subnational targets are of similar intensity. Kettnaker concludes that for the anti-GM campaign, "protest against national governments and the EU showed surprisingly little difference in frequency or intensity."

Comparing Contentiousness

Can we systematize our comparison of European and domestic contentious events over time? Drawing upon efforts in International Relations to quantify the degree of conflict inherent in different forms of political engagement, we assigned each of the nearly 10,000 contentious events identified in our data set—including the 490 EU events—a "conflict score."[7] We were then able to compare the levels of contentiousness of protest events launched against EU and non-EU grievances and also to follow changes in the contentiousness of these repertoires over time. As scored, relatively peaceful forms of protest—marked by low to moderate levels of conflict—register in the 400s, while scores in the 800s signal that protests included violence either against property or against persons. Along this scale, the overall mean conflict scores for both European and domestic events for our period of investigation are strikingly similar (674.6 for EU events and 675.4 for non-EU events). In the aggregate, this finding supports the argument that Europeans are employing similarly intense repertoires of claims-making against European grievances as they employ in domestic politics.

Over our period of investigation, however, the process of European integration has proceeded through a number of critical stages. How has the repertoire of contentious claims-making evolved in response? Employing our contentiousness scale, we are able to analyze changing forms of contentious claims-making over time. These results are presented in figure 2.2.

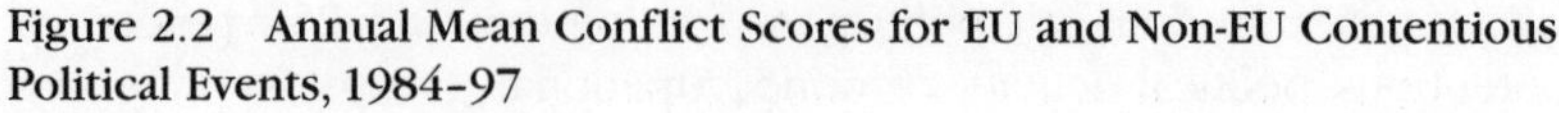

Figure 2.2 Annual Mean Conflict Scores for EU and Non-EU Contentious Political Events, 1984–97

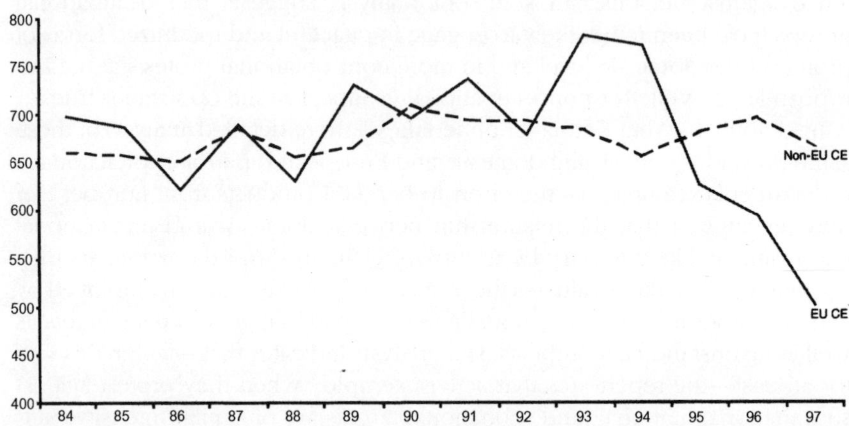

The trends presented in figure 2.2 suggest that the repertoire of European contention has passed through three stages of development over the past decade and a half. First, from 1984 through 1988, protesters were likely to employ repertoires of similar intensity against European and domestic targets. During the second period, from 1989 through 1994, there was a distinct rise in the degree of conflict inherent in protests against the EU. Finally, during the most recent period described by our data—between 1995 and 1997—contentious action undertaken in protest against EU issues and targets was *less* conflictual than the repertoire employed against domestic grievances.

How can we best place these findings in context? First, drawing upon our earlier findings concerning the frequency of European protest, we can say that—with time—European grievances are provoking *more frequent* but also *less contentious* protests. This pattern—in turn—suggests two possible interpretations. Either increased contention over EU-induced claims is beginning to produce an adjustment on the part of social actors to the more institutional routines that give them direct access to EU decision-makers—as Marks and McAdam predict. A second possibility is that once EU decisions are reached, the processes of both implementation and contentious opposition revert to the national sphere, where they become part of the familiar repertoire of domestic contention.

OVERALL FINDINGS

As the European campaign against genetically modified foods suggests, the development of a supranational realm of European government presents a series of new opportunities and constraints for domestic social actors. In this new world of transnational politics and supranational institutions, protesters not only undertake traditional domestic forms of contentious action, but they can also band together in cross-border actions with like-minded actors from across the continent.

But set against the rapid development of international institutions and policies, substantial barriers remain to launching contentious action in the transnational realm. Most individuals continue to have difficulty ascribing the sources of their grievances directly to the EU, and significant transaction costs impede their efforts to coordinate collective action across national boundaries. National governments continue to play a primary role in policymaking before the EU, and tried-and-true routines of collective action and familiar institutional patterns attach citizens to their national political systems.

Which groups of actors have been the most proactive in launching contentious action against EU policies? In addition to farmers, we have identified a substantial range of contentious actions launched by other occupationally based groups, including fishermen, construction workers, and miners. In short, those groups that have been forced to confront the painful realities of integration at first hand have had the greatest incentive to work to surmount the barriers to transnational engagement.

Moreover, our findings also suggest that, rather than seeing an immediate and direct displacement of contentious politics from the national to the supranational levels, we are more likely to see a range of social movement approaches to the European level of governance: transnational cooperation against domestic actors, collective European protests, and the domestication of European issues within national politics. On this last point, our evidence strongly suggests that the largest proportion of contentious political responses to the policies of the European Union takes domestic rather than transnational form. In other words, although Europeans are increasingly troubled by the policy incursions of the EU, they continue to vent their grievances close to home—demanding that their national governments serve as interlocutors on their behalf.

What are the likely consequences of this finding? For one thing, it allows Commission bureaucrats to live inside the Ring that surrounds Brussels in a charmed world in which protests are held at a great distance. Second, it deprives movement activists who have chosen to make their careers in Brussels-based NGOs of the weapons they need—in the form of national support—to back up their claims (Turner 1996). Third—and here we go well beyond our data—in the long term this process may lead to a partial transformation of national states from autonomous centers of sovereign decision-making to pivots between domestic collective actors who cannot reach the European level and European officials with no direct ties to European citizens.

In short, the empirical record we examine suggests that European integration, rather than provoking the transnationalization of European politics, is leading instead to the Europeanization of domestic politics and to the intermediation of national states.

When we turned our attention to the thesis that opportunities for political engagement beyond the state favor institutional over contentious forms of political action, we found domestic social actors engaged in a range of contentious efforts to influence European decision-making. We also found that—through the decade preceding Maastricht—protests were just as vigorous against European as against domestic grievances. Following Maastricht, however, their tenor appears to have begun to change. Whether this change is a result of the institutional logic of the EU or of the redirection of contention to national politics to confront the processes of national approval and policy implementation, we cannot say.

Finally, what are the implications of our findings for the changing role of social movements in an integrating Europe? The increasing share of Western European protests that concern the EU strongly suggests that a growing number of Europeans are ascribing the EU with responsibility for their grievances and that they are more likely than ever to respond through protest. But the location of this contention—in domestic rather than transnational venues—also suggests that social movements continue to operate where they always have: in domestic politics and against national governments.

In turn, our findings concerning contentious political action suggest that there will be a key role for national states to play for some time to come—not only in basic treaty negotiations and passage of EU directives, but in calibrating between partial domestic and collective national interests with respect to Europe. Not only are the majority of protests across the continent undertaken against domestic political issues, but even the largest share of those that are undertaken in direct response to the institutions and policies of the EU—to date—have taken familiar and domestic rather than transnational shape.

Our evidence also hints at the development of a new category of protests that do not conform to the traditional repertoire that grew up around the national state. Just as the consolidation of the national state in Europe produced a "new repertoire" (Tilly 1995a), organized around the growing power of centralizing states, the consolidation of a new European polity may be producing routines of contention that bridge the European center and subnational periphery by protesting against the national state and turning it into a pivot between irresponsible European decision-makers and mass publics that demand to hold someone responsible for their claims.

NOTES

We thank the participants in the conference on the Europeanization of Politics, Nuffield College, Oxford, June, 1999; the workshop on "Citizens, Parties, and Elections in the EU," Center for European Studies, University of North Carolina, Chapel Hill, August 1999; and the workshop on "Dimensions of Contestation in the European Union," University of North Carolina, Chapel Hill, May 2000, for helpful comments on earlier versions of this chapter.

1. For representative studies, see Kriesi et al. 1995, Rucht 1997, Tarrow 1989, Tilly 1995a and 1986, and White 1995.

2. For earlier reports on the research, see Imig and Tarrow 1999 and 2000, and Tarrow 1995.

3. The coal miners' strike was covered in numerous media sources the week of March 7–14, 1997. English accounts were found in the *Reuters Western European News Service, the Independent, Daily Telegraph, The Glasgow Herald, The Irish Times,* and *The Guardian.*

4. This category also includes more generalized demonstrations where the direct targets of contention are difficult to identify—reflecting high levels of confusion when it comes to untangling both the "true" source of European grievances and the appropriate role for national governments to play in resolving European concerns.

5. Pigs and blockades evidently have an affinity. A week later, a group of pig farmers blockaded two supermarket distribution depots in protest of cheaper foreign meat (Press Association Newsfile, 19 March 1999).

6. The largest share of this violent protest (38.8 percent of the total) was made up of the actions of a small number of nationalist groups, primarily associated with the Basque, Catalan, and Irish Nationalist movements. The second largest share of this category (33.2 percent of the total) escalated from more peaceful protests, demonstrations, and strikes to the point where there were major violent confrontations with the police. If we were to re-classify these events, violence against people would account for 9.1 percent of the contentious political action of nonoccupational groups in domestic politics. This figure would be comparable to the corresponding percentages for both occupational and nonoccupational groups operating against European issues, though still double that of occupational groups active in domestic protests.

7. Efforts to create scales to evaluate the contentiousness of political interaction events include Joshua Goldstein's Conflict/Cooperation scale, Will Moore and David Davis's International Political Interactions Conflict Scale, and the IDEA project, undertaken by the Project on Nonviolent Sanctions and Cultural Survival at Harvard University. These scales are built from expert evaluations of the intensity of conflict inherent in various political behaviors.

For this research, we drew from these scales to describe and array the repertoire of contentious political action. Principal modifications included removing state-generated actions (e.g., failure to form a ruling coalition in a legislature) and expanding the portion of the scale describing contentious political action.

Protest events are scaled between 400 and 900. The lower end of this range corresponds with peaceful protests and rallies. The upper extreme corresponds with riots, looting, and violent demonstrations.

2

EUROPEAN POLICIES AND NATIONAL RESPONSES

3

Trade Union Organizing at the European Level: The Dilemma of Borrowed Resources

Andrew Martin and George Ross

INTRODUCTION

Trade unions have developed in constant interaction with markets and states. Unions are hard-won organizations based upon the accumulation of "movement" resources such as shared values of solidarity, mass-mobilizing capacities, and supporter willingness to take risks for the cause. Unions have therefore been much slower to develop and change than the volatile markets that have continuously redefined the challenges confronting employers' power. Both the nature of those challenges and unions' capacity to meet them have in turn been decisively conditioned by the actions of states. States do so indirectly by shaping markets, both within and across their borders, and directly by inhibiting or facilitating union responses to changing markets. Unions have therefore also used their power to secure resources from national political institutions through support of political parties, binding legislation, resort to courts, and national identity itself. The extent of unions' success in extending the scope of their power across national market arenas has thus been coupled with their success in gaining influence in national state arenas, with resources from each reinforcing resources in the other.

For all of the internationalism in labor ideology, however, union movements have been thoroughly embedded in the institutional structures of national political economies. While this has been the source of their strength in the earlier postwar period, it has made them especially slow in adapting to the internationalization of markets. European unions have been confronted with this issue by the distinctive way in which the European states have created a single transnational market. They have transferred the regulation of product markets, including macroeconomic policy, from the national states to the new institutions established at the European level, while leaving the regulation of labor markets—including social policy as well as industrial relations—at the national level. This has put unions in a contradictory position. As the Europeanization of the markets in which companies operate progressed, it would have seemed logical, a priori, for unions to follow their market interlocutors toward Europeanization by developing corresponding strategies and structures.

There have been large obstacles, however, precisely because European unions were so deeply rooted in their national societies. The potential returns from the national use of their resources still seemed greater than any foreseeable returns from transnationalization, which might actually dilute declining national union power. Differences between national economic structures, union organizational patterns, industrial relations systems, and "cultures" (including languages) provided further reasons for unions to "stay home." The nature and structures of European institutions were themselves obstacles. Their largely intergovernmental character made domestic pressure on national governments the best way to try to influence Europe. Moreover, the approach to European integration, especially since its renewal in the 1980s, centered upon transnational liberalization and deregulation and discouraged the relocation of regulatory activities from national to European level.

This makes the development of the European Trade Union Confederation (ETUC) in recent years a puzzle (Martin and Ross 1999). It has become more powerful than anyone had reason to expect. And it has become so without replicating time-honored national development courses. Much of the explanation lies in the ways in which particular European institutions—especially the European Commission—have tried to induce unions to invest more at the European level. Because national union movements in Europe were reluctant to allocate resources and to grant it significant opportunities to acquire capacities on its own, the ETUC had to seek its building materials elsewhere, from friendly, but self-interested, European institutional elites. In effect, *incentives from outside have reinforced the efforts of those from within European unions who advocated further Europeanization of union strategies*. The confluence of these incentives and Europeanizing union actors' efforts, in the larger context of post-1985 integration, has been enough to produce a significant degree of union Europeanization, as this essay will explain.

EUROPE'S ECONOMISM AND UNION TRANSNATIONALIZATION

The 1957 Rome EEC Treaty created a customs-free zone, common external tariff, and Common Agricultural Policy (CAP). The resulting "common market" was compatible with the national models of economic development that flowered in the postwar boom years (Crouch 1999: chap. 6). Member-states retained their industrial and macroeconomic policy autonomy. Social policy and industrial relations remained at the heart of national politics. The EU began with little authority in the areas that mattered to unions, therefore. Its originators hoped, however, that policy interdependence would promote "spillover," reinforced by deliberately built-in tension between the EU's original mandate and the institutions set up to implement it.[1]

Enthusiasm for integration in the "common market" period stagnated, but energy for renewed integration briefly reappeared in the 1970s after French President Charles de Gaulle, the major obstacle, had departed the scene. Social matters were part of this revival. The Commission established a "Social Partners" office in 1972, giving European-level labor and business organizations access to Commission deliberations on social and employment issues. The 1974 Social Action Program was partially implemented toward the "less favored"—migrant workers and their families, the handicapped, youth, and the poor. There were also directives on gender equality and on workers' rights in collective layoffs (plant closures), changes in firm ownership, and bankruptcies (with this last providing that affected workers be informed and consulted, the first enunciation of a recurrent EU theme). Regional differences received heightened recognition through the creation of the European Regional Development Fund (ERDF) in 1975, although resistance to interstate transfers kept its resources small. Most important was the workplace health and safety area, and much legally binding health and safety regulation was enacted during the 1970s. New activity was short-lived, however. Growing pains from the expansion from six to nine member-states after 1973 created chronic budgetary conflicts that paralyzed decision-making. By the later 1970s, the Social Action Program was a dead letter. More broadly, integration stalled in the worsening economic circumstances after the 1973 oil shock. EU member-states retreated to particular national solutions, creating divergent economic policies and disparity among EU economies.

It was not until the mid-1980s that changing intergovernmental politics made resuming integration possible. In January 1985 the European Commission proposed the "1992" program to complete the internal market. To facilitate its enactment, the Rome Treaty was revised by the Single European Act (ratified in 1987) to allow decisions by a "qualified majority" (QMV) on most single market issues. The SEA also enlarged EU competencies—the legal basis for action—into research and development, the environment, foreign policy cooperation, and "economic and social cohesion" (regional policy), and made it easier to act in certain existing areas by extending QMV (Moravcsik 1991, Cameron 1992). While preserving unanimity over most social and labor measures, the SEA did allow QMV on health and safety issues to keep national regulations from being used as barriers to competition.

Commission promotion of "social dialogue" between capital and labor at the European level was encouraged. Finally, the European Parliament got new "cooperation" (amending) powers that proved significant when the Parliament's Social Democrat-Christian Democrat majority became a major proponent of enlarging the EU's social policy role.

The Social Charter and the Maastricht Social Protocol

"Market building" continued to take precedence, however. The 1992 program was well underway, the EU's budgetary system reorganized, and EMU deliberations started before the Commission turned to serious "market correcting" through the 1989 Community Charter of Basic Social Rights for Workers. This "Social Charter" was only a "solemn commitment" on the part of member-states—eleven, given British rejection—to a set of "fundamental social rights" for workers that referred to the often weakly enforceable social wording already in EU treaties. An Action Program followed in November 1989 and by January 1993, forty-seven different proposals had been submitted to the Council.

The already hurried pace of integration intensified after the end of the Cold War, marked by the Maastricht Treaty on European Union. Maastricht's main effect was to initiate movement to Economic and Monetary Union (Eichengreen 1993, Dyson 1994). EMU committed Europe to a restrictive macroeconomic policy regime to prevent inflation. Although *less noticed,* however, Maastricht also included a "Social Protocol" that expanded the EU's social policy authority. It specified subjects on which eleven member-states agreed that action could be taken through the normal EU legislative process without the participation of the British, who opted out (signing on in 1997 after New Labour's election success). It extended QMV to "working conditions" and "information and consultation." Moreover, it made negotiated agreements possible as a binding substitute for legislation, a provision remarkable because it made bargaining between European-level union and employer organizations a formal part of European social policy formation. Action could also be taken on social security and the social protection of workers, protection of workers whose employment contract is terminated, and the "representation and collective defense of the interests of workers and employers," including codetermination, but only by unanimity (Falkner 1996).

The first Social Protocol proposal, in 1993, was on the "information and consultation of workers" in multinational corporations through the formation of European Works Councils (EWCs). The social partners could not agree, however, and a 1994 directive mandated EWCs in all multinationals above a certain size with a European presence. A new try in 1995, on parental leave, led to the "first European bargain." The Commission then reopened the "atypical work" issue, leading to agreement on pro-rated parity in treatment for part-time workers in 1997 and the regulation of short-term contracts soon thereafter. A "burden of proof" provision (a Social Charter proposal about workplace sexual harassment); European Company Law, including "information and consultation"; and the extension of information and consultation to all EU companies of more than fifty employees were other issues explored (Arcq 1994).

The very rapid change in opportunity for the ETUC, coming mainly from European institutions' new social policy capacities and the Commission's willingness to use them to provide resources, challenged the ETUC and its national union confederation constituents to reconfigure the ETUC's own role. How complicated these changes turned out to be is the subject to which we now turn.

THE TENTATIVE EUROPEANIZATION OF TRADE UNION STRUCTURE

Trade union Europeanization is a story of interactions between European institutions seeking to stimulate Euro-level interest representation, a small number of unionists who perceived Europe as important, and the growing significance of European integration itself. From the beginning, the architects of European integration tried to promote transnational interest representation. Jean Monnet's functionalist strategy saw the development of Euro-level interest representation around the Commission and other EU institutions as a royal road toward policy "spillover" and full-fledged European political culture. In the case of unions, however, receptivity depended on Europe being salient and on the existence of well-placed unionists who believed transnationalization was essential.

In the first, Common Market, period, Europe was an adjunct to national political economies in which national unions were central players. Employers responded initially to integration more rapidly than labor, forming the Union of Industrial and Employers' Confederations of Europe (UNICE) a year after the Rome Treaty. Although some unionists also saw a need for organization geared to the EU, ideological and organizational divisions delayed the establishment of the European Trade Union Confederation (ETUC) until 1973 (Dølvik 1997: chaps. 6–7; Gobin 1998). By then, with the customs union fully implemented, initial discussion of Economic and Monetary Union (EMU), prospective membership for the four EFTA states, and growing Europeanization of business, the case for a labor counterpart to UNICE had become stronger. The new ETUC included EFTA and EU unions and was open to Christian and communist unions, not just those within ICFTU. In addition, it gave limited representation to the European Industry Committees (renamed

Federations, EIFs, by the 1995 ETUC Congress)—regional sectoral organizations of workers that corresponded at the European level to national federations, linked in some cases to the ICFTU's International Trade Secretariats.

Operationally, the new ETUC was a secretariat and a small staff (about twenty). Membership dues yielded just over a half million U.S. dollars, barely enough to pay for a Brussels office. The ETUC's resource poverty was a clear reflection of national unions' limited expectations for it. Between 1973 and the "1992" project the ETUC was as preoccupied with organizational principles as with establishing itself in the European arena. There was an important initial phase of ideological enlargement when Christian unions were admitted in 1974 and the Italian communist-affiliated CGIL in 1976. Cold War tensions persisted, however, and further admission of communist-affiliated confederations was blocked by their national counterparts.[2] By 1983 the admission of unions from new EU members (plus some from outside it) had increased ETUC affiliates from a founding seventeen (covering 36 million members in sixteen countries), to thirty-four (about 41 million members in twenty countries). The number of participating EIFs had also risen from six to ten.

The ETUC's purpose was to "represent and advance the social, economic, and cultural interests of the workers on the European level in general and toward European institutions in particular." The policy positions it took were not much more specific because, according to one observer, "claims had to be acceptable to a maximum number of members" without impinging "too much [on] issues of national controversy," while remaining "sufficiently relevant and mobilizing to legitimate the existence of a European union structure" (Goetschy 1991, Visser and Ebbinghaus 1992). The Executive Committee (elected by a triennial Congress) could decide by two-thirds majorities (weighted by membership), but consensus became customary. Nothing at all could be decided without the agreement of the two largest confederations, the British TUC and German DGB, and they themselves differed fundamentally over European integration. The ETUC thus concentrated on broad issues that it could pronounce on but not affect, such as employment, reduction of working time, training, and information and consultation in multinationals. It made a few efforts to mobilize its affiliates' members, a rare instance being a demonstration against unemployment by 80,000 unionists at the 1983 Stuttgart European Council. Beyond that, affiliates did not allow it room for serious action.

The ETUC's early attempts at exerting influence were confined to the Brussels arena, largely dissociated from the union members it nominally represented. This was encouraged by the European Commission when it set up its "Social Partners" unit plus sectoral tripartite bodies. The ETUC, initially hopeful, withdrew from most of these in 1978 after concluding that neither employers nor governments were interested in serious commitments. By then, Euro-pessimism had set in. The momentum of "1992" led to new efforts by European institutions to promote Euro-unionism, however, which combined with a heightened union awareness of the need for effective European-level action began a revitalization of the ETUC. The Single European Act signaled increased receptivity to European problem solving by member-states and business. Unions took this as a threat to national regimes of labor rights and standards and began strident warnings about "social dumping." The prospect of a single transnational market also fed a new willingness among unions, increasingly on the defensive nationally, to look to transnational strategies. The SEA offered some new opportunities, albeit limited, for doing so and the Commission actively encouraged the unions to make the most of them.

"SOCIAL DIALOGUE"

The Commission first focused on "social dialogue." The SEA required the Commission to "develop the dialogue between management and labor at [the] European level, which could, if the two sides consider it desirable, lead to relations based on agreement." There were formidable obstacles, however, in the imbalance between the social partners. Neither the ETUC nor UNICE had mandates to negotiate binding agreements. For UNICE, which sought to avert European-level regulation and bargaining, this was an asset. The ETUC desired European-level regulation, but like UNICE, it was an organization of national confederations. In resource terms, although UNICE was small, it was backed by employers' firm-level power and technical, legal, linguistic, and financial knowledge.

The initial discussions about large matters such as new technologies and employment broke down quickly. They were relaunched in 1989 after the Social Charter, but again discussion was frustrating (Goetschy 1991). This time the Commission was more determined. Given the evident differences in the social partners' positions, it decided upon an asymmetrical approach that sought first to encourage ETUC and national union movements to become stronger European actors. Recognizing that resources from national unions alone were unlikely to suffice, the Commission added EU resources as necessary. A more effective ETUC might then lead UNICE to reconsider its naysaying posture. Moreover, a stronger ETUC, partly dependent upon Commission resources, could also be an ally for the Commission in broader political matters.

Jacques Delors thus took to the union Congress circuit, announcing the Social Charter first to the 1988 Stockholm ETUC gathering. His address to the British TUC's Bournemouth Conference later that year prodded a major and formerly anti-European constituent organization of the ETUC to new European commitments. The Commission president also went out of his way to engage important unionists privately. His staff and DG V (Employment and Social Affairs) systematically encouraged the ETUC, not least by supplying money for the ETUC's internal activities to the tune of several million ECU per year (1 ECU = $1.10, depending upon exchange rates). The commission provided support for ETUC meetings in Brussels and elsewhere, for supported travel and translation; funded the European Trade Union Institute (ETUI, the ETUC research arm) and an organ called AFETT (set up in 1986) to train unionists about new technologies; supported ETUC health and safety activity through the Trade Union Technical Bureau (TUTB—1989); and helped to found the European Trade Union College (ETUCO) to train unionists for European-level activity. Commission support also allowed the ETUC to hire new personnel and build a larger, more autonomous, organization.

The Commission pushed social dialogue less actively at the sectoral than at the peak level, but, with the Parliament, it supported EIF efforts to organize worker representatives in multinational corporations (MNCs), initially for meetings pending adoption of a 1991 proposal for a directive on EWCs. When it became clear that the EWC directive was stuck in Council, the Commission decided to fund further EIF efforts to prepare EWCs proactively, leading to a new budget line set up by the European Parliament in 1992, which provided more than four times what the EIF budgets were at the time. The money covered meeting costs, but it also enabled EIFs to hire additional staff and achieve a higher profile and legitimacy within the ETUC, with their own member unions, and with workplace activists.

Organizing for Europe

Serious efforts to rethink ETUC organizationally began at its 1988 Congress. Delegates urged that the ETUC be given "increased means to become a united and coherent force" for "a true social and contractual European policy," through "strengthened structures and increased membership, enhancing efficiency both in terms of finances and staff," and increased cooperation among an increased number of EIFs. The 1988 Congress authorized the preparation of reform proposals for the next Congress in 1991. Only the national confederations could push reform through, however, and the German DGB, representing the most powerful European labor movement and dissatisfied with the ETUC's responses to the Single Market, became the prime mover. Its motives were not wholly European; by strengthening the ETUC in which it would have a powerful voice, the German confederation could help guard against European sectoral corporatism.

The DGB found allies in the Italian confederations, and together they promoted a working group on ETUC organization whose report, adopted in 1990, recommended that the ETUC "become a genuine confederation with appropriate competencies and tasks," implying "the transfer of some competencies from national to the European level," including "setting priorities but also executing them," to "coordinate collective actions, build up international trade union countervailing power and organize solidarity through actions promoting common objectives" (ETUC 1990). The report proposed changes in policy-making structure and enhanced power for the ETUC leadership. It also urged an increased role for the EIFs, making the ETUC, until then an organization of national confederations, one consisting of crossnational sectoral bodies as well.

The 1991 Congress ratified these recommendations, prioritizing European union action and emphasizing that the ETUC was the right vehicle for it. The role envisioned for the ETUC included formulation and implementation of joint strategies in collective bargaining and the representation of joint interests in the EU legislative arena. The Congress also approved changes to shake up the ponderous policy process, engage leaders of national member organizations more actively (rather than just sending international department bureaucrats to meetings), and facilitate consensus building in preparation for Executive Committee decisions.[3] A new leadership was also selected. The EIFs became member organizations more nearly equivalent to national confederations, moving the ETUC closer to a transnational rather than interconfederal organization.

There was no consensus on any underlying transnational vision, however. The Italians and Belgians pushed it vigorously, but the Nordics and the TUC opposed abandoning established "intergovernmental" practices, while the DGB itself—so instrumental to the reforms—could not support transnationalization because of opposition from its member unions. Deciding which competencies would be transferred from national to the European level was left to the ETUC Executive Committee, where the diverse interests of national constituents would retard change. The ETUC thus remained dependent on member confederations. Moreover, financially strapped member organizations were in no position to enlarge ETUC resources, and the ETUC remained a small organization (a six-member secretariat backed by a staff of thirty) dependent on additional funds from European institutions.

THE ETUC AS A EUROPEAN PLAYER? THE 1990S

Prior to Maastricht interaction between European institutions and the ETUC, reformers had strengthened the union side of social dialogue but insufficiently to make employers negotiate. UNICE would only bargain under constraint, and the Commission sought ways to provide it. The threat posed by the possibility of EU legislation was one way. Beginning in late 1990 the Commission produced a small flood of Action Program legislation, all the while consulting regularly and exhaustively with the "social partners." The employers were perplexed: they could expect that although much of the legislation would not pass, some would, and UNICE disliked what it could anticipate. From UNICE's standpoint, however well designed EU legislation might be, it was bound to be more constraining than no legislation at all or, second best, a bargained agreement. Worse still, there was always the chance that legislative precedent would further embolden the Commission and even lead to a broadened treaty.

Coalition at the Confederal Level

The path took a new turn in the 1990s—again because of European institutions—when the Commission's "legislative threat" strategy bore fruit in the Maastricht negotiating process. The Commission tabled an ingenious suggestion early in the game, proposing new clauses to expand the EU's social policy competencies and scope for QMV, plus a provision that the "social partners" be given a short period to negotiate on subjects on which the Commission intended to propose legislation if nothing should result from their negotiations. With Council approval, negotiated agreement could then replace legislation. The Commission's paper was quickly buried by member-states in the spring of 1991, but on 31 October 1991, after assiduous Commission work, the "social partners" agreed to re-propose it in their name. No one—and in particular, UNICE—really expected it to pass at Maastricht, but, given an unexpected turn of events at the very last minute, when the eleven members decided to go ahead without Britain on the Social Protocol, pass it did. For the ETUC, the Social Protocol was a breakthrough beyond anything it could have expected, abruptly making it a participant in EU social policy formation—a role that it maintained throughout the decade of the 1990s.

The Social Protocol's significance depended on how it was used. The Commission chose to test it first in 1993 with the European Works Council Directive.[4] The social partners agreed to talk but could not reach agreement, and the proposal returned to the regular legislative process to become, in September 1994, arguably the single most important piece of European legislation to date from a trade union perspective. But failure to get EWC agreement from the "social partners" left the Social Protocol's utility to be demonstrated, however, and the Commission decided to try again in early 1995 with a proposal on parental leave. This time agreement was reached on a "first European bargain" in December 1995 and was given legal force with a Council Directive in June 1996. As a result of it, all European employees gained a right to three months' leave to take care of a child at birth, adoption, or any time up to the age of eight, plus a right to leave for "urgent family reasons" (to be specified by member-states).[5] The agreement made but modest progress over what already existed in member-states, and this was why it was proposed. The important thing for the Commission and the ETUC was to establish the precedent of negotiated legislation under the Social Protocol.[6]

The Commission then started procedure on two directives on "atypical work" (e.g., types of jobs other than full-time and permanent ones). The first was on "flexible working time and worker security" and aimed at guaranteeing workers in "new formulae of work" the same rights and treatment as workers with full-time permanent jobs. The Commission presented the issue as a tradeoff, granting to employers more flexible work and to unions the need to "organize" and regulate such work. The basic principle was "nondiscrimination" between full- and part-time or other atypical work. ETUC and UNICE agreed to this second "European collective bargain" in 1997 (EU Commission 1997). Another atypical work agreement on conditions for shorter-term work contracts was hammered out a year later. These atypical work agreements were important precedents toward a greater Europeanization of labor relations because they concerned a more controversial matter than parental leave. The deals give national unions incentives to organize part-time workers and, hence, to strengthen themselves in new, heavily feminized sectors of the workforce. Unions, by signing, recognized the legitimacy of employers' quest for flexibility in employment patterns, however, and the agreement made it possible for national-level "social partners" to lower national barriers to part-time employment.

The Social Protocol and its "negotiated legislation" was an extraordinary culmination of the process begun so inauspiciously in 1985. The social dialogue structure provided the Commission with a forum in which to launch its "negotiate or we will legislate" initiative. But before doing so, it had already enlisted the ETUC in what amounted to a coalition to push a refractory UNICE into accepting a role as bargainer at the European level—a move that UNICE had fiercely resisted until then. This was a sharp reminder that while issues concerning the relationships between trade union structure and strategy can be debated within unions, they are determined quite as much by states and other actors. For the Social Protocol, the Commission's initiatives were decisive in opening an opportunity for ETUC to become a negotiating body at the European level—an opportunity that the newly installed ETUC leadership was eager to exploit.

Stagnation at the Sectoral Level

The Commission has not made comparable efforts at coalition building and involvement of the unions as European negotiating bodies at the sectoral level. At that level, employer resistance is facilitated because most European sectoral business organizations are industry-wide, rather than generalized employer associations, a fact typically invoked to justify refusal to enter social dialogue. UNICE tries to reinforce this virtual monopoly of representation by confining social dialogue to European-level intersectoral organizations. Social dialogue has been established with Commission support in a few sectors, typically where there are special EU programs (restructuring plans for economically vulnerable sectors, for example, where the Single Market created transition problems, often obligated negotiated distribution of EU training and R&D funds). In general, employers accounting for about half of Europe's jobs, including the core engineering sector, have not entered even minimal European social dialogue.

Some sectoral union EIFs, for their part, have aimed at drawing employers into discussions over issues with potential for precedent-setting agreements. These typically arise when employers expect more success at influencing Commission action by approaching it (or other bodies) jointly with unions, especially if they have insufficient access on their own, either directly or via their governments. This excludes large multinational companies that can make their voices heard directly or through sectoral organizations they dominate. Getting money from the European Social Fund and the European Regional Development Funds is another inducement. EIFs have been particularly successful on health and safety issues, where incentives to engage in social dialogue are strong for firms that cannot or do not want to avoid stringent national health and safety standards. Here, moreover, the legitimacy of union claims to a European-level voice is widely conceded. The effectiveness with which EIFs can pursue this strategy depends heavily on Commission actions, however, which have not been forthcoming often enough to make real differences. In general, national sectoral unions themselves are not always enthusiastic about sectoral social dialogue, a fact that may account for a certain ETUC timidity in this area.

Stirrings at the Periphery: EWCs and Cross-Border Collective Bargaining

While the sectoral level of European negotiation remains stagnant, European Works Councils are significantly extending the structure of European unionism down to the company level. Over 1,200 companies are affected by the directive (ETUI 1998). If all set up EWCs with 30 members (the maximum under the initial directive unless otherwise agreed) and if unions are involved, 36,000 workplace activists could be drawn into transnational union work, creating the bases for transnational linkages among union bases within companies. The ETUC (with Commission and Parliamentary financial help) has been generating the intellectual and financial resources to help train EWC members (through ETUCO and TUTB), and EIFs are developing the capacity to support them. On rare occasions, as in the abrupt closing of the Renault plant in Vilvoorde, Belgium, transnational solidarity has been facilitated by Works' Council contacts (see chapter 9).[7]

Of potentially greater importance than the still-nascent EWCs are current efforts by national unions and confederations to develop cross-border coordination of wage bargaining. Most such efforts have been within the Deutsche-Mark zone, led by IG Metall and its counterparts in neighboring countries. At the initiative of its North-Rhine Westphalia region, wage-bargaining officials from IG Metall and its counterpart unions in Belgium, Luxembourg, and the Netherlands sat in on each others' steel industry negotiations in 1997, for example, and IG Metall has since tried to extend this practice to its other regions. Through the European Metalworkers Federation (EMF), it has begun urging its counterpart unions in other countries, and European unions generally, to agree on a common norm for wage increases based on productivity growth plus the European Central Bank's (ECB) target rate of inflation (Schulten 1998). A September 1998 meeting of confederations and sectoral unions from Germany and the Benelux countries in Doorn, Netherlands, urged that such a norm be implemented so as to avert "bidding down" and agreed on a procedure for informing and consulting each other about wage demands.[8] The logic of this incipient coordination within the D-Mark zone could be extended once it is replaced by the Euro-zone. Built up piecemeal by national confederations and/or sectoral unions to head off what IG Metall refers to as "ruinous wage competition," such coordination could become the most likely route to a Europeanization of collective bargaining. The EIFs could play a role, as could the ETUC (which welcomed the Doorn meeting), though without itself engaging in any collective bargaining. Nevertheless, the process is still at an embryonic stage, and the conflicting interests of the diverse national unions' structures remain formidable obstacles.

PROBLEMS AND PROSPECTS: THE EMERGENT STRUCTURE OF A EUROPEAN LABOR MOVEMENT

No longer a "head without a body," the ETUC has tried to draw national and local union officials into transnational activities. As we have argued, however, this has been largely a top-down process, driven by the interplay of actors in European institutions and the ETUC more than by national and local unionists convinced of the need for European-level action. As one observer suggested, it has been a story of "structure before action" (Turner 1996). As a result, there is a bias in the ETUC's structure; most development has been at the intersectoral level, where ETUC's leadership operates—and furthest from the shop floor where unions have their traditional epicenter. It has also been significant at the Multinational Corporation (MNC) level, where EWCs are being formed. The least development has occurred at the intermediate, or sectoral, level, where the EIFs—except insofar as they have been involved in EWCs—have yet to make important breakthroughs. Employer resistance here is virtually complete, while Commission efforts thus far to overcome it have been meager. Underlying this idiosyncratic pattern of development lie several significant strategic dilemmas.

BARGAINING: WHAT EURO-LEVEL ROLE FOR THE ETUC?

The ETUC has consistently articulated an expansive vision of its bargaining role. It aspires to negotiate binding agreements with employers at the peak of a multitiered European industrial relations system and be a player in European-level policy formation. But events have propelled the ETUC toward this role by a distinctive route. If national unions historically acquired their power and position by mobilizing members, the ETUC—which had not really constructed its new position from its own resources—was in a very different situation. What could it do? Where would it get its bargaining power? What would its constituents—all more deeply rooted in dense sociopolitical settings than the ETUC—allow it to do? What resources would they provide for that purpose? How would the ETUC's new bargaining role be decided?

The most enthusiastic Europeanizing unionists hoped that social dialogue would give rise to true European-level collective bargaining. As a "genuine confederation with appropriate competencies and tasks," the ETUC would negotiate binding "framework agreements" with its intersectoral employer counterparts to be implemented at national and local levels. It would also coordinate European-level sectoral bargaining strategies. The ETUC's constituents did not universally share this vision, however. The Social Protocol forced this issue to the top of the agenda, precipitating a long internal controversy.[9]

In 1992 the ETUC leadership staked out an ambitious claim to a bargaining role. German and Nordic participants, stung by the ETUC Secretariat's autonomous conduct of the 31 October 1991 negotiations that led to the Social Protocol, opposed the claim.[10] The Germans argued for a "bottom-up" approach: negotiating presupposed bargaining power, so that national unions had to be strengthened before national collective bargaining could be coordinated and an "independent European trade union counterforce" developed. Since collective bargaining is sectoral, this counterforce would have to be created at the sectoral level. Finally, collective bargaining had to be distinguished from negotiated legislation under the Social Protocol. A compromise was reached in March 1993 that affirmed ETUC's negotiating role but confined it to intersectoral negotiations under the Social Protocol, only when given specific mandates and subject to strict and continuous control by the national unions. These basic points were incorporated into the ETUC's constitution by the 1995 Congress, which left the Executive Committee to "establish the internal rules of procedure" for intersectoral negotiations.

Controversy continued during the second half of the 1990s; in the end, the Secretariat got clear confirmation of its role as bargainer, but only in the very special context of negotiated legislation under the Social Protocol. This had already been established in practice in the negotiations over EWCs and parental leave, during which close contact between the ETUC's general secretary and affiliates was maintained. The part-time work deals were concluded under the newly adopted rules, including approval by a qualified majority of the executive over some opposition. The ETUC's bargaining role was thus institutionalized, and its leadership in forging common positions was accepted (leading very recently to the establishment of a permanent ETUC collective bargaining committee). Getting to this point also intensified national affiliates' involvement in European activity. Social Protocol negotiations, by demonstrating that significant matters could be at stake, compelled national union leaders with real power—responsible for collective bargaining at the national level—to become personally engaged, even if only to avert the perceived threats of rapidly changing European market situations. On the other hand, the ETUC did not come much closer to its vision of a European industrial relations system. As long as employers negotiate only under the shadow of law—which can only be cast over the narrow range of subjects within the limits of the EU's treaty prerogatives—the potential of Social Protocol negotiations is limited. Even then, everything depends upon the initiative of the Commission, which is unlikely to propose much new legislation in the foreseeable future.

Are prospects better for sectoral social dialogue? The Commission's failure to do much to overcome employer resistance is an obstacle. The ETUC's own ambivalence also stands in the way, though it could concede the sharp distinction between negotiated legislation and collective bargaining and back the EIFs' efforts more consistently. But the bottom line lies elsewhere: what brings employers to the bargaining table is trade union capacity to disrupt and regulate production by mobilizing members to strike and securing their compliance with agreements. Only national unions have such capacity, however diminished and uneven it may have become. To the extent that they retain or can restore it, they could do much to build European cross-border bargaining if they became convinced of its importance. Since the EIFs are directly controlled by national unions, they are the *only* part of the existing European trade union structure through which national unions might be willing to organize cross-border coordination of bargaining and—if this induces employers to engage in cross-border coordination—perhaps even to conduct it.

To be sure, unions might instead try coordinating cross-border bargaining selectively on their own, as IG Metall is doing, but the EIFs provide a readily available and institutionalized vehicle. If the EIFs' authority and capabilities were to be increased, so, too, would be their weight in the ETUC, shifting its emphasis from intersectoral toward sectoral bargaining and perhaps reconfiguring the ETUC's internal structure, along with its conception of its role in an emerging European collective bargaining system, perhaps also feeding new awareness of the centrality of Europe to rank-and-file concerns. But the EIFs could only move toward collective bargaining if their member unions authorized and backed them and—at this writing—national unions still seem unconvinced of the need for such a counterforce.

Perplexing Futures for the European Works' Councils

What would convince unions to use EIFs in cross-border collective bargaining strategies? One possibility lies in the situation that EWCs could create. The EWC directive left employers leeway to bypass unions in operating EWCs, perhaps integrating them into unilateral mechanisms for "direct communication" or "employee participation." Excluding unions is difficult if at least some subsidiaries are unionized, however. But whatever the union involvement, employers can minimize the use of EWCs, resisting anything more than the minimum requirements of one meeting a year, to "inform and consult" the workers in a mere "exchange of views." In most existing agreements, "managements . . . have successfully demarcated information and consultation from collective bargaining," as they are by law in countries like France and Germany (Hall et al. 1995: 44). Only a handful of agreements have provisions for consultation that are more meaningful, at least on paper. And in only one case, Danone, has an EWC gone beyond consultation to negotiation. A dynamic eventually leading to European-level company bargaining cannot be excluded, however, from among the multiple possible consequences of EWCs. EWC meetings facilitate cross-border communication among employee members, supported by cross-border networks that would otherwise not exist, allowing for an exchange of information beyond what management provides, enabling unions to verify local management claims, compare situations, and formulate demands. Beyond that, information can be fed back into national and local collective bargaining, calling bluffs, bolstering demands, and putting new issues on the agenda.

Central MNC managements could combat potential whipsawing by harmonizing contested conditions unilaterally and requiring subsidiaries to resist precedent-setting changes. Unions might in turn conclude that to make gains, they have to negotiate at the European level and so the pressure for a bargaining dimension at the European company level will intensify. Because integration of production across borders increases unions' bargaining power by enhancing their ability to disrupt production, the pressure could be difficult to resist. But company vulnerability could be minimized by keeping components or stages of production outside unions' strategic domain (via outsourcing techniques of one kind or another). Moreover, central management could undermine coordination among subsidiary workforces by making them compete for new investments. Accurate information through EWCs can make such "investment bargaining" more, rather than less, effective if it bolsters the credibility of threats to relocate investment and jobs.

The path that EWCs open toward real bargaining may be narrow, therefore. It is at least conceivable, however, that MNC managements could initiate bargaining and turn it to their own ends even if unions do not have the bargaining power to force them into it. "Framework agreements" with EWCs could even accelerate "the spread of best-practice methods, . . . with positive effects for both sides: better cost and productivity performance in subsidiaries as well as an improvement of working conditions through the entire Euro-company." Where such mutual gains are possible, cross-border "productivity coalitions" might emerge through EWCs, which could then become the means for company-specific Europe-wide regulation of industrial relations, strengthening the company's European corporate identity in the process. Unions, rather than employers, would then have reason to be wary of turning EWCs into collective bargaining bodies (Busch 1996). Were EWCs to foster cross-border identification with MNCs, their employees might readily support the decentralization of collective bargaining to a subsidiary level at the expense of multi-employer bargaining by national unions, reinforcing decentralizing trends in national industrial relations systems, further undermining national unions' ability to create national solidarity. In this scenario, EWCs could become the basis not for European collective bargaining, but for a transnational brand of micro-corporatism that would erode national regulation of employment relations.

It might only be possible for national unions to avert this danger by joining forces to reestablish regulation on a European basis, building structures for transnational labor representation at the cross-company level to link representatives in different EWCs with one another as well as with those in other companies, and to decide common norms for company-level practices and strategies for enforcing them. The EIFs, again, are the only available instruments for doing so, with links to EWCs by virtue of their role in establishing and assisting them. But they are still a long way from being effective instruments for regulating employment relations on a cross-border, cross-company basis. That could require authorizing the EIFs to negotiate binding cross-border multi-employer agreements or at least coordinate cross-border negotiations with individual employers by member unions in different countries and supporting such negotiations with cross-border industrial action. Few member unions are ready to cross that threshold from national to transnational bargaining strategy. The threat of transnational micro-corporatism could convince them that the risks of not "pooling their sovereignty" in European structures are greater than those of doing so. But this threat is still distant.

EMU and the Euro-Bargaining Imperative?

The coming of the single currency profoundly alters the context of collective bargaining. Governments will no longer be able to use changes in currency rates to offset the adverse employment effects of "asymmetric shocks" and other processes impairing the relative competitiveness of regions and sectors. These effects might be limited by "automatic stabilizers" or funds deliberately provided to adversely affected regions. Extensive EU fiscal federalism is quite unlikely, however, given the relatively small size of the EU budget (presently little more than 1 percent of Community GDP).[11] With little intra-EU labor mobility, adjustment will be concentrated almost entirely on labor costs, including the "social wage." If a deterioration in relative (unit) costs cannot be reversed by productivity improvements, unions in affected areas will be pressed to accept nominal wage reductions or low increases and cuts in nonwage costs, eroding bargained or statutory social benefits. This may happen even without shocks, insofar as employers (and governments) seek price advantages that are no longer attainable by currency depreciation through wage and benefit cuts. Given variations, regions with stronger unions could lose competitiveness to regions with weaker unions, increasing pressure on the stronger unions to accept cuts. Unions everywhere might thereby be drawn into a deflationary vicious circle of labor cost dumping that could cumulatively lower aggregate EU income, demand, and employment.

The dangers are great. National or sectoral trade unions that are able to dampen wage competition within labor markets separated by national currencies become regional unions in competition with one another in an emerging single European labor market. Common ground will be hard to find because such competition would be the only available mechanism with which to protect jobs. Creating a currency area too large for an effective wage cartel could thus produce a decentralized European wage bargaining structure with some strong unions but no coordination. The dangers are amplified by EMU's restrictive macroeconomic policy regime. With unemployment at near–Great Depression levels and governments locked into policies that may worsen it, unions are under enormous pressure to save jobs wherever they can, straining solidarities nationally, sectorally, and even within individual companies. Under these circumstances, the prospects for constructing common cross-border cross-company collective bargaining strategies, not to speak of mobilizing the bargaining power to implement them effectively, seem extremely slim (even if IG Metall and other unions have begun talking about doing it on a limited scale). The unions' responses to EMU may well be to try to shore up national collective bargaining structures rather than intensify the development of European-level structures (Rhodes 1997, Fajertag and Pochet, eds., 1997, Martin 1999).

The Political Arena

The ETUC has shared with EU leaders the faith that political integration could be achieved through successive installments of economic integration. But the gaps between such hopes for spillover and what has happened since the mid-1980s have underlined the dilemmas of relying on economic approaches to achieve political spillover. Far from being automatic consequences of economic integration, political and social union have depended on decisions made in arenas where the ETUC and its members have had little influence.

The ETUC has not been shy about criticizing and proposing. It welcomed the 1985 White Paper for its promises of growth and employment but opposed its "one-sided approach," which posed "serious dangers for workers" by failing to take into account "social realities and necessities." It then called repeatedly for measures to promote upward convergence of social and labor standards, as elaborated in its 1988 European Social Programme. To avert social dumping, the ETUC argued, rights had to be guaranteed at the European level both through legislation and negotiation. Legislation was needed to establish "fundamental social rights" to organize, bargain collectively, and strike; to social protection, health, and safety at the workplace; and to equal treatment regardless of gender. Needed as well were new standards such as the right to information or participation in the introduction and application of new technologies, cross-border representation structures in European multinational companies, a "framework for European industrial relations," and rights to training, recognition of credentials, and educational as well as parental leave. All rights should also be enforceable in the courts, with the possibility of appeal to the European Court of Justice," just as are the rights of those engaged in cross-border trade and investment." The Commission would then have to propose legislation to assure the specific rights.[12]

The ETUC's quest produced decidedly mixed results. The Social Charter was a solemn commitment rather than an enforceable set of rights. Since Action Program legislation was confined within the boundaries of EU legislative authority set by the treaty, there could be none assuring collective bargaining and social protection rights, while Maastricht explicitly excluded collective bargaining. The ETUC got better results on workplace health and safety, in part because it could participate in broader coalitions since there was support among economic actors and governments, particularly those with higher standards, for preventing regime competition in health and safety.

The ETUC did make a breakthrough in the 31 October 1991 Agreement that led to the Maastricht Social Protocol. Penetrating the theretofore exclusively intergovernmental arena of EU treaty-making, the ETUC succeeded in becoming a participant in policy formation, if only in the narrowly circumscribed area of EU social policy competence. In turn, this made possible the EWC directive plus the parental leave and atypical work agreements. The ETUC achieved these modest successes, once again, as part of coalitions, often led by the Commission, supporting policies that had substantial member-state support. But in the post-Delors period, the political constellations favorable to social policy advances of this kind largely disappeared. EMU's macroeconomic policy constraints then squeezed social policy between unemployment and the convergence/stability pact criteria. EMU limits policies against unemployment to supply-side "structural reforms" that supposedly increase the employment intensity of growth by increasing the labor market flexibility. This, in turn, will allegedly reduce the "reservation wage" by decreasing social benefit replacement rates, lower labor costs, especially of the less skilled, all at the cost of more inequality and reduced employment security. EU social policy itself has changed in response to this supply-side conception of employment policy (EU Commission 1994: 199).

Despite judging the design of EMU as fundamentally flawed, the ETUC continued to back it, arguing that it was needed politically to keep integration going. Accordingly, the ETUC's position has been not to reject EMU but to remedy its flaws. It called for EMU to start on schedule in 1999 to avert instability, for example. To realize EMU's potential contribution to recovery, however, governments had to abandon their "mechanical" application of the convergence criteria, especially for budget deficits, and adapt them to the changed economic conditions of the mid-1990s. The ETUC also reiterated its call to redress the imbalance between price stability and other goals built into EMU. Thus, in the context of the Amsterdam Treaty and its sequels, the ETUC agitated to make employment and growth explicit objectives, to establish institutions to achieve such objectives, and to provide a role for the social partners.[13]

In general, when the ETUC was able to break into EU-level political arenas on social policy, it was as part of coalitions with the Commission and some member-state governments. In the high politics of monetary union, however, there has been no coalition in which the ETUC could join to deflect EMU from the path it has criticized so consistently. The ETUC's criticisms and proposals thus had no discernible effect on EMU's design and the process of transition to it. This was largely because EMU was shaped in political arenas where labor was not present. Central bankers and finance ministers dominated all key venues—the Delors Committee, the EMS Monetary Committee, and ECOFIN (the Council of Economics and Finance Ministers). Along with the European Council, they have operated behind closed doors, insulated from direct political pressures. However EMU unfolds in the new political context, the position of critical support for EMU by the ETUC and its constituents has so far put them in an excruciating bind, tying them to a version of an economic approach to political integration that has brought high social costs and rising popular disenchantment, including among union members.[14] It is difficult for the ETUC and its constituents to express this disenchantment without seeming to abandon support for European integration, whose fate is linked to EMU. Commitment to the economic approach to integration thus confronts the European labor movement with a daunting strategic dilemma. Contrary to the functionalist hopes the ETUC has shared with many of Europe's builders, social and political union does not automatically follow from economic integration. Explicit political choices intervene. So far, the ETUC and its affiliates have had limited impact on those choices.

CONCLUSIONS

There has been more union transnationalization in European labor than one might have expected. The pattern of it is ambiguous, however. The ETUC was strengthened and reconfigured in response to market integration and the growing role of European legislation in regulating it. The results for European workers have been significant but far from sufficient to confront the deep changes that European integration has brought. The Maastricht Social Protocol spawned sporadic "negotiated legislation" dependent on Commission initiatives. Though this was symbolically important, it was not real collective bargaining and is unlikely to become so.

More disturbing was the very weak development of European collective bargaining at the sectoral and company levels, where initiatives by European institutions had not helped much. The ambiguous potential of European Works Councils may hinge more on building new trade union strategic capacity between company and intersectoral levels than on help from the EU. Building such capacity is up to the unions themselves. The degree of trade union Europeanization that has occurred thus seems seriously flawed: the structure is strongest at the top—where it is most easily influenced by the priorities of European institutions—and weakest where it needs to be strongest if there is to be real European collective bargaining.

Organizations, movements, and industrial relations systems are shaped by the interactions between strategic actors at historic junctures. Interactions between national European union movements, "Europeanizing" elements in them, and European institutions played the central roles in shaping the ETUC's structure, goals, and strategies. The process thus far is profoundly different from that which led to the formation of strong national unions in the late nineteenth and early twentieth centuries, when national unions developed in industrialization constructed their resource bases against the grain of elites through hard-nosed rank-and-file mobilization supported by appeals to ideological solidarity. The context of the ETUC's development, in particular the fact that it had to create itself in a setting where national union movements were deeply rooted in national political economies, has made it virtually impossible to pursue such a rank-and-file strategy. National union movements were reluctant to give the ETUC the resources and capacities to grow, thus it had to seek its building materials elsewhere. It did so, by and large, by accepting help from European institutional elites that were well-disposed toward labor but that also had their own political agendas. The most significant by-product of these interactions may have been the ETUC's commitment to a general vision of European integration close to the one held by the Commission and other key institutional players.

Identifying the tradeoffs built into this commitment has been central to our argument. The ETUC, prior to the "1992" period, was a small and weak Brussels lobby.

ETUC insiders, committed but critical "Europeans" to begin with, understood that accepting the resources offered by the Commission was one way to generate the prominence and strength that they needed to promote their urgent messages about the importance of transnational organization and action. They could then rely for additional support on their more "European" contacts in different national labor movements. In return for these resources, however, the ETUC was drawn into a coalition to advance the initiatives of those supplying them. In this exchange there was an implicit promise that the Commission's particular European strategies would lead to a real expansion in European social regulation and the foundation of a European industrial relations system. But the Commission was unable to produce anywhere near as much as it had promised. The result was that European trade unionism found itself restructured along lines that were only partly its doing and not always clearly to its advantage.

How could a transnational industrial relations system develop in Europe and what would one look like if it did? National industrial relations systems took a much longer time to take shape than the brief period we have surveyed. If the development of such national systems is a precedent, we must be careful to avoid premature conclusions. It may turn out that the trajectories begun so tentatively by the ETUC and its constituents will lead to something resembling a real European-level industrial relations system with capacities to protect and sustain workers' interests in the new global economy, even if this seems wildly optimistic now. A pessimistic outlook may be more realistic. What we can say is that, to this point, the development of the ETUC as a "movement" has not really followed the historic lines of most national labor movements. Instead it has developed largely by borrowing resources from European institutions at the summit of the European experiment to gain legitimacy with its own national constituents and by using the openings provided by these European institutions to try to elicit changes in the behavior of its opponents in management. The ETUC, in other words, has developed from the top down rather than as a mass organization built from below. EMU and the changes that it will engender offer different opportunities and new threats.

NOTES

1. The social provisions of the Rome Treaty were limited, excluding employment and remuneration issues except for equal pay for men and women (Article 119). The treaty prescribed free mobility of labor, paralleling free movement of goods and capital; this led to rules governing workers' rights to move across EU territory, residence and equal treatment in hiring and firing, remuneration, and other conditions for member-state nationals working outside their own country. National social security program differences aimed at securing competitive advantage were barred, leading to the first social legislation (in 1958) and Court of Justice litigation. The major "social" clause, Article 118, called for "improved working conditions and an improved standard of living for the workers" without establishing instruments for doing so beyond the "functioning of the common market." The Commission was empowered only to "cooperate" with member-states. Broad matters of "social citizenship" remained the responsibility of individual states, and the Common Market coexisted with as wide a variety of social policy and industrial relations regimes as it had members.

2. The Spanish Workers' Commissions were only admitted in the late 1980s, the Portuguese Intersyndical in the mid-1990s, while the French Confédération Génerale du Travail (CGT) remained outside until 1999.

3. A Steering Committee was established, composed of the president, general secretary, two deputy secretaries, and fifteen members chosen by and from the Executive Committee, that was to meet eight times a year to frame issues to be decided by the Executive Committee. The president and general secretary became full voting members of the Executive Committee, meeting quarterly. All member organizations would continue to be represented in the Committee, which would remain the authoritative policy-making body between Congresses.

4. The "information and consultation of workers" proposal had a long EC/EU history, stretching back to the failed 1980 Vredeling Directive. The Action Program proposed a similar directive. Council inaction on it prompted the attempt under the Social Protocol. Negotiations over EWCs offered prospects for success in achieving something of considerable symbolic value. By 1993 there was accumulated experience with works councils, the labor movement wanted them, and employers had learned that they were not very threatening.

5. The right is individual and nontransferable (to assure equal treatment of men and women). It also protects the right's users against discrimination, entitling them to the same or an equivalent job and acquired rights, while permitting some variation in compliance under special circumstances. Income during leave is left to member-states and social partners.

6. It added the right in only three countries, while adding to gender equity in more countries by making the right individual and distinguishing parental from maternity leave.

7. The European trade union bodies at intersectoral, sectoral, and company levels described so far are the main components of the transnational structure resulting from the interplay of European institutions and trade unionists. That interplay has spawned additional cross-border union linkages, but they can only be mentioned briefly. In regions where there are local cross-border labor markets, the ETUC has set up Interregional Trade Union Committees (ITUCs). There were twenty-eight ITUCs by the end of 1995, but significant activity in only a few, mostly concerning problems of cross-border workers due to differences in national labor law and social security and also economic development with EU regional funds. Of greater long-term significance is the ETUC's integration of unions in the Central and East European countries (CEECs) of the former Soviet bloc. This began with a framework for contacts, the ETUC Forum for Cooperation and Integration, and observer status for CEEC unions at the 1991 Congress. Since then, nine confederations from six CEECs have been admitted to full membership, and four additional confederations became observers. As in the past, the ETUC embraces unions from countries beyond current EU boundaries, particularly those likely to enter the EU in the future, which are effectively part of the European economy. From the ETUC's standpoint, the "development of autonomous industrial relations at the level of the 'European model' in Eastern Europe" is vital to the common interests of workers throughout Europe.

8. The meeting was the second of its kind, resulting from an initiative by the Belgian confederations in 1996.

9. The following account is based primarily on interviews and correspondence with participants in the deliberations. This material was gathered by the authors and by Jon Erik Dølvik, who generously shared his information. Dølvik 1997, chapter 9.

10. Skeptical even about this, the DGB was willing to allow the ETUC to proceed under case-by-case mandates. The Nordics, rejecting negotiated European labor market regulation altogether, insisted upon ordinary legislation, while most Latin participants and the TUC supported negotiations by the ETUC. This division corresponded roughly to strong and weak national unions, with weak unions looking to European regulation to compensate for their lack of power.

11. While central governments in the United States and Canada account for at least half of general government expenditures, the EU budget accounts for only 2 percent of such expenditures in the Community.

12. "European Social Programme," and "Community Charter of Fundamental Social Rights," adopted by the Executive Committee, December 1988.

13. The ETUC called upon the Intergovernmental Conference to revise the treaty by including a new employment chapter, establishing an Employment Committee "with the same standing as the existing Monetary Committee" and requiring both committees to consult the social partners (ETUC 1996c). See also Coldrick 1996.

14. "ETUC supports EMU, but—and this is becoming a big but—a growing number of our members don't." P. Coldrick, The European Employment Pact and EMU, speech, Rome, 16 May 1996.

4

Framing Contention: Dutch and Spanish Farmers Confront the EU

Bert Klandermans, Marga de Weerd, José Manuel Sabucedo, and Mauro Rodriguez

April 2, 1995, thousands of farmers flock through the ancient streets of Santiago de Compostela, the provincial capital of Galicia, Spain's most northern province. They are protesting at the doorsteps of the provincial government. They demand that the provincial and national governments raise the milk quota given to Galician farmers and urge that the government rather than the farmers pay the fines for overproduction of milk.

In that same period Dutch farmers are dumping dung at the doorsteps of the Ministry of Agriculture in The Hague. Later that year they occupy a provincial magistrate where the so-called "manure-rights" are registered. Both protests aim at the government's manure regulation, which in effect forces farmers to reduce their stocks or to invest in alternative ways of manure processing.

Here are completely different protests in two parts of Europe that apparently have nothing to do with each other. Yet they do have an important element in common. Farmers in both countries protest against their provincial or national government because they disagree with a measure taken by the European Union. To be sure, it is the national or provincial government that implements the regulation, but it is decided upon by the European Union. In fact, national governments have no choice but to implement the regulations.

Supranational entities such as the European Union create additional layers of policy-making above and beyond the nation-state. Within these supranational entities states, national and international political organizations, and citizens interact to define policy. Sidney Tarrow (1998a) coined the term *composite polities* for such multilayered political structures. A composite polity, according to Tarrow, is "a system of shared sovereignty, partial and uncertain policy autonomy between levels of governance, and patterns of contention combining territorial with substantive issues" (p. 1). Unlike what is sometimes suggested, such composite polities are neither new nor uniquely interstatal. Indeed, Tarrow borrowed the concept from Wayne te Brake, who used it to describe European politics in the sixteenth through eighteenth centuries. And, as far as interstatehood is concerned, different levels of governance exist not only between supranational entities and states, but also between national and regional governments, between city councils and provincial authorities, and so on.

The concept of composite polity is extremely useful in helping us to understand the dynamics of protest within multilayered political structures. In his *The Social Psychology of Protest* (1997: 190ff), Klandermans has argued that multilayered political structures imply both constraints and opportunities for social movements. Building on te Brake's work, Tarrow (1998b) developed a model of contentious politics in composite polities, which shows how complicated contention in these polities might be. The model illustrates that even the simplest structure of two "lower" authorities and one "higher" authority already generates complicated interactions. Policy-making, contention, and control can serve as three domains to illustrate the point. As far as policy-making is concerned, it is not uncommon for policy to be defined at the higher level but to be implemented and enforced at the lower one. Thus, the affected citizens must solve the problem of which authority is to be held responsible and where to go to protest a rule: to the lower authority that is enforcing the rule or to the higher authority that invented it? (see Klandermans and de Weerd 1998). As far as contentious politics is concerned, the two lower authorities may fight each other and attempt to mobilize their subordinates. Or, lower authorities may be both in conflict with the higher authority and trying to build an alliance while mobilizing their subordinates. Citizens may be in conflict with a lower authority while trying to win the support of the higher authority. A lower authority that has a conflict with its citizens may try to get the backing of the higher one. Citizens may be in conflict with the higher authority and try to forge alliances with lower authorities or expect that lower authorities will defend their interests vis-à-vis the higher authority. Finally, as far as policing and the control of contention are concerned, the most common arrangement in Western democracies is that lower authorities are responsible for law and order. But, higher authority may interfere because the lower authority fails or refuses to do so. Or, the higher authority may interfere on behalf of one of the parties in the conflict, usually on behalf of the authorities, but occasionally on behalf of the citizens (McAdam 1982).

In short, then, contention and protest in composite polities are complicated matters. As discussed in the introductory chapter, the European Union is a typical example of a composite polity. With the ongoing European integration a growing number of issues within the European Union are dealt with at the supranational level. That has raised the question of whether this development is paralleled by the development of transnational protest movements. The scarce systematic empirical work suggests that protest against the policy directives of the European Union has expanded but that most of it aims at the national rather than the supranational level. As Imig and Tarrow observe in chapter 2, the source of the protest may be supranational, but the target remains national most of the time. Bush and Simi (in chapter) arrive at a similar conclusion in a study that concentrates on farmers' protest between 1992 and 1997. To complicate matters even further, Bush and Simi also show that farmers are far more likely to engage in protests *against each other,* rather than coordinate protests across national boundaries. This finding adds yet another complexity to composite polities. Indeed, citizens of two communities may compete and fight each other either directly or by claims on their governments to take their side and defend their interests (see Tarrow 1999a, Imig and Tarrow 1998). The question is, why? Why is it that farmers' protests aim at national authorities or farmers in other European countries rather than the European Union, even if those protests originate in EU politics? That is the question we will try to answer in this chapter.

Within the European Union, agricultural policy is one of the domains where much of the actual ruling takes place at the European level. Farmers are confronted with composite politics par excellence—the European Union's Common Agricultural Policy. Therefore, farmers' protest as a typical example of contention in a composite polity must deal with all the complexities that have been discussed so far. In figure 4.1 we have tried to schematize the context of farmers' protest. Individual European countries such as Spain and the Netherlands are negotiating with the EU on behalf of their farmers. In doing so, the two countries may be allies or competitors. On the other hand, national governments are supposed to implement the rulings of the EU on their territories, whether they like it or not and whether their farming communities like it or not. The farmers, for their part, may try to influence the European Union directly through lobbyists or protests in Brussels, or they may use the same means at home to make their national governments act on their behalf. Like their governments they may compete or ally with opposite numbers in other countries of the European Community.

In this chapter we will take the perspective of the citizen in a composite polity or, more specifically, that of the farmer confronted with the EU's common agricultural policy. By interviewing farmers in the Netherlands and Spain, we try to get some insight into how farmers perceive the political structures they have to deal with. The question we will try to answer is: Why do farmers so seldom take the EU itself as the target of their protests? We are

Figure 4.1 Contentious politics and the European Union's agricultural policy

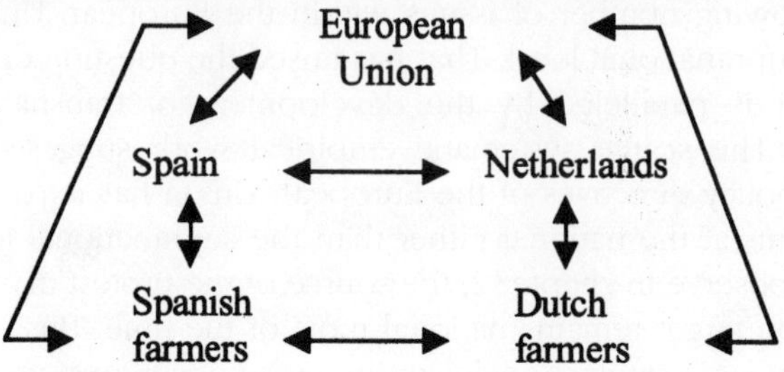

looking for an answer in two different directions. The first set of questions is about how farmers *frame* their political environments. Framing refers to the process of defining one's situation. In the social movement literature the framing concept refers more specifically to the process of acquiring a collective action frame (Snow et al. 1986, Gamson 1992, and see Klandermans 1997 and Tarrow 1998b for synthetic treatments of the concept). Collective action frames are sets of beliefs that legitimate collective action. A collective action frame defines inter alia grievances, responsible actors, and possible strategies to redress grievances. Relying on the collective action frame concept, we have posed the following questions: How do farmers perceive national and European agricultural politics? What do they know about both? Do they hold the national government or the European Union responsible for the state of the farming industry? Do farmers trust the national government to do a good job in representing their interests at the European level?

Our second set of questions concerns another possible reason why farmers' protest doesn't transnationalize, that is, a possible lack of *transnational solidarity*. To what extent have farmers in Europe developed a collective identity? Collective identity is one of the elements of a collective action frame. It defines a group or category of people who feel that they share a common fate (Melucci 1996, Taylor and Whittier 1992, Kelly and Breinlinger 1996). Social movement literature has hypothesized that collective identity is a requirement for collective action to take place.

The answers we will give to these questions are based on a longitudinal study we conducted between winter 1993/1994 and autumn 1995 in the Netherlands and Galicia, the most northwestern province of Spain. Galicia and the Netherlands are opposites in many ways. Spain entered the European Union many years after the Netherlands, which was one of the founding members of the original EEC. As a consequence, the Spanish people are less familiar with the EU than the Dutch people, for whom the European Community has been part of everyday political life since the 1950s. The first decades saw Dutch farming at the receiving end; for the farmers in the Netherlands the Common Agricultural Policy has been a profitable matter for many years. When Spain entered the Community, agricultural policy was already geared toward controlling all kinds of surpluses and downsizing agricultural subsidies. Farming in Galicia to a large extent consists of small farms that have yet to modernize. It is precisely these small farms that have an uncertain future under European governance, because the official policy is one that aims at modernization and upscaling. On top of that, Spanish politics have been scandal-ridden during the past years, generating a level of political cynicism unknown in the Netherlands. In terms of our questions regarding the framing of the political environment and the development of transnational solidarity, we may therefore expect farmers in Galicia to differ considerably from their Dutch colleagues. As Spain entered the EU much later than the Netherlands, Galician farmers might be less familiar with the ins and outs of the EU as a political structure. Also, in all likelihood they have developed a European identity to a lesser extent than Dutch farmers. Moreover, because Spain entered when the European agricultural policy already had become more restrictive, we may expect Galician farmers to be more skeptical about the EU than Dutch farmers. At the same time, we expect less trust in the national government among Galician farmers than among Dutch farmers.

METHODS

Design. The research reported here is part of a larger study on farmers' protest. We interviewed a sample of 167 Dutch farmers and 295 Galician farmers three times, namely in the winter of 1993/1994, winter 1995 (1995/1), and fall 1995 (1995/2). Galician and Dutch farmers have to deal with the same agricultural measures from the EU but in different national political contexts with different historical backgrounds. In a way, our study can be conceived as a natural experiment, as a paired comparison of unlike cases, trying to study in a comparative way the impact of European policy in two different areas. We have chosen the Netherlands and Galicia because they are similar as far as agricultural products are concerned but opposites as far as agricultural development is concerned. In both countries the same kind of farmers were involved, mainly from dairy, arable, and mixed farms, but on modern and large-scale enterprises in the Netherlands and old-fashioned and small-scale farms in Galicia. Trained interviewers at the respondents' homes conducted face-to-face, computer-assisted interviews. The interviews lasted on average three quarters of an hour.

Subjects. The subjects interviewed resulted from samples drawn from selected farming communities. The criteria used to select communities were: (1) a large enough population of farmers, and (2) an average size of farms in the community similar to the national average (Netherlands) or the provincial average (Galicia). Farmers from the selected communities were asked for their cooperation.

The mean age of the respondents in the two samples was approximately the same: forty-six years in the Netherlands and forty-nine in Galicia. Level of education and size of farm illustrate the opposite character of the two areas. In the Netherlands the vast majority of the respondents (70 percent) had completed secondary or higher agricultural education, whereas most farmers had average- to large-size farms (70.7 percent). In Galicia we found the opposite: 90 percent of our respondents had only a primary education, whereas 77 percent had small farms.

Measures. Three groups of the variables included are relevant for our discussion. (1) *Framing the political environment* as a concept was broken down into several separate measures meant to assess people's opinion about the European Union and their national government. *Knowledge:* in each interview we included a set of questions on some basic facts about national and European agricultural politics in order to assess our respondents' knowledge of such politics. *Responsibility for the state of farming:* we asked who in the eyes of the respondents is responsible for the state of the farming industry. The answers to the open question were coded. For our discussion three codes are relevant: "don't know," "the national government," or "the European Union." We also added a structured questionnaire. It asked respondents to indicate on a ten-point scale to what extent specific factors or actors were responsible for the state of farming. Three actors are relevant for our discussion: the national government, the Ministry of Agriculture, and the European Union. *Assessing the European Union:* in the third interview we included a set of evaluative questions about the European Union and the role of the national government in the Union. Factor analysis revealed three evaluative dimensions: the significance of the EU to farmers, the representation of farmers' interests in the EU by their national governments, and the influence of the national government on EU policy. Based on the factor analysis and on scale analyses, three scales were constructed: *evaluation* (Cronbach's alpha: .71), *representation* (Cronbach's alpha: .71), and *perceived influence* (Cronbach's alpha: .60). *Trust in government:* from the second interview onward, we included a set of questions about trust in government. Factor analyses and scale analyses produced a single dimension (Cronbach's alpha: .69 and .73 in the second and third interview, respectively). In addition to these variables, four more political variables were included: (a) *Powerlessness*—a scale based on four questions taken from the powerlessness-scale developed by Neal and Groat (1974) (Cronbach's alpha: .70, .64, and .72 for the three interviews, respectively. (b) *Political identification*—we used the classic "left-right self placement" as a measure of identification with the Left or the Right. (c) *Interest in politics*—people were asked whether they were interested in politics and whether they talked regularly about politics. The answers to the two questions were highly correlated (.74, .72, and .76 in the three interviews) and were combined into a single measure. (d) *Talking about agricultural politics*—we asked our respondents whether they talked about agricultural politics with members of their family, other farmers, or other people in general. The three answers were highly correlated and were combined into scales (Cronbach's alpha: .85, .89, and .89 for the three interviews).

(2) *Identity* was assessed by asking our respondents to what extent they identified (1 = not at all, 4 = very much) with farmers at each of three levels of inclusion: regional, national, or supranational (European).

(3) *Action preparedness and action participation.* We assessed the subjects' preparedness to take part in four forms of collective action that were part of the action repertoire of farmers in those days—demonstrations, blockades, symbolic actions (such as dumping dung on the doorsteps of the Ministry of Agriculture), and refusal to pay taxes. For each of these action forms, we asked whether respondents would participate if they were to disagree completely with an agricultural measure or with agricultural policy in general. The answers to these questions were taken together into a scale of *action preparedness*. Cronbach's alpha of the scale at the three points in time was satisfactory: .75, .74, and .75. During the first interview, we asked the same question for four more action forms. We closed that section of the interview by asking our respondents whether they had taken part in any of these actions in the past. The answers to this question we took together into a measure of *action participation in the past* (0 = "none" to 8 = "all eight"). In the second and third interview we asked whether the respondents since the previous interview took part in any collective action directed at agricultural measures or policy (yes/no). The answer to this question was used as a measure of *action participation since the previous interview.*

FRAMING THE POLITICAL ENVIRONMENT

Both national governments and the European Union are players in the arena where the common agricultural politics is defined. How do farmers in Galicia and the Netherlands evaluate their national governments and the European Union? Table 4.1 presents a few basic parameters for this assessment. The table opens in Panel a. with factual knowledge about agricultural politics, both at the national and at the European level.

Two outcomes immediately catch the eye: knowledge about national and European agricultural politics is very limited in Galicia, and national politics is better known than European politics in both samples. In both countries those farmers who are better informed about national agricultural politics are

Table 4.1 Evaluating the European Union and the National Government

	Galicia			*Netherlands*		
	1993/9	*1995–1 4*	*1995–2*	*1993/9*	*1995–1 4*	*1995–2*
a. Knowledge about Agricultural Politics (Means on a Scale 0–1)						
National	.21	.11	.10	.61	.59	.59
EU	—	.05	.04	—	.37	.43
b1. Responsibility for State of Farming Industry (Percentages)						
Don't know	23.7	10.2	20.0	4.8	1.2	3.0
National government	60.7	52.2	50.2	22.2	21.6	29.3
EU	4.4	4.1	2.7	40.7	15.0	24.6
b2. Responsibility for State of Farming Industry (Means on a Scale 0–10)						
National government	—	8.42	7.45	—	6.08	6.21
Ministry of Agriculture	—	8.06	6.78	—	6.68	6.91
EU	—	7.44	5.63	—	7.59	7.31
c. Assessment of the European Union (Means on a Scale 1–5)						
Evaluation	—	—	2.44	—	—	3.18
Perceived influence	—	—	2.68	—	—	2.33
Representation	—	—	2.36	—	—	2.82
d. Assessment of National Government (Means on a Scale 1–2.5)						
Trust	—	1.40	1.34	—	1.94	1.94

also better informed about European agricultural politics (Pearson *r*: .21 and .32 in the Netherlands and .56 and .73 in Galicia). Within each country, it is the farmers with an interest in politics and who talk with their friends and colleagues about agricultural politics who are better informed. In Galicia, being informed is also related to political identity. Those farmers who identify with the political left (self-placement) are better informed than those who identify with the right.[1]

To what extent in the eyes of our respondents are national government and the European Union responsible for the state of farming as an industry? Panel b. presents data relevant for that question. The first part refers to the answers to an open question, "Who is in your eyes responsible for your situation as a farmer?" The most interesting finding is perhaps that very few farmers in Galicia respond by mentioning the European Union. If they do hold some political actor responsible, it is their national government. Dutch farmers, on the other hand, hold their national government and the European Union equally responsible and, unlike their Spanish colleagues, very few have no opinion at all.

These figures are confirmed by the answers to the set of structured questions. In Galicia, it is national politics that is held more responsible than the

European Union; in the Netherlands, the European Union is held more responsible than national government. At the individual level, the answers to the two questions are correlated: farmers who mention national government in response to the open question more often also hold the national government and the Ministry of Agriculture more responsible in response to the structured questionnaire. Similar findings can be reported with regard to the European Union. In both countries, farmers who are better informed about agricultural politics more often hold the European Union responsible for farm policy and less the national government.

How do farmers evaluate the EU and how well their national governments represent the farmers' interests? Panel c. presents the figures for three evaluative dimensions: the significance of the EU to farmers, the representation of farmers by their national government, and the influence of the national government on EU policy. The farmers in the two countries differ in a significant way. Farmers in Galicia are less positive about the EU than farmers in the Netherlands but perceive their national government as more influential than their Dutch colleagues do. However, Dutch farmers are more content than Galician farmers with the way national government represents their interests at the European level.[2] In both countries, being more knowledgeable about agricultural politics both at the national and at the European level makes farmers more positive about the European Union but less positive about their national government's influence in the European Union. Being informed has no impact on how farmers evaluate their government's performance as a representative of farmers' interests.

Whether citizens trust their government to represent their interests depends, of course, on whether they trust their government altogether. If farmers don't feel like trusting their government, they won't have much confidence in government as their intermediary in Brussels either. Panel d. in table 4.1 presents the mean scores of Galician and Dutch farmers on our trust in government scale. Obviously, farmers in Galicia hardly trust their government. Levels of trust in the Netherlands are much higher ($p<.001$ for both years). In a way, this does not come as a surprise. At the time when we conducted our interviews, Spanish politics was struck by one scandal after another. It would have raised serious questions about the reliability and validity of our survey had we not found this difference. What is important for our argument, though, is that trust in government correlates with the farmers' assessment of the European Union and especially of the role of their own government (table 4.2).

Table 4.2 provides a summary of six regression analyses with the assessment of responsibilities and of the EU at time 3 as the dependent variables and country and trust in government at time 2 as the independent variables.

The effects are net of the differences between the countries. Table 4.2 reveals that the less farmers trust their national government, the more they

Table 4.2 Trust in Government and the Assessment of the European Union: Standardized Betas

	Attribution of Responsibility (Time 3)			*Assessment of European Union (Time 3)*		
	National government	*Ministry of Agriculture*	*EU*	*Evaluation*	*Perceived influence*	*Representation*
Trust in government (Time 2)	.22	.24	.15	.10	.17	.10
Country (Netherlands = 2 Galicia = 1)	.12	.16	.41	.47	.30	.27

Note: All coefficients are significant, $p < .05$.

hold it responsible for the state of the farming industry. Interestingly, this doesn't mean that they hold the European Union less responsible; on the contrary, they hold the Union more responsible as well. Furthermore, less trust in national government means more negative evaluations of the EU, less perceived influence of the national government on the EU, and a more negative evaluation of the government's performance as protector of the farmer's interest.

In both countries, political identification and feelings of powerlessness influence trust in government. The more farmers identify with the political right and the more powerless they feel, the less they trust their national government. In Galicia, trust in government is also related to interest in politics and to the extent to which people are talking about politics: farmers who are not interested in politics but nevertheless talk about it trust Spanish government the least. Among Dutch farmers, we found a similar pattern but that did not reach statistical significance.[3]

In sum, knowledge about the agricultural policy of the European Union is relatively scant, certainly if one takes knowledge of national agricultural policy as a standard of comparison. Knowledge among Galician farmers was close to zero. Their Dutch colleagues were better informed, but also among Dutch farmers EU knowledge was significantly lower than the comparison standard. Moreover, in the eyes of our respondents the EU is certainly not the only responsible or even most responsible player in the arena where agricultural policy is defined. In Galicia, the national government is perceived to be the one and only responsible actor; in the Netherlands, national government and the EU are held equally responsible. In terms of the evaluation of the EU and the role of the national government in the EU, we found more negative evaluations of the EU and the national government as the representative of the farmers in Galicia than in the Netherlands. On the other hand, we found more positive evaluations of the influence of the national government on the EU in Galicia than in the Netherlands. Assessment of responsibility and evaluation of the EU and national government were related to levels of trust in national government. The less farmers trusted their national government, the more they held their government responsible for the state of farming as an industry. And not only that, they also evaluated the EU and the role of their national governments less favorably than farmers who trusted their government.

Overall, these findings confirm our expectations with regard to the difference between the two countries. In view of these results, it may not come as a surprise that Galician farmers aim their protests at their national government. They have no idea about the EU as a political structure, and they hold the Spanish government primarily responsible for the state of farming. Although their attitude toward the EU is not very positive, they feel that their government could have an impact, if only it represented them better. Indeed, they don't trust their government at all. Among Dutch farmers, the picture is more complex. They know the EU's agricultural policy much better than their Galician colleagues do, and at least a fair proportion holds the EU and not national government responsible for the situation of the farming industry. They are less negative about the EU and the way their government represents their interests but are doubtful about the impact their government has in the European political arena. On average they trust their government more than their Galician colleagues do, but, obviously, the less they trust government, the more negative they are about its role in the EU and the less confident they are about its role as protector of their interests. On the basis of these results, one could understand why Dutch farmers—though not all of them—also aim their protest at the Dutch government rather than at the EU.

TRANSNATIONAL IDENTITY

To what extent have farmers in Europe developed a transnational identity? That is to say in terms of our study, to what extent do farmers in Galicia and the Netherlands identify with farmers in Europe? The social psychology of protest not only points to the way in which someone frames his or her political environment as a potential determinant of protest participation but to *collective identity* as well. After all, most political protest is *collective* action—that is, action on behalf of groups people identify with. Preparedness to take part in collective action and, following from that, actual participation develop because people identify with their companions in adversity.

When it comes to contention in composite polities, a key question becomes, At what level do people locate their companions? Phrased within the context of our study, the question becomes, With whom do farmers feel solidarity, with farmers from the same region, with farmers from the same country, or with farmers in the EU? If no farmer identifies with his fellow-European farmers, it is unlikely that we will see farmers engage in transnational protests at the European level. Brewer (1991) has argued that group identification will be stronger the more exclusive a membership group is. Following her reasoning, we may expect that identification with farmers in the same region will be stronger than identification with farmers in the same country, which again will be stronger than identification with farmers in the European Union. This is exactly what we found (table 4.3).

Table 4.3 presents the means of the answers to the question of to what extent our respondents identify with farmers in the same region, the country, and the EU.

Obviously, the more inclusive the group becomes, the lower the levels of identification we found. This is true for both Galicia and the Netherlands. Comparison of the three levels of inclusiveness for the two countries reveals

Table 4.3 Identity: Means on a Scale 0–2

	Galicia			*Netherlands*		
	1993/9	*1995–1 4*	*1995–2*	*1993/9*	*1995–1 4*	*1995–2*
Regional	1.23	.79	1.12	1.28	1.31	1.28
National	.59	.40	.40	1.00	1.01	.97
European	.31	.17	.24	.49	.59	.60

that the levels of regional identification were more or less the same in the two countries (except for a dip in identification in the second interview in Galicia).[4] National and European identification, on the other hand, are much lower in Galicia than in the Netherlands. Seeing that levels of European identification are so low, it must once again not come as a surprise that we observe so few instances of transnational collective action by farmers in Europe.

In both countries, national identification correlates strongly with European identification (Pearson correlation ranging from .35 to .70), while correlations between European identity and regional identity are much lower or even insignificant (.10 to .24). The correlations between national and regional identity fall in-between: .27 to .46. Apparently, some farmers are inclined to identify with farmers at any level, but on the whole, identification with farmers in someone's region does *not* guarantee any transnational identification. Obviously, to many farmers, identification at the national level is as abstract as identification at the European level and therefore equally unlikely, certainly in Galicia.

We found no systematic correlation between attribution of responsibility for the state of farming, on the one hand, and patterns of identification, on the other. In a way, that is interesting because it suggests that levels of identification are not so much determined by the way farmers frame their political environment. Indeed, there doesn't seem to be a feeling of shared fate connected to identification at a national or transnational level.

Among Dutch farmers, levels of identification were higher among farmers who talked frequently with other farmers about agricultural politics. This relation was found for all three types of identification, but more strongly for national and European identification than for regional identification. That makes sense. After all, identification is not an abstract category but is rooted in social interaction. This is, of course, in line with social movement literature that defines collective identity as a social construction generated in interpersonal interaction. Talking about agricultural politics has made some Dutch farmers more aware of the fact that they are in the same situation as other Dutch farmers, as well as with other European farmers. We did not find the same correlations in Galicia, but remember that farmers in Galicia talk much less about agricultural politics than farmers do in the Netherlands.

ACTION PARTICIPATION AND ACTION PREPAREDNESS

What about protest? Do the differences in framing and identification that we found, produce differences in the preparedness to take part in protest and in actual protest participation? Let's start our analyses by simply describing to what extent our respondents have actually taken part in protest on behalf of farmers and whether they are prepared to take part in such protest in the future. Table 4.4 presents the relevant figures.

Panel a. gives the percentages of the respondents who have taken part in farmers' protest. The first column concerns protests in the past; the two other columns concern protests in the period since the previous interview. For obvious reasons, the first column has much higher percentages than the remaining two. After all, the past refers to many years, whereas the period since the previous interview is at most a year. It is clear from the table that the farmers in Galicia have participated far less in protest than the farmers in the Netherlands. This holds both for the longer and the shorter periods.[5]

Panel b. presents the mean scores on action preparedness. The same pattern emerges: low scores in Galicia and far higher scores in the Netherlands. Panel c. reveals, however, that this is predominantly a matter of differences in past experience. Broken down into those who have never participated in any protest in the past and those who have participated at least once in protest before, action preparedness in the two countries is the same. People who have taken part in farmers' protest in the past are equally prepared to take part in protest in the future, no matter which of the two countries they are from.

Participation in the past impacts on participation in the future, as path analyses demonstrate (figure 4.2).

These analyses exploit the fact that we have panel data. Participation in farmers' protest is regressed on action preparedness and reported participation in the *previous* interview. Indeed, participation is determined by action

Table 4.4 Action Participation and Action Preparedness

	Galicia			*Netherlands*		
	1993/4	*1995–1 4*	*1995–2*	*1993/9*	*1995–1 4*	*1995–2*
a. Action part.	37.3%[1]	3.1%[2]	1.7%[2]	86.8%[1]	11.4%[2]	17.4%[2]
b. Action prep.[3]	1.88	1.80	1.96	2.80	2.63	2.59
c. Action Preparedness by Participation in the Past						
Did part.[3]	2.96	2.70	2.54	2.68	2.57	2.63
Did not part.[3]	1.89	1.79	1.98	1.78	1.89	1.80

[1] participation in the past;
[2] participation since the previous interview;
[3] means on a scale 1–5.

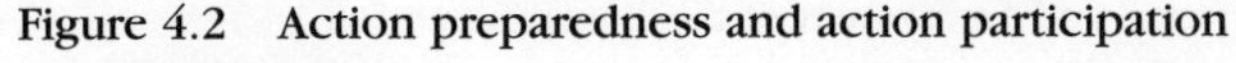
Figure 4.2 Action preparedness and action participation

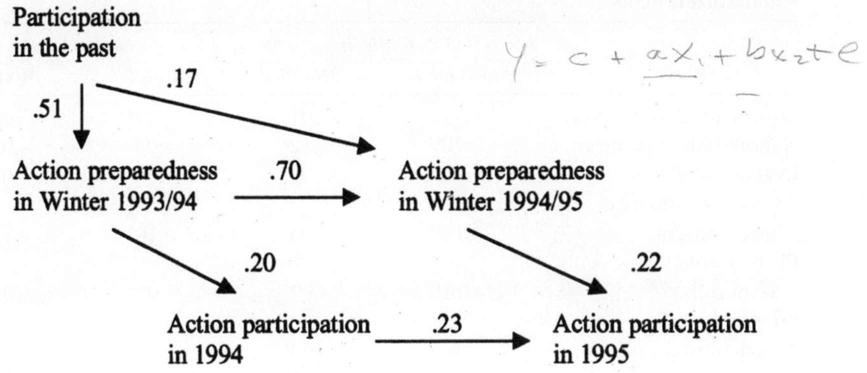

preparedness and past action participation. However, only recent action experience has this direct impact on action participation. Long-term experiences, as indicated by our question about participation in the past, impact on action preparedness but not on action participation.

Thus, participation in the past explains a substantial proportion of today's readiness to take part in collective action, which in its turn explains actual participation. That raises the question of the correlates of such past experiences. To what extent are framing of the political environment and the presence or absence of some transnational identity an influence on people's readiness to take part in collective action? In order to investigate that matter, we ran a series of regression analyses. On the basis of these analyses we reduced the number of independent variables by only taking those variables that reached significance in at least one country. Table 4.5 provides the results of regression analyses for each country with the remaining variables. Two models were tested: Model 1, encompassing the framing and identification variables; Model 2, adding knowledge of agricultural politics. Significant and theoretically important differences can be observed between the two countries.

Let's look at Galicia first. Farmers who have participated in protest in the past identify with Spanish rather than European farmers and are less inclined than other Galician farmers to hold the EU responsible for the state of farming. Moreover, they evaluate the EU more positively but are not convinced of their government's influence in the EU. These results suggest that the Spanish government rather than the EU is more likely to be the target of protest by Galician farmers.

In the Netherlands we find a similar pattern with regard to the evaluation of the EU and the perceived influence of national governments within the EU. There is, however, one important difference in comparison with Galicia:

Table 4.5 Past Participation and Assessment of the European Union: Standardized Betas

	Galicia		*Netherlands*	
	Model 1	*Model 2*	*Model 1*	*Model 2*
European identification	–.14*	.01	.21*	.13
National identification	.20**	.12*	–.03	–.02
Evaluation EU	.18**	.01	.13	.05
Perceived influence government	–.18**	–.06	.19*	–.13
EU responsible for state farm policy	–.14*	–.09*	.03	.03
knowledge of agricultural politics	–	.60***	–	.32***
R^2	.13	.42	.09	.18

Note: * p < .05, ** p < .01, *** p < .001

in the Netherlands, farmers who have protested in the past are the farmers who identify *more* with European farmers rather than less. Meanwhile, identification at the national level appears to be irrelevant. This suggests a greater likelihood that among Dutch farmers, the EU could become a target of protest.

In both countries, including knowledge of agricultural policy in the equation not only increases the variance explained considerably but also reduces the correlations with some of the other variables substantially. This finding suggests that a fair part of the correlation between framing the political environment and identification, on the one hand, and reported action participation in the past, on the other, is due to knowledge of agricultural policy or the lack thereof. Indeed, farmers who in the past have taken part in protest are better informed about agricultural politics both at the national and the European level, and they continued to be better informed throughout our study. This is not surprising because in both countries it was those who were interested in politics and talked about agricultural politics who had taken part in protest in the past.

In sum, we found the expected differences in action participation and action preparedness between Galicia and the Netherlands: much less action participation and action preparedness in Galicia than in the Netherlands. This is in line with the other differences we found between Galician and Dutch farmers. If we look at our study as if it were a quasi-experiment, the results confirm our hypotheses about the link between framing the political environment and identification, on the one hand, and protest participation, on the other. But it is difficult to decide which of the many differences between farmers in Galicia and the Netherlands are responsible for the differences in action participation and preparedness, and therefore it is important to also have the longitudinal data. Action participation and action preparedness to a large extent appear to be continuations of behavior in the past. Those farmers who participated in protest in the past are more likely to participate in protest in the future. Interestingly, participation comes with more knowledge about agricultural politics. And being knowledgeable in its turn influences the evaluation of the EU and identification with other European farmers. Although we don't have any direct evidence about the possible targets of protest, our data on framing of the political environment and transnational identity suggest that if protest is to take place, it is more likely to aim at the national government than at the EU.

DISCUSSION

In this chapter we have tried to find an answer to the question why farmers so often chose national governments as targets of their protest, despite the fact that the EU is to a large extent responsible for the state of the farming industry in the European Community. The EU's Common Agricultural Politics is a composite polity par excellence. As a consequence, farmers all over Europe must sort out the political context they encounter. Our findings indicate that this is not always easy. Many a farmer simply seems to lack the necessary knowledge to understand national and European agricultural politics. This is especially true in Galicia. As a consequence, farmers don't know where to attribute responsibility for agricultural politics, or they take for granted that the national government is responsible for the state of farming. Even if they are aware of the distribution of responsibilities between the EU and national governments, they still may feel that their government is not defending farmers' interests adequately in Brussels. Trust in government is a crucial factor in this respect. Farmers who do not trust their government are less positive about the EU and feel that their government is not protecting their interests.

In short, the way farmers frame their political environment has a strong influence on how they react to the EU's agricultural policy. Knowledge about agricultural policy and trust in government are the two factors that determine the assessment of the EU. This assessment in its turn impacts on action preparedness and action participation. These effects hold both in comparisons between Galicia and the Netherlands and in analyses within these countries.

Equally important is the influence of processes of identification. Farmers identify primarily with other farmers in their region. In the Netherlands they also identify with other farmers in the country, but this is not the case in Galicia. Identification with other farmers in Europe is not very common. In Galicia, a European collective identity is virtually nonexistent. In the Netherlands, such identity is less unusual but certainly not omnipresent. On the contrary, also among Dutch farmers a European collective identity is rare. Hence, not only do most Dutch and Galician farmers frame their political environment such that protest at the European level will not be the first thing that comes to their minds; most of the time they also lack the transnational identity needed for such collective action. Our framing argument is, of course, in line with the argument made by Imig and Tarrow, that people are more likely to protest close to home because that's where they are offered the better political and institutional opportunities. In addition to these factors, we have pointed here to the significance of transnational solidarity.

In both countries, action participation was strongly influenced by being knowledgeable about agricultural politics. Farmers who in the past had participated in protest were better informed and throughout our study continued to be better informed about agricultural politics than farmers who never participated in protest. At the same time, being better informed meant identifying more strongly with other farmers in Europe and holding the EU more often responsible for the situation of the farming industry. Both being informed and having participated in farmers' protest in the past appear to make people more prepared to take part in future protest. Action preparedness, in its turn, was the best predictor of action participation. Therefore, the link between protest participation, on the one hand, and assessment of the EU and identification with farmers in Europe, on the other, depends on how well informed farmers are. The better-informed farmers are more likely to identify with farmers in Europe. They are also more likely to hold the EU responsible for the state of farming and they are more likely to take part in protest.

What do these findings suggest for the future? On the basis of our data this is difficult to say, but if the trends we have observed continue, one would expect that both the Dutch and the Galician farmers might begin to look more European, the former probably earlier than the latter. Already in the course of our project, some of this could be observed among the Dutch farmers. Furthermore, processes of identification are context dependent. Measures taken by the European Union might make the European identity of farmers more salient. Much depends, on the other hand, on the policy of the national governments. They could choose to defend their farmers' interest and form an alliance with their farmers to put pressure on Brussels. Or, they could choose a European stand and alienate their farmers. Under those circumstances, farmers will protest at home, because they feel betrayed and abandoned by their own government.

NOTES

1. This is based on regression analyses with knowledge at time 2 and time 3 as dependent variables and political interest, talking about agricultural politics, and political identification at time 1 as the independent variables.

2. All these differences are significant at $p < .001$

3. These are results from regression analyses with trust in government at time 2 and 3 as dependent variables and left-right identification and feelings of powerlessness in the previous interview as independent variables. All beta's are significant at $p < .05$.

4. A possible explanation for this dip is that campaigns for local elections were taking place shortly before we conducted our second interview. Because of the campaign, political cleavages between farmers were more salient than their common fate. As a consequence, the level of identification with farmers in the region dropped.

5. Elsewhere, we have further analyzed the increase in protest participation in the Netherlands between the second and third interview (de Weerd and Klandermans 1999). As these fluctuations are not central to our argument here, we will not discuss that specific finding.

5

European Farmers and Their Protests

Evelyn Bush and Pete Simi

> "Euro-Disney under Siege—French Farmers Storm the House of Mickey Mouse!"
>
> (*Reuters,* 26 June 1992)

On June 26, 1992, thousands of families were thwarted in their efforts to visit Euro-Disney by a huge traffic jam organized by the notoriously theatrical French farmers. Arriving at dawn, the farmers barricaded the Euro-Disney parking lot with more than three hundred tractors and lifted the blockade only after the lunchtime news broadcasts gave prominent coverage to their protest. Meanwhile, another sixty farmers overran the grounds of EC commissioner Jacques Delors's home near Auxerre, southeast of Paris, and sprayed the area with defoliants.

The blockade of Euro-Disney marked the culmination of two straight weeks of protest during which French farmers disrupted road and rail traffic and dumped manure and unsold vegetables in front of government buildings (*Daily Mail,* 27 June 1992). The blockade and the accompanying protests were organized to coincide with the European Community's summit in Lisbon and the pending implementation of reforms to the European Common Agricultural Policy (CAP). Among these reforms were measures that would reduce the economic protectionism that had characterized Western European agriculture since the CAP was first implemented in 1958 (European Union Commission 1995: 10). Proponents of the reforms argued that the EC's generous farm subsidies distorted world trade and were the "major stumbling block to a settlement in the five-year Uruguay round of international trade talks under the General Agreement on Tariffs and Trade"

(*Reuters,* 28 June 1992). Farmers, meanwhile, feared that the potential loss of subsidies and protective tariffs would mean a significant reduction in their standard of living. Predictably, farmers took to the streets in protest. But why blockade Euro-Disney?

First, the park was selected to garner optimum media coverage. As one farmer explained: "The other day we blocked a motorway and caused a fifteen-mile traffic jam. The news didn't even mention us. This way, we are sure of being talked about" (*Daily Mail,* 27 June 1992). Second, from the French farmers' perspectives, Euro-Disney symbolized an unwanted and excessive American presence in European affairs. The American amusement park came to typify an increasing "cultural encroachment," as well as what was perceived as an unfair amount of American influence in European politics and economics. Consider the following statements made by leaders from the FNSEA—the French National Farmers' Union—the largest farmers' union in France:

> Many farmers were chased away when thousands of acres of good agricultural land was taken over. This land is among the most productive in France. We do not want a France covered by Euro-Disneys. (Luc Guyau, FNSEA leader, *Daily Mail,* 27 June 1992)

And again:

> We chose Euro-Disneyland because it is a symbol. It is built on agricultural land. It also symbolizes America. Without American pressure, the reform of the European agricultural policy could have been different. (Jean-Louis Colas, FNSEA, *Reuters,* 27 June 1992)

Targeting Euro-Disney was not an exception: other symbols of commercial America, such as McDonalds and Coca-Cola, became popular targets during the 1990s. While Disney reacted by downplaying the significance of the blockade, McDonalds took advantage of the opportunity to respond to farmers' protests:

> We are in no way responsible for their problems, in fact quite the opposite. . . . We understand the concern of farmers who want to defend their interests. . . . But we are surprised to see they are channeling their discontent against certain McDonald's restaurants. . . . All the produce sold in our restaurants comes from French and European suppliers. . . . Our minced meat is from Orleans, potatoes for the chips from Lille and salad ingredients from the southwest. . . . (*Reuters,* 22 November 1992)

The French campaign against the CAP reforms is just one among hundreds of instances where farmers have taken to the streets to protest decisions made through international agreements over the past decade. What can these protests tell us about how international institutions shape contentious politics? As authority is transferred from sovereign nation-states to international bodies, to whom do average citizens voice their grievances? And with whom does the responsibility and power lie for addressing them: National governments? Multinational corporations? International institutions? Foreign competitors? With such a plethora of actors from which to choose, and with the ambiguity that accompanies fundamental and widespread institutional change, it can be difficult to predict the reactions and expectations of ordinary citizens as they attempt to make their voices heard in transnational political arenas.

In this chapter, we explore how the establishment of the European Union has influenced the face of contentious politics within European agriculture. Specifically, we analyze agricultural protests that occurred between 1992 and 1997, in order to gain a better understanding of how national governments and citizens have responded to changes brought about by European integration. Our first set of questions corresponds to issues raised by Imig and Tarrow in the introductory chapter of this volume. In particular, we are interested in the forms that European farmers' protests have taken, with an eye for evidence of "Europeanization," "domestication," and "transnationalization" of protest. Our results provide a picture of the forms European farmers' protests have taken since the MacSharry reforms in 1992.

The bulk of our analysis, however, addresses Imig and Tarrow's preliminary conclusion in chapter 2 that "the consolidation of a new European composite state may . . . turn the national state into a pivot between irresponsible European decision-makers and mass publics that demand to hold someone responsible for their claims." We focus on three high-profile protest campaigns that occurred in Greece, Great Britain, and France. As we will demonstrate further on, the governments in these three countries had different ways of carrying out the brokerage role described by Imig and Tarrow—and with very different outcomes for the farmers involved. Their differences in negotiating style, we will argue, are influenced by two variables: economic strength relative to other EU member-states and the domestic political opportunity structure that serves as the backdrop for each series of protests. First, however, we turn to a discussion of the forms of protest that farmers have used in Western Europe since 1992, as revealed by our analysis of reported contentious political events.

EUROPEANIZATION, DOMESTICATION, OR TRANSNATIONALIZATION?

In their introduction to this volume, Imig and Tarrow hypothesize that "a move from national to supranational institutions might lead social actors to shift their claims from the national to the European level." Have farmers' protests increasingly involved the institutions and policies of the European

Union? For those cases in which farmers' grievances are EU-based, have farmers become more likely to frame their protests against the EU directly or to put pressure upon national representatives who are expected to intercede on their behalf? In short, can we identify a pattern of either Europeanization or domestication in contentious action launched by European farmers?

We operationalize "Europeanization" as an increase in protest that targets the EU directly. To measure "domestication," we look for instances of protest provoked by EU decisions but targeted at national governments. After considering the issue of domestication, we turn to the question of "transnationalization." We ask whether or not supranational institution building has facilitated cooperation among farmers across national boundaries. Over the past few years, researchers have been gathering evidence that suggests that transnational activism is occurring among some nonstate actors, particularly in the environment, peace, women's, and human rights movements (Chilton 1995, Marks and McAdam 1996, Pagnucco 1997, Smith 1997, Keck and Sikkink 1998). Have farmers, likewise, increasingly cooperated in protest actions across national boundaries in unified attempts to influence EU policymakers?

Data and Measurement

In order to address these questions, we turned to the set of media reports found on the *Reuters* newswire in order to construct an events data set on agricultural protests. We began by conducting an exhaustive search for all potentially relevant reports of agricultural protests in the more than 200 data sources that are included in the *Reuters* textline service. Through this process, we unearthed some 1,791 articles that were likely prospects for finding information on protests by farmers. We then read the full text of each of these articles, coding those that were relevant and eliminating irrelevant or duplicate articles. In this way, we compiled and coded a set of reports of 184 contentious political actions undertaken by farmers in the EU member-states between January 1992 and June of 1997. In one respect, in constructing this data set we followed the example of Imig and Tarrow, by focusing on instances of contentious political action, rather than on more institutionalized forms of political activity undertaken by farmers and their unions, such as lobbying or voting. But our method differs from that undertaken by Imig and Tarrow in several significant ways. First, we focused on a smaller set of actors (e.g., farmers rather than all contentious actors), and on a shorter period of time (some five and a half years rather than the fourteen covered by Imig and Tarrow's data). In exchange for less breadth of coverage, we believe we gained the advantage of much greater depth: not only is our analysis based on the full text—rather than the introductory section—of each media account, but our method also allowed us to combine information found in multiple accounts in order to compile a greater level of detail about each event reported in our data set. Our method yielded a total of 184 discrete contentious events that were launched by farmers across the European Union. Figure 5.1 illustrates the aggregate trend line for contentious events between 1992 and 1997.

Looking across the trendline, we see that the largest share (*N* = 25) of these farmers' protest events occurred in the last quarter of 1992. Over half of these instances involved French farmers protesting against changes in the CAP and the implementation of the General Agreement on Trade and Tariffs (GATT). In 1996, the number of events reached its second highest peak (*N* = 21). More than half of these protests were waged by beef farmers whose grievances were related to the international crisis surrounding Bovine Spongiform Encephalopathy (BSE, a.k.a. Mad Cow Disease).

Our next task was to operationalize the concepts of Europeanization, domestication, and transnationalization. To do so, we developed a set of codes indicating whether: (a) the sources or targets of contention were subnational, national, supranational, international (foreign government), or multinational (corporation, foreign economic competitor); or whether (b) each protest event was coordinated transnationally.

To ascertain the targets of farmers' protests in the context of European integration, we turned to the subset of events in which the European Union was the source of farmers' grievances. We coded grievances as EU-based if they concerned EU regulations such as changes in subsidies, quotas, tariffs, or compensation to farmers *or* if the grievance concerned international competition—since market liberalization was a major policy objective, and therefore an outcome, of the CAP reforms. Following these criteria, fully 90 percent of all the events in our data set were EU-based. What follows is a breakdown and discussion of the targets of these 128 Europrotests.

Figure 5.1 Count of European Farmer Protests, Yearly Totals, 1992–1997

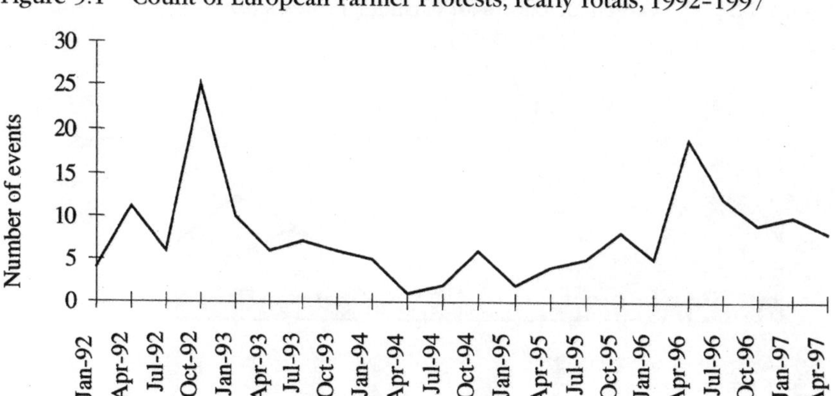

Europeanization and Domestication

We divided our EU-based events into three categories: "EU protest," "national protest," and all others. An "EU protest" is one in which farmers directly target the EU, taking Euro institutions and personnel as their objects of protest and explicitly stating that they expect their grievances to be addressed by the European Union. For instance, a group of farmers that storms the European Parliament building, shouting, "Down with the EU!" in protest of EU regulations, is clearly taking the European Union as its target. EU protests accounted for 24 percent ($N = 31$) of our Europrotest events. During the five-year period that we examined, the yearly proportion of all protests launched by farmers that targeted the EU increased over time, although the yearly number of EU-targeted protests remained relatively constant.

The majority of the protests against EU policies and decisions, however, fit within Imig and Tarrow's category of "domestication"—for example, they did *not* directly target the European Union but were instead aimed at national governments and occurred within domestic political space. Since all of the protests in this portion of the analysis were in response to EU policies, we infer from their predominantly domestic focus that farmers expected their national governments to do a better job of representing their interests before the EU. For example, although the EU establishes policy determining agricultural aid and reform, in 1992 Spanish farmers who were angered by these reforms protested against their own government (*Reuters,* 11 April 1992). This dovetails with the findings of Bert Klandermans and his collaborators (chapter 4) concerning Dutch and Spanish farmers' attitudes. Spanish farmers' statements to the press suggested that although the Spanish government insisted its hands were tied and that the causes of farmers' grievances were beyond its control, the farmers continued to hold their national representatives responsible (*Reuters,* 12 April 1992).

Figure 5.2 The Targets of European Farmers' Protests, 1992–1997

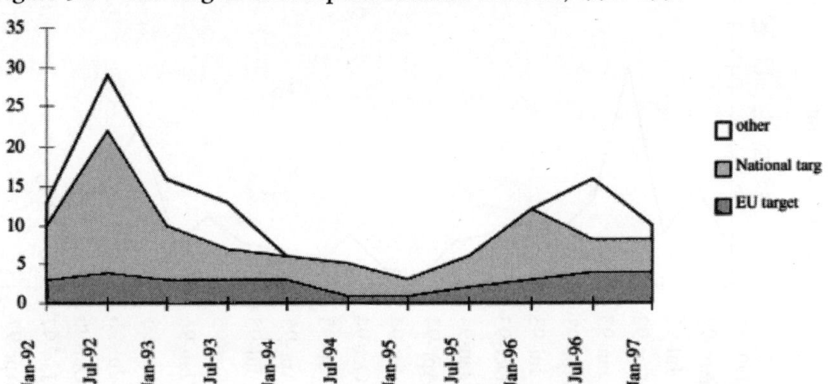

Figure 5.3 The Percent of Farm Protests Targeting European, National, and Other Targets, 1992–1997

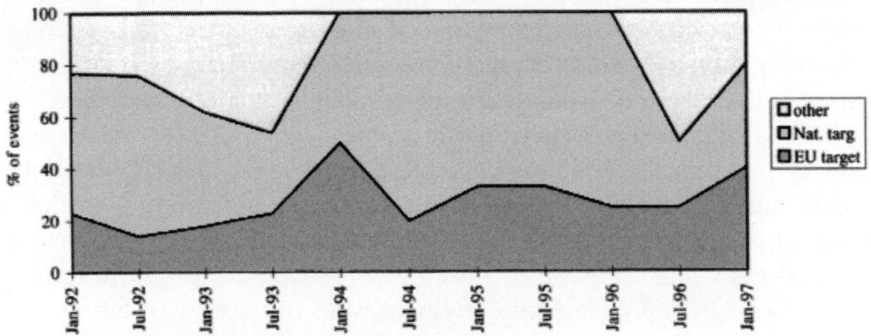

Whereas the number of EU-targeted protests remained constant over time, the number of events with national targets varied considerably. In particular, we noted two peaks in activity; the first coincided with protests against CAP reforms; the second occurred at the height of the BSE crisis. Why, then, during peak periods of Euro-based protest, do we only see increases in national, and not in European Union, targets? From a resource mobilization perspective, this domestication of protest might be a result of the significant transaction costs and the greater difficulty of coordinating and targeting the European Union directly, as well as the comparative ease of targeting domestic actors. It also may be the case that farmers target national governments because such a strategy is part of a historically developed repertoire of contention that revolves around domestic institutions (Tilly 1986, Tarrow 1998b). To the extent that this pattern of protest has been institutionalized, we would expect it to continue for some time, regardless of whether or not EU-centered tactics might be better fitted to the context of European integration.

Consistent with Imig and Tarrow's findings in chapter 2, then, our analysis of agricultural protest targets suggests that, although the EU is the source of 90 percent of the farmers' grievances, it does not necessarily follow that we will see a decreased role for the state in the face of European integration. Rather, a new role for the state may be emerging, one in which domestic protesters demand that governments negotiate more vigorously on their behalf (Marks and McAdam 1996). The fact that the greatest proportion of protests—in some years as high as 80 percent—was directed at national political actors supports this prediction. Yet this is not the entire story. By measuring event targets, we were, in effect, measuring only the expectations that citizens have of their national governments. How state representatives go about performing this pivot function is another issue, which we address in the second half of this chapter. But first we consider the issue of the transnational coordination of farm protest for the period we studied.

Transnational Protest

Has European integration been accompanied by transnational alliance formation among nonstate actors? For European farmers the answer seems to be no. Farmers from different countries were much more likely to protest *against* each other than they were to work together against shared antagonists.

If international institutions provide a forum for collective expression of grievances, as they do for actors in some other social movement sectors (e.g., women, human rights, and the environment), then alliances might develop among farmers from multiple countries seeking to form a transnational, united front. On the other hand, a primary objective of the CAP reforms was to liberalize agricultural markets, reducing the protection of farmers from their competitors in other countries. In response, some farmers have lashed out against persons and property (e.g., foreign truck drivers and the produce they are hauling).

Among the 141 protest events for which a target was identified in our set of newswire reports, 37 involved nonstate actors from two or more countries. But of those, we found only 8 instances of cooperative transnational protest (6 percent of the total). On the other hand, there were 29 competitive transnational protest events (21 percent of the total)—in which farmers physically targeted other countries' citizens or property in order to express opposition to competition from foreign farming industries. In short, when protests involved farmers from two or more countries, they were more than three times as likely to protest against each other than they were to form transnational alliances.

Why the lack of cooperation? First, the CAP reforms did not have uniform effects on all European farmers. One of the stated purposes of the reforms was to correct inequities that had purportedly been aggravated by the CAP. Therefore, owners of large, capital-intensive farms might be more adversely impacted by the reforms than would owners of small farms, insofar as the reforms reduced incentives for large-scale production (Zanias 1994: 114). This would suggest that farmers in countries with predominantly large, capital-intensive farms might have interests that diverged from those of farmers in countries characterized primarily by smaller farms and less capital-intensive farming industries (Maraveyas 1996: 106). Interests may also vary across farming sectors. Subsidy cuts to citrus growers, for example, may offset subsidy increases to the dairy industry. These types of differences are likely to preclude transnational cooperation.

Another reason for the lack of cooperation may be that European farmers compete with one another more directly than other types of actors. For example, unlike European industrial workers, who have occasionally coordinated transnational campaigns against employers (see chapter 9 by Lefébure and Lagneau), European farmers do not typically work for large, centralized, transnational organizations with branches in several states. They usually work for themselves. If their incomes are low, it is not due to decisions made by readily identifiable employers against whom they can collectively strike. Rather, it is due in a far more direct way to market-related policies that render farmers more vulnerable to competition from producers in other countries. Perhaps, then, attacking a competitor can be thought of as a proxy for attacking "competition" in the abstract.

Finally, a sense of national identity may play a role in determining whether or not farmers cooperate transnationally. Interestingly, of the few (n = 8) events that were cooperative, most were framed in response to the actions of either the United States or U.S.-based multinational corporations. For example, in one case, farmers targeted the U.S.-based McDonalds corporation by occupying different restaurant locations and offering free hamburgers. In another, they directed their anger toward the United States, in part by burning an American flag and decrying the American role in the process of European integration (*Reuters,* 18 November 1992).

Although low numbers make generalization problematic, this tendency to cooperate across national boundaries in opposition to the United States may suggest that transnationalization of protest is more likely to develop in the presence of a shared antagonist against which all European farmers can rally. The United States, in particular, is a ready target. Not only was it highly influential in the Uruguay Round of GATT negotiations, but it is also a symbol of the increasingly competitive economic conditions that farmers often designate as a source of their grievances. The round of incidents in 1999 in which French farmers ransacked McDonalds' restaurants dramatically illustrates this point (c.f., *New York Times,* 29 August 1999).

GOVERNMENTAL RESPONSES TO DOMESTICATION

As we have shown, farmers angered by EU policies and regulations were disproportionately likely to target their national governments and other domestic institutions when they launched protests. This finding suggests the emergence of a pattern of protest wherein European politics is domesticated rather than remaining the exclusive jurisdiction of the European Union and its institutions. Furthermore, farmers tend to form alliances with nonstate actors within their national boundaries, rather than forming transnational alliances. So if European policies are contested domestically, how do national governments balance the often-opposing demands of their domestic constituencies and their foreign counterparts in Brussels? And what circumstances are likely to influence representatives' strategies?

Imig and Tarrow suggest that—as integration proceeds—individual nation-states are increasingly likely to act as intermediaries between their domestic constituencies and the EU. But what are we to make of this hypothesis in practice? Certainly, the degree to which a government chooses to play this role, and its ability to do so, will vary as a function of both domestic and external opportunities and constraints.

We can gain some measure of the variation in individual states' responses to farmers' protests by evaluating three comparable protest campaigns by farmers in Greece, Great Britain, and France. In each of these three cases, farmers mounted volatile and extended protest campaigns over grievances that either directly or indirectly were prompted by EU policies. In addition, these three cases in comparison are useful because they vary in ways that allow us to begin specifying the conditions that determine how aggressively and effectively governments negotiate on behalf of their domestic constituencies. We explore two dimensions of each case: the economic strength of the country relative to other EU member-states and the country's level of domestic political support for European integration.

Our rationale for focusing on the first variable is that the economic position of any particular state within the EU may be related to how much leverage its national government has with which to actually negotiate. As explained by O. F. Hamouda, "In an economic union, economic strength is the most crucial factor in determining social preference. [Economically weaker] member nations will thus always find themselves at a disadvantage, if not in the discussion process of political decisions, then undoubtedly in the shaping of economic trends" (1994: 199). Rather than assuming that supranational and international institutions influence all parties equally, we ask if some EU member-states might be better positioned to negotiate on behalf of their citizens as a condition of their economic power. Table 5.1 provides information on some relevant economic characteristics of the three cases.

The second variable we consider is the domestic structure of political opportunities confronting each protest campaign. In particular, we are interested in the strength of political opposition toward incumbent governments' positions on European integration. As the strength of domestic political opposition grows, so should pressure on incumbent governments to demonstrate both national allegiance and strength of leadership in EU negotiations to the voters. For example, if domestic politicians uniformly promote European integration as necessary or in the interests of domestic constituencies,

Table 5.1 Basic Indicators of Agriculture in the European Union (1989)

Characteristics	*Greece*	*France*	*U.K.*
1. Percentage of Workforce in Farming	26.3	6.4	2.2
2. Farm Production as a Percent of GDP	16.4	3.2	1.4
3. GDP per capita in ECU	9,303	18,567	18,182
4. Average Farm Size (Area in ha)	6.4	43.3	93.9

Sources: EUROSTAT, The Situation of Agriculture in the Community (Brussels, 1990). Commission of the E.C. The Situation of Agriculture in the Community (Brussels, 1987–1991).

then incumbent governments may experience relatively weak political pressure to challenge EU policies. Conversely, in domestic contexts in which integration is highly contested, and especially when elections are approaching, national representatives might experience greater pressure to demonstrate their loyalty to domestic constituencies by challenging EU directives. As we will demonstrate further on, in domestic contexts where European integration is highly contested, negotiations with the EU often become the object of domestic scrutiny, as political parties publicly differentiate themselves in terms of their positions on integration.

Greece, the United Kingdom, and France enjoyed different levels of economic strength and domestic consensus on integration during the period when each series of protests occurred. Furthermore, we can identify protest campaigns in each of these countries of sufficient duration and intensity to generate extensive news coverage, allowing us to assess how each government responded to the strategic need to mediate between a powerful domestic voting bloc and the EU.

Greece: Anti-Austerity Protests 1996–1997

Greece, the poorest of these three countries, also has the greatest percentage of its population in farming. Farm products in Greece account for a relatively large percentage of the country's GDP when compared to the UK and France (see table 5.1). As a result, we might expect Greece's national government to be supportive of its farmers' demands, not only because of their importance to the national economy, but also because of the relatively large voting bloc that farmers potentially comprise. On the other hand, Greece desperately wanted to qualify for entry into the European Monetary Union (EMU)—for which a "stability pact" required cuts in budget deficits from all the EU members. As we demonstrate further on, this latter concern carried considerably more influence than did the farmers' grievances in determining the government's performance of the brokerage role hypothesized by Imig and Tarrow.

In December 1996, Greek farmers embarked upon a series of highly disruptive protests against their national government, stating that "Farmers can't go to Brussels to protest. That's the government's job" (*Reuters,* 4 December 1996). Their grievances included economic hardship as a result of the liberalization of agricultural markets and austerity measures imposed by the Greek government, measures that had been implemented in order for Greece to meet the monetary requirements for EU membership (*Reuters,* 3 December 1996). Embattled farmers faced growing imports of products in which Greece traditionally had been self-sufficient, cuts in EU subsidies, diminished national subsidy programs, growing debts, and health scares (*Reuters,* 4 December 1996). In response, farmers demanded price supports, lower fuel costs, a reduction in the VAT on farm equipment, an increase in the EU milk quota, and a rescheduling of farm debts owed to the state agricultural bank.

This protest campaign was particularly disruptive, resulting in significant damage to Greece's economy. During two separate events in December 1996 and January 1997, each lasting between two and three weeks, thousands of farmers blockaded the main highway running north and south through Greece. Only two weeks into the first event, the barricades erected by farmers were reported to have resulted in $500 million worth of damage to the Greek economy, as exports plunged by 42 percent (*Reuters,* 11 December 1996). The protests led to substantial property damage and bodily injuries, as well as violent clashes with foreign truck drivers and the police.

In spite of the damage inflicted by the farmers' roadblocks, and regardless of the fact that farming families represented 26 percent of Greece's population (Maraveyas 1996: 99), the Socialist government, led by Costas Simitis, held fast to its economic program and refused to offer farmers concessions. In explaining his refusals, Simitis repeatedly claimed that he was powerless to make changes and that the EU was the true source of the farmers' grievances. According to the Greek government: "The market is controlled by European rules and . . . we have commitments with the EU that have to be met" (*Reuters,* 7 March 1996). There is little evidence to suggest that the national government sought further EU concessions for its farm industry. As one official explained, "A course is set for the country towards EU convergence. The government cannot and is not allowed to turn back from this course, no matter how just the demands" (*Reuters,* 3 December 1996). Throughout the campaign, the government claimed that it had no independent authority to enact domestic economic policies (*Reuters,* 3 December 1996).

Meanwhile, the farmers were not alone in their opposition to austerity. They were one "among a long list of groups protesting or striking a 1997 budget described as the toughest in 15 years, and against strict incomes and tax policies" (*Reuters,* 9 February 1997). Teachers, industrial laborers, civil servants, and others were reported to have been protesting with such frequency that "protest rallies clog traffic almost daily in the Greek capital" (*Reuters,* 9 February 1997). Public opinion was overwhelmingly on the side of the farmers. Eighty percent of Greeks believed that the farmers were justified in their demands (*Reuters,* 29 January 1997).

Despite the public's outcry, the government's decision to aggressively pursue economic convergence with the EU largely escaped challenges from opposing political parties. Although the Conservatives accused Simitis of making "false promises to the farmers" (*Reuters,* 5 December 1996) and of failing to respond effectively to the farmers' blockades (*Reuters,* 5 December 1996), opposition parties were largely silent when it came to the government's austerity measures. Furthermore, even if strong criticism had existed, "[Simitis] controlled 163 seats in the 300 seat parliament with no hints of defection among socialist deputies and no opposition capable of exploiting the situation. The conservative New Democracy Party [was] split and without any charismatic leader to challenge Simitis' policies" (*Reuters,* 18 December 1996). Greece was the only one of our three cases in which domestic political parties did not publicly pose a significant challenge to the incumbent government's decisions to comply with EU mandates.

In the end, Simitis's austerity budget was passed by a vote of 160 to 136 (*Reuters,* 22 December 1996). The few concessions to farmers included a two-year freeze on farmers' debts and a debt-rescheduling plan. In response to the farmers' roadblocks, Simitis implemented an "anti-blockade" plan that allowed for deployment of riot police to dismantle them. These measures brought an end to the farmers' roadblocks. In January, the government dispatched approximately 5,000 police (with permission to use tear gas and fire hoses) and helicopters to prevent farmers from blocking the highways as they had in December (*Reuters,* 6 February 1997). According to the police, they disabled the farmers' tractors by deflating their tires. The farmers, however, reported that the police also destroyed radios, cut electrical cables, threw sugar in petrol tanks, smashed windshields and headlights, and cut ventilator belts (*Reuters,* 7 February 1997). On February 9, 1997, *Reuters* reported, " . . . many of [the farmers'] tractors are immobilized and the government hopes the protests will ease as farmers will have to return to their fields in two weeks for seasonal work" (*Reuters,* 9 February 1997).

The necessity of meeting the EMU's economic convergence requirements appears to have had a strong influence on the Greek government's refusal to negotiate with the farmers. The relevance of EMU entry was highlighted by Simitis's repeated emphasis on it in his statements to the press. "Simitis has said that sacrifices must be made by everyone to meet economic convergence targets with EU partners and that failure to do so would be a disaster for Greece" (*Reuters,* 5 December 1995) and that failure "would mean Greece's international isolation" (*Reuters,* 22 December 1994).

Domestically, the situation in Greece was characterized by an absence of effective, organized opposition to EU membership among Greece's political parties (*Reuters,* 13 December 1996). This lack of any substantial challenge to the ruling government is likely to have been a factor in its refusal to make concessions to farmers. Such opposition surely was not lacking in the British and French cases.

Great Britain: The BSE Crisis

In the spring of 1996, British farmers launched a protest campaign against an EU-imposed international ban on British beef exports. The ban was imposed due to suspicion of a "link between bovine spongiform encephalopathy (BSE), or Mad Cow Disease, and its fatal human equivalent, Creutzfeldt-Jacob Disease (CJD)" (*Reuters,* 26 March 1996). Throughout the course of the BSE crisis, farmers in multiple countries waged protests. But it was British farmers who were the most adversely affected and the most active. At the advent of the crisis, British farmers' protests were nondisruptive and primarily symbolic. They included peaceful marches and public beef giveaways. As the crisis continued, however, the protests increased in intensity. Nonetheless, we found no evidence that they were anywhere near as disruptive as the Greek farmers' protests.

Along several dimensions, the British BSE protests were quite different from the Greek anti-austerity campaign. Unlike their Greek counterparts, British farmers generally owned large, capital-intensive farms and were backed by a powerful farmers' union (*Reuters,* 12 October 1996). Furthermore, as Sheila Jasanoff points out, Britain's Ministry of Agriculture, Fisheries, and Food (MAFF) "was known to favor agricultural interests over consumer and even public-health concerns, and thus was committed to down-playing risks that might undermine consumer confidence and harm its major political clients" (Jasanoff 1997: 226). Operating in a context where farmers enjoyed considerably greater government support than was the case in Greece, British farmers were quick to name the EU as the primary source of their grievances and as the institution responsible for alleviating the hardships caused by the ban on British beef exports.

The British and Greek cases also differ in terms of our two focal variables: state economic strength and domestic political opposition toward the incumbent governments' handling of EU mandates. Britain has far more economic clout in the EU than Greece (Zanias 1994, Maraveyas 1996), and its Conservative electorate and part of the ruling party were extremely skeptical of the virtues of EMU membership. In contrast to the Greek case, British politicians during the BSE scare openly declared that the UK had nothing to gain and much to lose through EU membership (*Reuters,* 10 May 1996). To the extent that similar sentiments were prevalent among the electorate, as the chairman of the 1992 Committee of Tory MPs observed, "adopting a harder stance with the European Union would win votes" (*Reuters,* 6 May 1995). These factors contributed to a relatively sympathetic environment for British farmers among the Conservative leaders of the day.

From the time the international ban on British beef was imposed, British Agriculture Minister Douglas Hogg attempted to persuade the EU to lift the ban, claiming that it was not based on sound scientific evidence. When his persuasive powers proved ineffective, the British government quickly moved to challenge the ban in the European Court of Justice (*Daily Telegraph,* 17 April 1996). In addition to this legal maneuvering, more radical measures were advocated by members of the Conservative Party, such as "withholding Britain's contributions to the EU budget" (*Reuters,* 23 April 1996) and a retaliatory ban on European imports (*Reuters,* 23 April 1996; 6 May 1996). Although John Major did not follow through with these suggested options, the existence of political pressure to do so may have influenced the hard-line strategy that he eventually chose to follow. Specifically, Major pursued a "policy of non-cooperation" with the EU, in which he persistently used the veto to block EU decision-making (*Scotsman,* 25 May 1998; 14 June 1996). Although Major's tactics did not secure the end of the beef ban, they were significantly disruptive. In the period from late May to mid-June, Great Britain blocked more than 70 EU policy decisions (*Reuters,* 21 June 1996).

Britain's refusal to cooperate was strongly denounced by other members of the EU. For example, Belgian Prime Minister Jean Luc Dehaene recommended that the EU "find 'mechanisms' to sanction countries which engage in British-style blocking tactics. He proposed that the powers of any member-state to use the veto should be reduced, or that such countries should lose EU funding" (*Independent,* 22 June 1996). Nonetheless, in mid-June, at the Florence summit, the EU offered Major a face-saving deal in which Great Britain would be permitted to export beef to non-European countries, on a case-by-case basis, with the approval of the EU (*Independent,* 22 June 1996). In exchange, the British government agreed to a selective cattle-culling scheme through which farmers would be compensated per head of cattle incinerated (*Western Morning News,* 31 July 1996). This agreement marked the end of Major's policy of noncooperation.

In the months that followed, the British cooperated and implemented the cattle-cull scheme, with the hope that the EU would gradually lift the ban. However, due to a lack of sufficient facilities to incinerate the large number of cattle that were doomed to the slaughter, the scheme ended up causing problems for farmers whose cattle could not be incinerated quickly enough. In effect, farmers could neither sell the cattle on the market nor receive compensation for culling them. In addition, they had to bear the costs of keeping alive the cattle that were to be incinerated. The failure of the cattle-cull scheme resulted in further protests from farmers. This wave of protests, however, was targeted more directly at Great Britain's national government, particularly John Major, than at the EU. In some regions, farmers publicly called for the resignation of Agriculture Minister Hogg (*Reuters,* 6 September 1996). In addition to the increased focus on domestic accountability, farmers' protests became more disruptive, as they launched blockades to prevent foreign beef imports and delivered a truckload of cows to the offices of the Ministry of Agriculture in Exeter (*Reuters,* 6 September 1996).

In September 1996, under intense pressure from British dairy farmers and their unions, as well as continued pressure from within the Conservative Party, Major backed out of the Florence agreement, halting the cattle cull. He cited as justification a scientific study from Oxford University, claiming that BSE eradication was not contingent upon the scheme (*Reuters,* 22 April 1996). As a result, beef farmers in Ireland and Scotland—where the beef industry is highly export-driven—stood to suffer losses due to decreased consumer confidence in beef. Major was harshly criticized for abandoning the Florence agreement and for bowing to the "powerful and traditionally pro-conservative farm lobby" and the anti-Europeans in the Conservative Party (*Reuters,* 22 September 1996).

While Great Britain did not make many friends in the EU during the BSE crisis, its tactics were not entirely ineffective. Major managed to obtain substantial EU assistance for Great Britain's farmers, including compensation for culled cattle at prices that were high enough that, at one point, French farmers were actually having healthy cattle sent to Great Britain to be slaughtered rather than selling them on the domestic market (*Western Morning News,* 31 July 1998).

The British/Greek comparison is instructive. In Greece, the economic need for inclusion in the EU was repeatedly cited by Prime Minister Simitis as taking precedence over the demands of any particular domestic group (*Reuters,* 4 February 1997). In contrast, Great Britain's representatives felt themselves, at best, only marginally beholden to the European Union. Major engaged in tactics that went beyond negotiation with the EU, making explicit attempts to interfere with the EU policy-making process and abandoning an international agreement to which he had committed. As Jasanoff points out, "British ministers and scientists appeared in Brussels looking like petulant children unwilling to play by grown-up rules" (1997: 224). Great Britain's favorable economic position was evident in its threats to withhold financial contributions from the EU and its threat of retaliatory trade sanctions against European imports.

The more immediate influence on each government's response, however, was the domestic political configuration in each country. In Greece, parties agreed on the need for monetary union, even if they opposed some of the details regarding how convergence was to be achieved. In Great Britain, such consensus was absent. Not only did domestic challengers advocate radical measures against the EU to force a lifting of the ban, but there also existed significant anti-EU sentiment more generally among Great Britain's political parties. Therefore, Major had an added incentive to play "hard-ball" with the EU. In fact, the newspapers interpreted much of Major's "policy of noncooperation" as an effort to publicly promote himself as an adherent of an anti-EU political platform (*Scotsman,* 26 May 1998).

France: The Campaign against CAP/GATT

Economically, France is more similar to Great Britain than to Greece, with a similar GDP, a comparable proportion of the population involved in farming, and many large, capital-intensive farms (see table 5.1). But regardless of the objective characteristics of their agricultural sector and the diminishing percentage of the French population involved in agriculture—which fell by a third between 1979 and 1990—the mythic image of the hardworking French farmer toiling away at the land is as strong as ever (*Daily Telegraph,* 16 September 1993). This traditional image of the farmer is deeply embedded in the French national identity and provides farmers with the cultural capacity to generate popular support, enhance the legitimacy of their claims, and increase the resonance of their grievances.

French farmers also benefit from a solid base of power within domestic political institutions. Nearly one-third of the country's 36,500 mayors are farmers, most parliamentarians represent rural seats or country towns, and a large proportion of the National Assembly deputies and Senate members sit on communal and departmental councils (*Reuters,* 15 September 1993). These advantages should enhance farmers' ability to effectively mobilize support against EU policies that they oppose.

French farmers are also well organized. The most powerful farmers' union is the FNSEA, which has significant institutional ties and a well-developed sensitivity to European farm policies (Roederer 1999). On the Right, the newest and most uncompromising union is the Coordination Rurale, which became an official union in 1993, although it had existed as a "coordination" since 1991. The Coordination Rurale is known for using sensational tactics such as the attempted blockade of Paris, as well as being quick to voice loud opposition to the larger unions' relationships with the state (*Reuters,* 28 June 1992). On the other end of the political spectrum is the left-wing Confederation Paysanne (CP), which was formed in 1987. Our media data suggests that the Confederation Paysanne's activity during this campaign consisted mostly of vocal opposition to agricultural reform, such as demands for the "reorganization of the fruit and vegetable market" (*Reuters,* 6 August 1992). If they were active in organizing disruptive demonstrations, such activities drew much less attention from our media sources.

The French agricultural unions were unanimous in their opposition to proposed cuts in agricultural subsidies. However, this consensus crumbled in terms of each union's view of what the French government should do. While the FNSEA tentatively welcomed the aid packages, the Coordination Rurale and Confederation Paysanne rejected them outright. According to Coordination Rurale leader Philippe Arnaud, the plan "was ridiculously insignificant," while Confederation Paysanne leader Henri Ricard responded to the plan by saying: "We're heading for a new explosion of anger next autumn" (*Reuters,* 21 July 1992). In the face of agricultural reform, the unions attempted to represent farmers' interests at the national level, which, as we will see, resulted in a "tug-of-war" between domestic political parties trying to demonstrate their capability of negotiating on behalf of farmers in Europe.

French politics is characterized by vigorous party competition, and the early 1990s were no exception. As our British and French cases demonstrate, within this competitive environment, political parties often define themselves in terms of their support for or opposition to international policies and agreements. Such rivalry encourages the use of pressure tactics that challenge national representatives to demonstrate their allegiance to domestic constituencies when negotiating with international institutions (Schmidt 1997).

Early in the 1990s, a Socialist president presided over a Center-left government that was increasingly under attack from an aggressive Center-right bloc. Eventually, the latter was politically victorious, subsequently taking power and responsibility for farm and trade policy. Partisan maneuvering in this context was in no small part influential in shaping France's response to the protests of its farmers. These protests occurred in two waves, the first against an initial set of CAP reforms proposed in May 1992, and the second against the GATT negotiations, which followed shortly after the approval of the 1992 reforms.

Although farmers across Europe immediately protested the CAP reforms of 1992, French farmers were its most outspoken opponents. Their protests accounted for over half of the events recorded in the last quarter of 1992. The initial explosion of political contention began in May of that year and was framed in response to the CAP reforms that were agreed upon in the Maastricht Treaty. In spite of widespread agricultural protests, the reforms were finalized and were soon followed by the GATT negotiations (*Reuters,* 22 May 1992). As a result of the pending international agreement that was being negotiated, farmers were threatened with increases in land set-asides and decreases in agricultural subsidies that went beyond reductions approved in the earlier CAP reforms. Predictably, GATT was a popular target for farmers' protests. This time, however, the perceived instigator of the GATT deal, the United States, became the new enemy. And in contrast to their previous protests against the CAP reforms, French farmers found a strong ally in their national government as they began their protest campaign.

In both instances, the anti-CAP and anti-GATT campaigns, the French government was expected to represent the interests of its farmers, on the one hand, and show support of the EU, on the other. In the former instance, France's rhetorical strategies for performing this brokerage role were similar to those employed by the Socialist government in Greece. Although the French government expressed some opposition to the initial reforms of the CAP, it ultimately insisted the changes were necessary in order to remain competitive in a global economy. And in some cases, government officials dealt with farmers' anti-CAP protests by using coercive action (e.g., an attempted blockade of Paris in June of 1992 was outlawed and riot police were sent to disperse the protesters). However, the response was not entirely adversarial, as less than a month after the announcement of the reforms French Prime Minister Pierre Beregovoy promised tax breaks to "soften the impact" (*Reuters,* 21 June 1992).

After the initial CAP reforms were finalized, French farmers turned their attention to the impending GATT agreement. This shift was accompanied by a change in the dynamic between the French farmers and their national government. Once farmers' protests were squarely aimed at the GATT and the United States, French national representatives began advocating strongly on their behalf. The newly appointed agriculture minister, Jean-Pierre Soisson, expressed the state's commitment to farmers as the GATT talks resumed: "I will not let French agriculture be pushed off course to allow [U.S. President George] Bush's re-election" (*Reuters,* 8 October 1992). Farmers responded tentatively but favorably to the government's promise of support: "I can say that I am satisfied by the firmness. Now we will judge the government, the opposition, and parliament on its acts" (Luc Guyau, FNSEA, *Reuters,* 25 November 1992). And, if words weren't enough, farmers demonstrated their support through action. During a French National Assembly meeting, farmers gathered outside, claiming, "The farmers did not want to attack parliament, you understand, they wanted to 'guard' it and show their support for the government's tough line in the GATT dispute" (*Reuters,* 29 November 1992).

In the months leading up to the general national elections of March 1993, the ruling Socialists met with increased political pressure to oppose the GATT. Following the reform of CAP, the opposition neo-Gaullist UDR suggested bringing a no-confidence motion against the government. Then, some four months before the general election, the UDR party accused the Socialists of an incompetent handling of GATT negotiations and demanded that the government use the veto in order to "defend French agriculture" (*Reuters,* 26 May 1992; 21 November 1992). The neo-Gaullists skillfully exploited the GATT negotiations by pressing for a hard line against any GATT deal that would weaken French agriculture. Skeptics suggested that "Conservatives may privately prefer to let the Socialists take the heat for accepting a GATT deal rather than inherit the problem themselves" (*Reuters,* 22 November 1992).

The UDR, however, would have no such luck. When the parties of the right scored a landslide victory at the polls in March 1993, GATT was still unresolved. While the farmers originally supported the right, this amicable relationship was not to last. In the summer of 1993, against farmers' wishes, the French state accepted changes in oilseed production policy—an important stumbling block in the GATT negotiations up to that point (*Reuters,* 8 June 1993). Farmers responded in fighting fashion, staging protests throughout France and making it explicitly clear that they were holding their national government responsible. They smeared French Foreign Minister Alain

Juppe's office with yellow paint, the color of rapeseed, and wrote the slogan "Juppe traitor" alongside. Farmers also ransacked the offices of parliamentarian Philippe Auberger and dumped manure outside government offices in Normandy (*Reuters,* 9 June 1993). To make matters worse, the ruling neo-Gaullists were now being dubbed by the Socialist Party as having "capitulated to Washington" (*Reuters,* 9 June 1993).

Over the next few months, French farmers took to the streets, blockading Euro-Disney and demanding that their national government reject the GATT. But the protests declined as government aid packages assuaged farmers' concerns and the prospects of a GATT veto seemed dismal. With France's signature to the GATT looming on the horizon, one farmer worriedly explained, "We're very, very much afraid of these international or European meetings because we're under the impression the [French] government will give in little by little" (*Reuters,* 7 July 1993). Meanwhile, the anti-GATT political rhetoric that contributed to the right's electoral victory was gradually replaced with far more moderate language as a GATT agreement approached. For example, elected officials, such as French Prime Minister Edouard Balladur, began "testing the waters" in preparation for an upcoming EC/U.S. meeting: "We're going in with a very open mind. We must not reject everything that's proposed" (*Reuters,* 16 September 1993).

While the prime minister gradually moved toward a GATT agreement, the French government granted aid packages to farmers worth some $506.7 million (*Reuters,* 25 November 1993). The coincidence of the aid packages and cooperation with the GATT led some to speculate, "The deal between the government and farm leaders seems to be: 'We give you money for you to remain quiet; don't hassle us and we'll try to do what we can on GATT'" (*Reuters,* 25 November 1993). As the GATT deadline drew near, massive farmers' protests that were anticipated by the press failed to materialize. The FNSEA staged some "symbolic" protests, which were said to ". . . cool down the pressure because it knows the results of GATT talks are inescapable" (*Reuters,* 25 November 1993). Others pointed to the success of the government aid: "People just got their direct aid. It's going to be hard to mobilize farmers again" (*Reuters,* 25 November 1993).

After further negotiations, the prime minister announced that France would sign the GATT agreement along with 117 other countries (*Reuters,* 15 December 1993). While the announcement was met with a few small protests, for the most part farmers were quiet. Suggesting that the government aid packages had placated the farmers, an adviser to President Mitterrand commented, "The same politicians who encouraged the farmers to go out and riot with their inflammatory statements suddenly had an interest in calming them down. . . . The arsonists became firemen" (*Reuters,* 15 December 1993). Shortly after the right's electoral victory, "hard-line" rhetoric against the GATT began to gradually diminish.

Ironically, the proud and independent French state provides us with the best example of a government functioning as a broker between domestic and transnational audiences. On the one hand, the French government negotiated on the farmers' behalf and provided financial assistance to alleviate farmers' concerns; on the other hand, it ultimately cooperated with the international institutions whose policies were the sources of farmers' grievances. The government was locked in the middle, signing the controversial GATT agreement with one hand and providing substantial assistance to farmers with the other. While farmers exert considerable influence in French politics, the importance of "keeping pace" with European economic integration ultimately appears to receive at least equal, if not greater, consideration by the French national government.

VARIATIONS IN STATE STRATEGIES

In each of the cases we have examined, the state was caught between the requirements of EU membership and the demands of its own citizens. However, the strategies that each government actually used to negotiate between the two poles varied. At one end of the spectrum, we find the Greek austerity protests, where citizens' demands were virtually ignored in favor of continuing on a course intended to satisfy EU requirements. At the other end, we have Great Britain, with its blatant attempts to derail the EU decision-making process on behalf of one of its domestic industries. In between, we find the French governments' nuanced attempts to negotiate on their farmers' behalf.

Two different political structures must be considered in order to understand the forms that negotiation takes for any particular nation-state. First, the European Union is a political structure composed of economically unequal partners that vary in terms of the resources that they bring to the negotiating table. Although domestic political structures appear to have a more immediate influence on government responses to protest, it may be that a favorable international economic position is a prerequisite for creating domestic political opposition to cooperation with the EU.

Yet, as Schmidt (1997) points out, it is apparent that all member-states of the EU are under pressure to adjust to the various institutional and economic changes brought about by integration. An important task that each member-state must complete, Schmidt asserts, is "to construct national discourses that project country-specific visions of how the nation fits into Europe and the world, which at the same time serve to justify the Europe-related economic and institutional changes" (Schmidt 1997: 169). She then argues that "Although all European member-states are subject to these self-same European pressures, differences in economic profile, institutional organization, and ideational pattern have ensured that they have not felt their weight equally or responded in the same ways" (Schmidt 1997: 169).

Our evidence supports Schmidt's position that the characteristics of domestic contexts are important determinants of the rhetorical strategies that national representatives use when attempting to simultaneously satisfy their EU partners and their domestic constituencies. Where we go beyond Schmidt, however, is in our emphasis on how domestic political conflict influences the vigor with which national governments choose to represent domestic grievants in Brussels.

Incumbent governments may indeed use rhetorical strategies to redefine the relationship between the nation-state and its changing international context. But equally important are domestic political challengers, who have less of an interest in creating a coherent discourse than in exploiting the difficult position in which ruling parties find themselves during this historical transition. These continually shifting conflicts play a large role in shaping national strategies.

Our evidence suggests that the extent to which government officials defend their citizens' interests in Brussels is a function of the level of domestic political opposition at a given time. It is clear, especially from the British and French cases, that political parties publicly define themselves and opposing parties in terms of their orientations toward the European Union. There exists within their rhetoric an implicit distinction between national and European interests, with politicians typically insisting that their party alone represents the former, while accusing political competitors of capitulating to the latter.

In addition, the extent to which politicians take a "hard-line" pro-EU or anti-EU stance varies temporally as well as geographically. As the French case illustrates, political parties voice stronger opposition to the EU when they are not in power and therefore can avoid accountability for their anti-EU rhetoric. France's UDR was quite vocal in its opposition to the impending GATT agreement prior to its electoral victory. After taking office, however, its inflammatory rhetoric began to cool. National politics, as well as each country's international posture, determined how its government mediated between its domestic structure and its European positions (Risse-Kappen 1995).

CONCLUSIONS

In this chapter, we set out to investigate the forms that both protests and governmental responses take when social and economic policies are determined through supranational institutions. First, we asked, to what extent do farmers target the EU as opposed to their national governments? Second, do supranational institutions create opportunities for cooperation for this group of nonstate actors across national boundaries? Finally, what strategies do national governments use to negotiate on their citizens' behalf in Brussels, and how do these strategies vary across contexts?

In response to the first question, the data from the period we studied indicate that the proportion of farmers' protests directly targeting the EU increased between 1992 and 1997. However, the proportional increase was due to periodic decreases in protest targeting the nation-state or "others." Fluctuations in protest are felt most by national and international targets, while the number of protests aimed at the EU appeared to remain constant over this period of time.

The frequency of protest overall did not follow a linear pattern but largely coincided with significant political events such as the CAP negotiations and the BSE crisis. However, during the last two years of our data, we began to see an increase in protest over more general EU-related agricultural issues. For example, Greek, Italian, and Spanish farmers in 1995 and 1996 increasingly protested over issues that were explicitly related to market liberalization, subsidies, incentives, and protective tariffs. Perhaps as the EU becomes further institutionalized and protesters become more adept at targeting it, EU-targeted protest will increase.

In response to our second question—concerning the transnationalization of protest—we found little evidence of cooperation among European farmers for the period we studied. Between 1992 and 1997, transnational protest was three times more likely to be competitive than cooperative. Certainly, there were notable examples of cooperation across borders, such as the 1992 farmers' rally in Strasbourg against the GATT, which drew delegates from across Europe and from as far away as Japan, South Korea, and Canada (*Reuters,* 1 December 1992). However, these were rare occurrences: cooperation was the last thing on French farmers' minds when they blocked the cross-Channel ferry port of Calais, vowing to "throw the English into the sea" (*Reuters,* 12 December 1992).

In this respect, patterns of farmers' transnational protest deviate from patterns found in some other social movement sectors, such as the environment and human rights. This variation may suggest that supranational institution building promotes transnational cooperation only within certain sectors of civil society or in certain contexts. The features that produce this variation have—so far—only been suggested, such as the role of economic competition or that of different international institutions or third-party states (Keck and Sikkink 1998). Researchers might examine how institution building modifies the relationships among nonstate actors, in particular, how institutions create incentives and disincentives for transnational collective action and how this varies across sectors and institutions (Tarrow in press).

For example, many farmers perceive EU policies as threats to their economic survival, since such policies often increase competition from farmers in other countries. It is much easier to take competitors as objects of protest than it is to attack "free trade." Consequently, theories of emerging "global civil societies" and "antisystemic movements" must take into consideration the fact that current international institution building entails, in part, the institutionalization of competitive practices for some sectors. Consequently, in sectors where economic considerations dominate, it should come as no surprise that there is little transnational cooperation among nonstate actors. For sectors such as the environment, human rights, or peace, however, supranational institutions may bring otherwise isolated actors together, therefore encouraging an increase in transnational cooperation.

We found that most of the cooperative transnational protest among farmers occurred when the United States was a source of the farmers' grievances. This finding suggests the need to further explore the role of identity in facilitating transnational cooperation. It appears that farmers are most likely to overcome nationally specific interests when they can identify a common enemy. However, all of the instances where we found transnational cooperation were rather short in duration. That is, they were rarely sustained beyond one brief gathering, unlike competitive transnational protests, which were far more likely to continue for several days or weeks.

Turning to the strategies national governments use to negotiate on their citizens' behalf in Brussels, our evidence suggests nontrivial variation among the strategies used by different nation-states. Judging from the three episodes we examined, domestic political variables, especially the degree of consensus toward EU membership, influence the amount and type of effort governments expend in defending national citizens in Brussels. But it is difficult to decipher whether governments that play "hard ball" with the EU do so because of a genuine intention to win concessions for their citizens or merely as a response to opportunistic opposition parties that frame incumbents' cooperation with the EU as an abandonment of national interests.

The fact that representatives of economically stronger countries appear to have greater negotiating power than weaker ones also should not be ignored. Within the political opportunity structures established by the European Union, political power may be determined by a number of variables, including national economic strength and the presence of international allies with similar interests. Our analysis only begins to scratch the surface of this issue, but it suggests an interesting relationship between political struggles at the national level and those that occur among nation-states in the European Union. Domestic debates over EU policy or membership vary according to how dependent national governments perceive themselves to be on EU membership. At the same time, domestic political actors strategically use EU policy issues to define themselves against one another—thus shaping the content of national political strategies. European farmers provide a vigorous example of how an emerging international realm of decision-making intersects with the face of popular political participation.

3

LOBBIES OR MOVEMENTS?

6

Lobbying or Protest? Strategies to Influence EU Environmental Policies

Dieter Rucht

Brussels, 23 March 1971: While the ministers of agriculture from the then six member-states of the European Economic Community were discussing the future subsidies for agricultural products on the thirteenth floor of an administrative building, a massive crowd of 75,000 to 100,000 angry farmers filled the inner city. The vast majority of them were from Belgium, but contingents from the five other states also took part in the event that was organized by the Belgium farmer association. The four-hour demonstration, which was supposed to be contained by 2,500 policemen, ran out of control. It was only the next day, after the dust had settled, when the full picture of the "battle" became visible to the public: one farmer was killed by a gas grenade shot by the police, at least 160 people were injured, several trams and automobiles were set on fire, and countless windowpanes of shops, telephone boxes, and traffic lights were smashed. The damage amounted to several million dollars. According to the Paris-based paper *Combat,* this was the first European farmer revolt.[1]

Twenty-eight years later, Brussels again became the site of a large farmer demonstration. On 22 March 1999, a crowd of 27,000 (according to the police) to 50,000 farmers (according to the organizers, the European Farmer Alliance—COPA[2]) poured into the streets. At the same time, the ministers of agriculture of the now fifteen EU[3] member-states were debating the Agenda 2000, a reform program that envisaged cuts of subsidies up to 30 percent for some products such as beef, wheat, and milk. This time, police and the local shopkeepers were better prepared. Some 5,000 police were concentrated in the Belgium capital. In the so-called European Quarter, all schools and most shops were closed. Barriers and barbed wire protected the key buildings hosting European institutions. Nevertheless, some groups within the crowd resorted to violence, causing considerable damage and attacking the police, who, in turn, responded with the use of tear gas and water cannons.[4]

In the days around each of these two events in Brussels, a number of additional protests were staged in various countries, including large demonstrations of regional farmer associations and blockades of several crossings of national borders in spring 1971 and a massive demonstration of 40,000 farmers in Madrid, another 10,000 in Strasbourg, and several other minor events in spring 1999. In the periods before, between, and after these hot springs, farmers were also far from being silent (see Bush and Simi, chapter 5). They blocked highways,[5] airports,[6] and border crossings; dumped overproduced agricultural products in the streets; destroyed public property; violently clashed with police; and organized peaceful mass demonstrations that, on several occasions, attracted large numbers of people. For example, financial sanctions in response to the violation of EU quotas on milk production in Italy provoked demonstrations that, in November 1997, mobilized half a million farmers in about one hundred cities.[7] According to the data of Imig and Tarrow (2000), the farmers staged 200 out of 490 protests against the EU in twelve member-states during the period from 1984 to 1997.

These numerous and often spectacular protests targeting EU institutions were paralleled by ongoing but largely unnoticed lobbying activities of the farmer associations, ranging from the regional to the EU levels. These associations are extraordinarily strong, with organizational rates of 90 percent in Germany and 80 percent in Britain (Allum 1995: 267). They are also well-staffed, experienced, and closely connected to the policy-makers in the agricultural domain, forming the so-called "iron triangle" together with the agricultural ministers and the agriculture officials in the Commission (Hix 1998: 253).

The combined strategy of massive and sometimes disruptive street protest, on the one hand, and tenacious lobbying, bargaining, and negotiating in conference rooms, on the other hand, could not prevent the economic death of millions of—for the most part—small farms across Europe. However, this strategy of national farmer associations and their Europe-wide alliance COPA[8] was effective insofar as, over decades, huge amounts of money, both from national and EU budgets, were spent to directly or indirectly subsidize farms. Even today, nearly half of the EU budget (total: 92.45 billion ECU in 1999) is devoted to agriculture while the contribution of agriculture to the GNP is only about 2.5 percent (Hix 1998: 255). Only the constant pressure of the farmer associations secured this flow of money, which, ironically, is completely at odds with the free market ideology embraced in principle by most European leaders. In addition, this flow of subsidies was, and still is, fostering a notorious overproduction at the cost of the taxpayer.

***

Compared to the farmers, other troubled economic groups, such as the miners, steel workers, and small shopkeepers, were less effective in defending their interests. Obviously, different social and economic groups targeting EU institutions and policies do so by investing different amounts of resources, using different strategies, and having differential impacts. This chapter, however, focuses neither on farmers nor on miners or shopkeepers. Instead, it concentrates on the environmental groups targeting the EU. Yet the mobilization of the farmers, as exemplified in the introductory examples, can serve as an instructive reference point to study the environmentalists. When compared to the farmers' mobilization, the attempts of environmental groups to influence EU policies look strikingly different. The question of why is of a more general theoretical and political interest, insofar as in the process of European integration, decision-making power is gradually shifting from national to EU institutions. Consequently, many interest groups and social movements that try to directly or indirectly influence the process of policy-making in Brussels (or Strasbourg or Luxembourg) are faced with the problem of where and how they invest their energies.

Regarding national and subnational mobilization, environmentalists share with farmers the fact that they are very active in terms of both protest politics and conventional lobbying. Similar to the farmers, environmentalists have established their lobbyists in the national capitals. Though starting later than the farmers, environmental lobbyists have become quite active and professional as far as the larger national organizations are concerned. They use essentially the same kinds of channels and tactics to contact and influence the policy-makers. Also similar to the farmers, environmentalists apply a broad protest repertoire, ranging from peaceful mass protests to disruptive and sometimes violent action. In terms of the numbers of protests and participants, it appears that in most EU countries, environmentalists do not lag behind the farmers. Hence, at the national and subnational levels the forms of activities of farmers and environmentalists do not differ significantly, although both rely on different organizational structures and, of course, social groups. Whereas the farmer associations exhibit a fairly centralized, formal, and corporatist or monopolist structure that represents a well-defined clientele, environmentalists typically rely on a heterogeneous and loosely coupled network of groups and organizations that, in principle, do not represent particular social or economic groups and thus are socially mixed (although being mainly part of the new middle class).

When looking at the activities in Brussels, however, we find a striking difference between farmers and environmentalists. While both groups are strongly engaged in essentially the same range of lobbying activities, though based on different structures (one central office for the farmers, but several for the environmental groups), the environmentalists exhibit a suspicious lack of protest activities at the EU level. To be sure, some transnational environmental protests did occur in Brussels (or Strasbourg). For example, actions of Greenpeace, Friends of the Earth, members of Green Parties, and animal rights groups were reported during the 1990s. However, these were scattered, rare, and small, and consequently did not attract much media attention unless, as in the case of animal rights groups around the mid-1990s, a celebrity such as Brigitte Bardot participated.[9] In my—certainly incomplete—search for environmental protests based on German newspapers and interviews with experts in the last two decades, I did not come across one single transnational environmental protest in Brussels or Strasbourg that was large and/or violent, thus resembling many of the domestic environmental protests.[10] So why do environmental groups, unlike farmers and workers,[11] not protest in Brussels? After all, they have proven their capabilities as trouble-makers and as "professional protest organizations" (Diani and Donati 1999). Moreover, a growing number of relevant environmental policy decisions are actually developed by EU institutions (Hey and Brendle 1994, Weale 1996) and environmentalists are aware of this fact. According to a 1998 survey of environmental groups in Britain, "a significant majority of the groups (60 percent) agreed that the EU was now more influential in the environmental sector than the national government" (Ward and Lowe 1998: 157; see also Roose 1999).

Although the puzzling absence of environmental protest in Brussels is addressed at the center of this chapter, an answer requires a fuller understanding of the strategic options available to environmental groups and the context in which they operate, including the situation in both their home countries and in Brussels. These aspects will be explored first before coming back to the key question. Given the current lack of systematic empirical research, this chapter does not provide a definite answer. Instead, I will develop some grounded hypotheses that, in a future step, will be submitted to closer empirical investigation.

TARGETING THE EU: STRATEGIC OPTIONS

Strategic choices to influence EU policies can be classified along two dimensions: the kind of strategy and the geographical level at which strategies are applied. Interest groups and social movements have a broad range of theoretically available strategic options and related tactics to advance their cause. In practice, this range of options is narrowed by various factors. One of these is the very type of movement and the issues at stake. Some movements are predominantly bound to an identity-oriented logic of action. They tend to focus on cultural aspects and/or seek for personal changes, thus favoring strategies of reformist divergence, subcultural retreat, or countercultural challenges of ways of life. Other movements are predominantly power-oriented. They prefer to engage in the realm of politics and, in particular, conflicts with state authorities. Still other movements typically combine both types of logic, promoting or resisting to similar degrees both personal and institutional changes (Rucht 1988).

Though the environmental movement also tries to change individual attitudes and behaviors, I would argue that this movement essentially belongs to the second category insofar as the issues it raises are predominantly regulated by the state. This is indicated by the fact that within a relatively short period, a full-blown environmental policy with its own governmental departments, agencies, laws, and other regulations was established. Propagating ecologically sound lifestyles and consumer behaviors based on arguments and appeals can complement, but not supplement, a regulatory policy founded on law, control, and coercion. Correspondingly, most of the movement's activities directly or indirectly target state authorities. Following power-oriented logic allows more specific strategic options to be identified, such as institutionalized participation, bargaining, pressure, and confrontation. These specific strategies, in turn, can be differentiated into more specific forms of action (Rucht 1990).

By *institutionalized participation,* I mean the use of formal channels of expressing demands, influencing, or partaking in political decisions, for example, via expert commissions, public hearings, procedural complaints, and referenda. *Bargaining* occurs in either formal or informal settings where the actors are dependent on each other because each of them controls a particular set of resources that is needed to jointly reach a solution. Bargaining takes place, for example, in public-private partnerships in which the state may supply money, whereas private groups offer other resources such as expertise or volunteers. *Political pressure* refers to the potential or actual use of nondisruptive means that are intended to have a negative impact on the addressee. For example, interest groups may threaten to mobilize their adherents or the wider public in demonstrations against the government unless the latter makes concessions in favor of these groups. Finally, *confrontation* is understood as a direct and explicit challenge to an actor defined as an adversary by more or less disruptive means, ranging from extremely harsh verbal attacks to civil disobedience to physical violence. Obviously, these categories empirically overlap and therefore cannot be clearly separated from each other. For example, pressure and verbal confrontation may occur in a bargaining setting.

The second dimension of strategic choices is the geographical level—ranging from the local to the international—at which the strategies are employed. Some issues, by their very nature, are strictly local, national, or international, whereas others are regulated, or have impacts, on all these levels and consequently also attract mobilization at various levels.

Regarding environmental movements, it is obvious that, in a more general perspective, they tend to employ the full range of theoretically available options (Rucht 1993, Princen and Finger 1994, Wapner 1996, Rootes 1999a). However, not each group employs the full strategic repertoire in each issue and at each level. Some groups have specialized in particular strategies, and certain strategies are more frequently used in some countries, types of conflicts, and periods than in others, as comparative research has demonstrated (Kitschelt 1986, Flam 1994, Rucht 1994, Kriesi et al. 1995).

The central question of this chapter is which strategies are used at which level, and why, to influence EU environmental policy. We cannot expect that all EU-related environmental activity is concentrated in Brussels for the simple reason that EU politics is a multilevel game (Grande 1996). Moreover, in a "composite polity" (see Imig and Tarrow's introduction to this volume) we find a complex web of horizontal and vertical relationships between decision-makers, implementing bodies, and nongovernmental actors, where policy decisions, even if formally made in a committee at the highest level, are strongly influenced by a plethora of other actors, notably at the national level. As long as individual governments have a strong position or even a formal veto power in EU decisions, it may be more effective and efficient to directly target national governments that, under pressure from domestic groups, then pursue these groups' interests in Brussels (Tarrow 1995, Klandermans et al. in chapter 4). Instead of trying to directly influence national or EU administrations, another strategy is to sensitize the wider public by protest actions that attract the attention of the mass media and thus may exert an indirect pressure on the decision-makers on the respective levels. We may also find the use of combined strategies when, in an implicit or explicit division of labor, some groups act nationally and others internationally, or some engage in bargaining while others prefer confrontation, thus indirectly strengthening the bargaining position of the moderate groups. The situation can become even more complicated insofar as some national groups in some issues may primarily focus on EU institutions, which, in turn, put pressure on the national government because the latter lags behind the standards of other countries or remains unresponsive to direct intervention by domestic groups (see the boomerang model of Keck and Sikkink 1998).

THE ACTUAL USE OF STRATEGIES TO INFLUENCE EU ENVIRONMENTAL POLICIES

As indicated earlier, the full range of strategic options familiar to the environmental movements is not applied on each level when it comes to targeting EU-institutions. What patterns can be found at the subnational, national, and EU levels? Ideally, we would have to analyze the activities of environmental groups of the fifteen EU member-states. This is, of course, not only beyond the scope of a single chapter but also beyond the knowledge of any individual author.[12] A major comparative study on environmental activism in seven EU member-states is underway (see Rootes 1999b) and will provide many insights. However, it is still too early to empirically determine the amount and patterns of EU-related activities of environmental groups. Given the current lack of broad and systematic information, I will limit my observations to two aspects: (1) the EU-related activities of environmental groups in Germany (for which some data is available) and (2) the transnational structures and activities of environmental groups in Brussels.

The Role of EU Environmental Policy within Domestic German Movement Activities

The German environmental movement is one of the strongest in Europe and probably elsewhere (van der Heijden et al. 1992, Kriesi and Giugni 1997, Rucht and Roose 1999). It is well known for its broad range and high level of activities and its considerable resources; its political influence is represented by, among other things, the strength of the German Green Party. Moreover, the movement can hardly be said to be narrow-minded in focusing only on domestic environmental problems. Indicators for this are the considerable resources of the German sections of internationally oriented organizations such as Greenpeace and the World Wide Fund for Nature.[13] Moreover, it appears that public awareness regarding the relevance of EU politics is relatively high in Germany, given the country's role as one of the driving forces in the process of European integration. Thus, it is unlikely that EU-related environmental activities, in both absolute and relative terms, are below the average of the EU countries. Nevertheless, scattered empirical information suggests that surprisingly little activity in Germany is devoted to influencing EU environmental policies.

It is certainly hard to assess the number of EU-related activities of German environmental groups in terms of lobbying and bargaining. So far, no studies on these activities are available. If we assume that social movement organizations usually gain their strength in virtually every respect, including their position in lobbying and bargaining, from public resonance and support, then we cannot conclude that much lobbying activity regarding EU environmental policies takes place at the national level in Germany. When we look at the range of themes and issues raised by environmental groups, European issues are certainly present, but only to a minor extent. We have no systematic empirical information on precisely that aspect, but analyses of the environmental discourse (Brand et al. 1997), as well as my own close reading and paper clipping over the last fifteen years, do not suggest a particular emphasis on issues related to and/or regulated by the EU. National and subnational issues by far dominate the protest agenda (Rucht 2000). It also appears that very few people within domestic German environmental groups have specialized in EU policies.[14]

Better indicators for which we do have quantitative information are the issues raised in environmental protests in Germany (including East Germany since 1989). Based on the data from the Prodat project, which covers a large sample of protests drawn from two nationwide newspapers from 1950 through 1994 (Rucht and Neidhardt 1998), we can determine the relative weight of environmental and antinuclear protests as a proportion of all protests. Moreover, we can calculate the relative weight of matters that refer to EU-related environmental concerns. For the period from 1970 to 1994, environmental protests (N = 542) account for 5.7 percent of all registered protests in this period (N = 9,497). In addition, mobilization against nuclear power (N = 603) accounts for 6.3 percent of all protest events registered in Germany.[15]

Within the category of pro-environmental protests, few are geared toward EU policies. When "European" environmental protest is broadly defined—that is, relating to one or more foreign European countries (with the exception of the former Soviet Union, but including non–EU member-states)—the proportion of these protests is 10.5 percent. This number also includes local or regional environmental problems across borders. If, however, we narrow our focus to strictly EU-related problems—that is, protests targeting explicitly EU institutions or EU policies—their proportion is extremely marginal. Out of a total of 542 environmental protests, only 4 (0.7 percent) match this criterion. The number of EU-related antinuclear protests is even lower because programs and regulations on nuclear power have hardly become a matter for EU policies.[16] Thus, one of the most active and radical branches of the broader ecological movement is not targeting the EU.

In conclusion, it seems safe to state that EU-related protests do not play a significant role in either the domestic discourse or protest mobilization on environmental matters in Germany. In some other EU countries, particularly the smaller ones, the proportion of such protests may be higher but, according to my assumption, still remains low when compared to national and subnational issues. This is also confirmed by preliminary analyses of this aspect in seven EU countries (Rootes 2000).

Representation and Activities of Environmental Groups in Brussels

One could argue that the absence of significant EU-related environmental activity within the respective national territories is possibly a consequence of an actual shift of activity to Brussels as the center of EU policy-making. If this assumption would hold, we would find significant lobbying and/or protest activities of environmental groups in Brussels. At first glance, at least the former seems to be true (Mazey and Richardson 1992). A number of trans- and supranational groups have established permanent offices in Brussels, most important the Europe-wide umbrella organization European Environmental Bureau (EEB),[17] Greenpeace, World Wide Fund for Nature, and Friends of the Earth. This initial "Gang of Four" has broadened into a group of eight, internally referred to as the G-8 (by adding the Climate Action Network Europe, CNE; The World Conservation Union, IUCN; the European Federation for Transport and the Environment, EFTE; and Birdlife International; see Long 1998, Webster 1998, Rootes 2000). In addition, there are Brussels-based representatives of a few additional organizations such as the ecologically orientated European Farmers Coordination (Confédération paysanne européenne—CPA) and issue-based alliances, such as the European Campaign for Clean Air.

A closer look, however, reveals that these environmental lobbyists are not powerful (Ruzza 1996, Rucht 1997). Even the offices of the larger groups are only moderately staffed. Taken together, the environmental groups are said to employ no more than thirty full-time staff people in Brussels (Long 1998). This is small compared to the size of their national headquarters. For example, the German section of Greenpeace in Hamburg employed 130 people in 1999. The environmental staff in Brussels is also modest when compared to the number of lobbyists of farmers, as well as to those in the automobile, chemical, and pharmaceutical industries.[18] In addition, the environmental groups, unlike a number of groups in other policy domains, are not formally represented in the preparatory stages of environmental decision-making. It remains at the discretion of the European Commission, and notably the Directorate General XI (Environment), whether or not it wants to obtain the opinion and advice of environmental groups, even though—for years now—there have been declarations of intention to grant these groups a more formal standing in councils and committees. When compared to the European Commission, it appears that the European Parliament, particularly its members from Green parties, is more supportive of the environmental groups. But so far, this has not changed their structural weakness because the Parliament still has little competency.

Patterns of Environmental Mobilization

Drawing on the categories presented in the first section, we can now try to roughly assess which kinds of strategies are used at which level to influence EU environmental policies.

As a rule, activities at subnational levels (local, district, region/state), which may be crucial for decisions referring to subnational and national environmental matters, are hardly relevant when it comes to EU environmental policy-making. Although many regions try to directly influence EU policies and have established their own lobbying offices in Brussels (Marks, Hooghe, and Blank 1996), they do so primarily to foster economic development and growth, not to protect the environment. Both in terms of lobbying and protest, the local and regional levels do not provide a promising leverage to influence EU environmental politics since these levels are not represented in the environmental policy-making process in Brussels.

However, targeting the national government, which, via the Council of Ministers or other national representatives, can have an impact in Brussels, may be an effective strategy. The previously established links between the national lobbyists and policy-makers can be used equally to influence decisions at the EU level, particularly when the national governments still have a formal veto power or, as is the case with Germany, can play a strong role because of their economic weight and the size of their financial contributions to the EU. While we can assume that lobbying national governments to influence decisions formulated in Brussels is important, the same cannot be said for institutional participation of citizens' groups at the national level. With few exceptions, such as the referenda held in some countries on whether or not to join the EU or to sign a fundamental EU treaty, no such opportunity exists domestically with regard to EU policy-making. A substitute for this missing opportunity could be the pressure exerted by demonstrative and confrontational protest. However, as we have seen, these forms of mobilization are important for national policies but not for those of the EU. To a still lower extent, protest activities of environmental groups occur in the places that host the major EU institutions (while at the same time negotiating and lobbying in Brussels is widely used). Nor are there many opportunities of institutional participation at the EU level, with the exception of appeals to the European Court of Justice—an opportunity that is extremely rarely seized by environmental groups.

We can summarize these assumptions and observations in a table, which presumably represents a pattern valid not only for the German environmental groups (table 6.1). The most striking aspect of this pattern is the absence of environmental protest in the form of political pressure and confrontation. This feature particularly calls for an explanation.

EXPLAINING THE ABSENCE OF ENVIRONMENTAL PROTEST IN BRUSSELS

In the following section, I discuss eight arguments that may account for the lack of protest in Brussels. Some of these arguments are of a more general nature, whereas others are specific to the domain of environmental policies. At a later point, I wish to conduct a more systematic empirical investigation

Table 6.1 Relevance of Strategies to Influence EU Environmental Policies

Kind of activity	*Subnational*	*Level of activity* *National*	*EU-Level*
Institutional participation	Absent	Less important	Less important
Bargaining	Less important	Important	Important
Political pressure	Less important	Less important	Absent
Confrontation	Less important	Less important	Absent

that will confront representatives from both national and EU-wide environmental groups with these considerations and assumptions.

A first and trivial reason for the absence of environmental protest in Brussels could be that the role of EU environmental policies is very minor relative to the national policies. If so, environmental groups would have little reason to shift their activities to Brussels. This argument, however, is not convincing in light of several facts. For one, according to the consensus of the literature on environmental policy in Europe, the EU has acquired significant competencies in this policy domain. Although national policies still carry more weight than those of the EU, a growing number of environmental questions are regulated by EU institutions (Liefferink et al., eds., 1993; Liefferink and Anderson, eds., 1997; Höll, ed., 1994; Jordan, Brouwer, and Noble 1999). This fact is acknowledged by most leaders of national and international environmental organizations, who are aware of the importance of EU policy-making (Brand et al. 1997: 231f, Hey and Brendle 1994, Ward and Lowe 1998, Roose 1999).

Second, even when acknowledging the importance of EU environmental policies, one could argue that this would not result in a growing mobilization in Brussels as long as the use of domestic channels of influence is more promising. Indeed, domestic pressure on the national government was, and in part still is, the preferred strategy of many interest groups that ultimately seek to influence EU policies. This may also be the reason why not all politically active interest groups "associate in Euro groups despite the fact that they are influenced by EU decisions," as a case study on Denmark demonstrates (Sidenius 1998: 86). As long as national governments have a strong say, let alone a formal veto power in joint decision-making in the EU, it may be not only more convenient but also more efficient to pressure their own government instead of trying to directly influence EU institutions. Time and again, domestic pressure has proved to be effective obtaining or maintaining privileges for particular interest groups (most notably the agro-business) or to prevent regulations that would have negative effects on them. In the last ten to fifteen years, however, this strategy proved to be less effective, particularly since the principle of consensus has been gradually replaced by a "qualified majority vote" in EU policy-making (Hix 1999: chap. 3). Thus, there is a risk that EU institutions, despite strong resistance of one or more countries in which environmental pressure is hard and successful, will eventually make decisions against the interests and activities of those who relied only on domestic mobilization.

Therefore, it seems safer to complement, or even substitute, domestic mobilization with mobilization that directly targets the EU. Given the shift of the locus of control to the supranational level, together with a move toward the majority rule in EU institutions, it is no wonder that the number of Brussels-based lobbyists has considerably increased, reaching an estimated 10,000 in the early 1990s (Secretariat 1992).[19] This general trend is also reflected in the growth of environmental lobbyism, which is another fact to reject the first two arguments presented earlier. However, the growing presence of environmental groups' offices does not translate into an increase of environmental protest in Brussels. Hence, we have to look for more specific arguments to explain this phenomenon.

A third and probably more convincing reason for the absence of environmental protest in Brussels might have to do with the possibility that lobbying EU institutions is by far more adequate and effective than the kind of unconventional protest action that is so common at national and subnational levels. One might even argue that confrontational action could undermine the position of the environmental groups that have gained recognition as "serious," "responsible," and "calculable" players. For instance, a Brussels-based representative of a European antiracist network stated that protest is not their business but rather a "job of our base organizations" in the individual countries (Ruzza 1999: 21).

One should also note that the Commission financially supports some environmental groups in Brussels. In the case of the European Environmental Bureau (EEB), which received over 400,000 ECU from the Commission in 1995, this was the main source of income (Webster 1998). This generous stream of money, which goes along with the privileged access of the EEB to the Commission, would hardly continue if the EEB promoted radical action.

It is also important to recognize that the representatives of environmental groups in Brussels are probably a special breed. One can hardly imagine that charismatic and passionate figures striving for direct action are attracted to the kind of paperwork and "shoptalk" that is required in Brussels. Rather, we find there administrators, experts, and people with diplomatic gifts who, while promoting the environmental cause, may also advance their chances for a future career within the EU administration.

Hence, career ambitions of lobbyists, together with their potentially negative perception of protest activities and—in some cases—financial dependence on the EU Commission, may be factors that, unlike the first two arguments presented earlier, could be valid reasons why protest is absent, regardless of whether this reluctance toward protest is "objectively" justified.

From the more detached perspective of an observer, it is not obvious why more confrontational action should undermine the position of environmentalist groups in Brussels. As a rule, demonstrative and confrontational protests that combine "appeal and threat" strengthen rather than weaken the cause (see Turner 1969, Gamson 1990). A probable exception to this is the outbursts of violence that may be counterproductive at least for some groups, though not necessarily for the farmers, whose actions, similar to those of fishermen and truck drivers, are met by an amazing degree of tolerance. Several studies have shown the advantages of the "radical flank effect" (Haines 1988), particularly when some groups retain their position of moderate negotiators while others concentrate on direct action. The environmental movement is diversified enough to allow for such a division of labor. So prima facie, there are no reasons to assume why such a combined strategy should only work at the national level and below. Also, one representative of a Brussels-based environmental group told me in an interview conducted in 1993 that they would welcome protest activities to strengthen their position (see also Lahusen 1999). It seems, however, that this is not the mainstream opinion.

Fourth, some characteristics of interest representation at the supranational level could make protest politics more difficult. Whereas the use of very different strategies in a national context may work well across different groups and organizations, it may be less effective when, in more general terms, interests and strategies vary greatly from country to country. International politics requires consensus and compromise across countries. Differences between the national sections of a given umbrella group tend to block any strong intervention and thus favor the status quo, as exemplified by the relatively toothless and sometimes even immobile European Environmental Bureau (EEB) in Brussels. Compared to smaller but more homogeneous and determined groups such as Greenpeace, the EEB has a low profile, especially when we look at the media reports. As long as environmental groups from some countries fight for stronger regulations, whereas groups from other countries find the current regulations fully satisfactory, and the voices of counter-lobbies from virtually all countries seek to soften even the existing standards, there is little chance of advancing the cause of EU policy-making, which is ultimately based on an aggregation of national positions.

As a matter of fact, it has been argued that environmental groups in the European Union have distinct national policy styles, with, for example, the German groups tending toward more radical demands and tactics, while the British are moderate and feel comfortable with the prevailing style of soft lobbying (Hey and Brendle 1994). Also, the fact that environmentalists, unlike farmers, are represented by several offices representing different groups hinders rather than facilitates the task of mounting a large protest, for which the organizers would have to agree on flyers, slogans, speakers, and the like.

With growing interaction across countries and groups, however, it appears that these differences are diminishing. Hence, we could expect at least a moderately growing readiness to open conflict, including protest action, in Brussels. The latter, however, is not happening as far as environmental groups are concerned.[20] So there is a likelihood that additional reasons work against a tendency toward protest politics.

A fifth reason for the lack of protest could be the notorious scarcity of resources in face of the numerous tasks. As previously indicated, the environmental groups retain most of their resources within their home countries so that their EU offices tend to be understaffed and, in addition to their main task of lobbying, have little energy to organize protest activities. This lack of resources probably exists not only because group leaders feel that the resources are needed more in the national arena, but also because it may be difficult to justify a significant transfer of resources to Brussels vis-à-vis the rank and file who are essentially focused on national and subnational issues. To them, EU policy-making is something distant and far more difficult to understand than national politics. Hence, they may not be supportive of a stronger engagement in Brussels at the cost of national presence and activity. Moreover, creating and maintaining transnational networks among heterogeneous groups is a difficult and time-consuming task that, in addition, is not appealing to some of the major players such as Greenpeace, which are keen to keep their own distinct trademark.

Sixth, related to the aspect of scarce resources and the problems of creating dense networks are the difficulties in motivating activists to protest in Brussels. One reason for this is simply the physical distance and the obstacle of traveling abroad (for reasons other than holidays). Another motivational hurdle may be the perception of the EU as a bureaucratic apparatus that is difficult to access and influence. Though a true bureaucracy, to an outsider EU structures rather resemble a jungle. Due to the fragmented and partly arcane policy-making process, it is difficult to determine who is really responsible and who should be addressed via which channels. In consequence, even environmental protests targeting the EU from domestic grounds are surprisingly rare. Moreover, when it comes to direct actions that interrupt routine activities, it appears that, compared to Brussels, it is easier to organize and to legitimate these in the home country where the protesters know the conditions and major players, speak the language, and can interact easier with target groups and bystanders.

Seventh, even though Europe exists as a set of political, economic, and administrative institutions, there is, in the foreseeable future, neither a chance for a postnational citizenship (Koopmans and Statham 1998) nor the possibility of a truly European public that could serve as an overarching sounding board for the demands and arguments of the protesters (Gerhards 1993; Eder, Hellmann, and Trenz 1998). Virtually all communication via mass media remains within the boundaries of national languages and discourses.[21] Journalists located in Brussels report only for the national papers of their respective home countries. They also complain that EU issues do not get the necessary space and attention in relation to their "objective" relevance. So it is likely that an EU-related protest in Brussels attracts less media attention than even a smaller EU protest in the domestic capital.

The last two aspects—structural difficulties in mobilizing protesters to go to Brussels and the absence of a strong European identity and European mass public—are by no means specific to environmental politics. Even the additional aspect of scarce resources is applicable to many groups in other policy domains, which, however, appear to generate more protest action in Brussels or Luxembourg.[22] Thus, we cannot assume that the previous three arguments provide a sufficient explanation. This brings us to a final argument. Taking the mobilization of farmers or workers as a reference point, it is obvious that these groups raise issues that are more obtrusive and more consequential to people's lives than most environmental topics. Whether or not an emission standard is tightened, whether or not the criteria for defining nature reserves are changed, whether or not one can assign to a product an eco-label approved by the EU—all of this has a relatively small impact on people's lives in relation to the threat of losing a job or being forced to sell a farm that is no longer economically viable. Moreover, as far as agricultural politics is concerned, national governments sometimes successfully use the EU as a scapegoat to divert criticism that otherwise might be directed to them. In such cases, concern, frustration, and anger appear strong enough to outweigh the obstacles against protesting in Brussels. Nevertheless, we should not forget that in addition to environmentalists, farmers also protest mainly in their home countries rather than Brussels (see Klandermans et al. in chapter 4 and Bush and Simi in chapter 5).

CONCLUSIONS

This chapter dealt with an apparent paradox: Regardless of the importance of environmental policy-making at the EU level, we find only a modest representation of environmental groups in Brussels and, more striking, an absence of environmental protest in the European "capital." Eight arguments have been presented and discussed that could account for the low profile of protest. In general, it appears that there exist considerable barriers to mounting protest action in Brussels, though most of these are not specific to environmental policy. Compared to other issues, particularly those in the domain of agriculture that do generate protest in Brussels, it seems that environmental matters do not have an impact on people's lives that is obtrusive, direct, and personally consequential enough to inspire people to surmount the obstacles. Because these obstacles are of a structural nature and will hardly change in the short term, there is little reason to expect a major strategic shift of environmental groups facing the EU. Lobbying will prevail over protest. Only when the general awareness about the actual—and increasing—relevance of EU environmental policy grows considerably, and when the limitations of the strategies of bargaining and lobbying become more apparent, will there be a chance that environmentalists will wage confrontation in Brussels.

NOTES

This is a considerably revised version of a paper presented at the conference of the European Sociological Association, Amsterdam, August 1999. I wish to thank Sidney Tarrow and Jochen Roose for their helpful comments on an earlier version and Amanda Dalessi for editorial assistance.

1. This brief account is mainly based on newspaper reports from the *Frankfurter Rundschau* and the *Süddeutsche Zeitung* in the days after the event.

2. Comité des Organisations Professionelles Agricoles, founded in 1958 with support from representatives of the European Communities.

3. EU denotes the European Union and, for pragmatic reasons in this chapter, all of its institutional predecessors bearing different names.

4. *Die Tageszeitung,* 23 February 1999, p. 5. For the description of this event, I also relied on reports from Agence France de Presse, for which I wish to thank Eric Lagneau.

5. At two occasions in Greece, the blockades lasted for two and three weeks, respectively. See Louloudis and Maraveyas (1997) and Bush and Simi in chapter 5.

6. In January 1997, farmers blocked for several days the airport in Milan to protest sanctions for exceeding the milk quotas set by the EU (see *Die Tageszeitung,* 20 January 1997, p. 6).

7. *Die Tageszeitung,* 26 November 1997, p. 5.

8. Besides, COPA exists as an alliance of agricultural cooperatives (Comité Général des la Coopération Acricole de la Communauté Européene—COGECA, founded 1959), which shares its fifty staff secretariat with COPA (Egdell and Thompson 1999: 124).

9. See *Die Tageszeitung,* 30 March 1995, p. 24.

10. According to the survey of Dalton (1994: 183) conducted in winter 1985–1986, a significant proportion of environmental groups in Europe ($N = 69$) did participate in "demonstrations, protests, or other direct actions": 25 percent did so often, 23 percent sometimes, 28 percent rarely, and 23 percent never.

11. On March 16th, 1997, 70,000 to 100,000 workers from various EU memberstates protested in Brussels against Renault's plans to close the plant in Vilvoorde, Belgium (see Imig and Tarrow 2000).

12. For a detailed analysis of the major environmental groups in the EU memberstates during the mid-1980s, see Dalton (1994).

13. The German WWF claimed to have about 185,000 donors in 1997 and Greenpeace about 530,000 donors in 1998. The importance of Greenpeace Germany is in-

dicated by the fact that roughly half of the money for international campaigns comes from Germany (27.7 Mio. DM), followed by the Netherlands (6.5 Mio. DM) and the USA (6.3 Mio. DM). See *Die Tageszeitung,* 10–11 July 1999, p. 8.

14. One of the few exceptions is Sascha Müller-Kraenner from the Deutscher Naturschutzring (DNR), the major umbrella organization of environmental groups in Germany. Constantly, but with moderate success, he argues to pay more attention to EU environmental matters. More recently, the DNR has established a small office in Berlin to cover EU environmental policies.

15. A total of thirty-eight environmental protests and three protests against nuclear power occurred before 1970.

16. When defined broadly, 5.5 percent of the antinuclear protests in Germany have a European dimension—that is, referring to at least one other European country. However, none of these protests is explicitly directed toward EU institutions.

17. The EEB, created in Brussels in 1974, was the front runner. Around the mid-1990s, it represented 132 organizations from 24 countries, including the 15 EU member-states.

18. The Union of Industrial and Employers' Confederation of Europe (UNICE) has more than 50 working groups (Schmitter and Streeck 1991). By the mid-1990s, the union represented 33 national associations in 25 countries. The Brussels secretariat has a staff of 40, but the organization can mobilize, if needed, a network of 1,500 experts in the specific federations (Lahusen and Jauß 1999: 79). The European Federation of Pharmaceutical Industry Associations alone had a staff of 20 people in the early 1990s (Greenwood and Ronit 1994: 38). For an overview on lobbyism in Brussels, see Mazey and Richardson, eds., (1993), Van Schendelen (1993), Pedler and Van Schendelen (1994), and Lahusen and Jauß (1999).

19. This figure did not include lobbyists focusing particularly on the European Parliament. In general, available figures on lobbyists vary greatly. "The Commission (1996) lists 637 pan-European non-profit-making organisations with which it deals[,] 118 (19 percent) of which are agriculture or food related" (Egdell and Thompson 1999: 122). Greenwood (1997) assumes the existence of 1,800 lobbying groups in Brussels, including representatives of single companies. Buholzer (1998, cited in Lahusen and Jauß 1999: 56) counted 828 European interest groups, 320 representations of firms, 131 national interest groups, 135 representations of regional and other subnational bodies, 142 advisers and 160 law offices, 46 chambers of commerce, 14 think tanks, 177 representations of non-EU countries, and 86 representations of international organizations.

20. According to Imig and Tarrow (1999: 124), the number of EU-related protests has tripled over the last decade in twelve Western European nations. This may be partly due to the fact that during the period discussed in that study (1983–1993), two states—Spain and Portugal—joined the Union in 1986. By contrast, data on three specific countries, including Belgium, indicate that there was no increase of European protests in Belgium from 1980 to 1995 (Reising 1999). If we divide this period into two halves, 229 protests occurred in 1980–1987 and 225 in 1988–1995. Assuming that most of these protests took place in Brussels, it is unlikely that EU-related protest in Brussels has increased.

21. Not surprisingly, efforts to create a truly European journal either have failed or, as in the case of *The European Voice,* a "Brussels-based weekly newspaper," attract only a small readership.

22. For example, at the occasion of an EU Summit about 35,000 people demonstrated in Luxembourg in November 1997 to demand EU measures to secure employment (*Die Tageszeitung,* 21 November 1997, p. 4). During the Summit in Amsterdam in June 1997, some 50,000 demonstrators required a policy to reduce unemployment and social marginalization. Among them was a French group of unemployed that had undertaken an eight-week march to Amsterdam (*Die Tageszeitung,* 16 June 1997, p. 3)

7

Multilevel Action Coordination in European Contentious Politics: The Case of the European Women's Lobby

Barbara Helfferich and Felix Kolb

The European Women's Lobby (EWL)[1] was created in 1990 and developed over the next ten years into an agency of representation of women's interests, recognized not only by affiliated organizations but also by European institutions. Today, the EWL has more than 2,700 affiliates in the fifteen member-states of the European Union, spanning the whole ideological, cultural, social, and economic spectrum of women's interests.[2] The EU plan to set up an Inter-Governmental Conference (IGC)[3] in 1996 and to amend the Treaty of the European Union provided a good occasion for the EWL to run its first major political campaign.

The EWL took advantage of this opportunity to work for the integration of a new gender equality clause into the Treaty of the European Union to overcome the absence of non–work-related issues in the EU's equal-opportunity policies at the time.[4] The Amsterdam Treaty, signed in 1997 and ratified in May 1999, would add important provisions to gender equality, including provisions for fighting discrimination outside of the labor market.[5] As we will show in this article, the amendments passed in Amsterdam were at least partly the result of a coordinated lobbying campaign of the European women's movement, spearheaded by the European Women's Lobby (see also Helfferich 1998). This policy change provides us with the possibility of examining the conditions in which public interest groups can influence policy—in light of the otherwise strong evidence that they more often fail to have much impact (Piven and Cloward 1977).

In attempting to analyze the impact of transnational public interest groups in the social policy field in Europe, our chapter draws on two intellectual strands: research focusing on the outcomes of social movement campaigns (cf. Giugni 1998) and the research tradition on policy change (cf. Keeler 1993).[6] We have chosen to investigate the campaign of the EWL, because it is one of the few European public interest groups in the social policy field that was successful in having its demands taken up by the governmental representatives negotiating the new Treaty of the European Union. The campaign, which was coordinated and run by the EWL—as well as by its national and European affiliates—included a variety of different strategies and activities, from informational and educational efforts to lobbying actions and activities on the European as well as on the national levels, plus the occasional protest mobilization.[7] While there may be a temptation to focus on the campaign activities themselves, we believe that it is equally important to look into the factors that created an environment that allowed the organization to conduct concerted actions in the first place. In the first section, we will describe the political context in terms of a *window for reform.* Our analysis will show that the success of the EWL can be attributed to the opening of the political system to public interest groups through the enlargement and integration of three northern countries into the Union and because a single group was able to take advantage of this political opening at the European, the trans-European, and the national levels. As we show in the second section, *multilevel action coordination* was the key to its success. In the third section, we turn to the actual campaign, analyzing the development of the EWL strategy and describing its activities during the Amsterdam campaign. In the conclusion, we will summarize our findings and suggest that success was a product both of the EWL's strategic action and of a favorable "window for reform."

THE POLITICAL CONTEXT: A "WINDOW FOR REFORM"

In this section we describe and analyze the political context in which the Amsterdam campaign of the EWL was carried out, before elaborating the hurdles the EWL had to overcome and its strategy and activities in its campaign. We believe that in order to understand the success of the EWL, we have to account for both the strategy and the context of the campaign separately. On the one hand, groups often fail to use opportunities provided by their environment (Banaszak 1996, Roose 1999) and, on the other hand, they sometimes apply previously successful strategies that will not lead to success when the political context is unfavorable (Kitschelt 1986). To capture the latter point, social movement scholars have developed the political opportunity structure approach. The basic idea of this approach—mainly developed in the United States (McAdam 1982, Tarrow 1998b) but also in Western Europe (Kitschelt 1986, Kriesi et al. 1995)—is that the dynamics, strategies, forms, and outcomes of interest representation are shaped by different characteristics of the local, national, and international political context (cf. McAdam 1998). The relative openness or closure of the institutionalized political system, the stability or instability of broad elite alignments, the presence or absence of elite allies for social movements, and state capacity for repression are some of the variables often used to operationalize the political opportunity structure of a given political system (McAdam 1996).

Recently, some scholars have argued that—due to the process of European integration—a new supranational level of political opportunities is developing, which is shaping both contentious politics on the European level and reshaping domestic conflict (Imig and Tarrow 1997, 1999; Marks and McAdam 1996, 1999). This work has largely focused on the institutional—and thus the most stable—parts of the European political opportunity structure. We argue that to understand the success or failure of groups involved in the process of European policy-making, we have to account for the more *fluid* aspects of political opportunity structures (cf. Goldstone 1980). To capture these factors, we apply the idea of a *window for reform,* as suggested by John Keeler (1993) in his study of "extraordinary policy-making." Keeler's central claim is that successful policy innovations are only possible when the various constraints that normally prevent policy changes give way to a policy window. We will argue that the EWL's activities surrounding the Inter-Governmental Conference (IGC) were embedded in just such a window for reform.

Keeler argues that two kinds of factors can act separately or in combination to open a macro policy window: first, "the size of mandate that the government enjoys" and, second, "the severity of crisis present during a would-be reform government's election and its first crucial months in office." (Keeler 1993: 436) He explains the influence of the size of mandate on the possibility of policy innovations using three different causal mechanisms:

- the *authorization mechanism,* which allows the government to appear authorized by the public to enact its program and thus reduce political and institutional opposition to policy innovation;
- the *legislative empowerment mechanism,* which empowers a government to implement its program by providing a large majority for the governing party or parties in the legislature; and
- the *party pressure mechanism,* which may create so much pressure from party activists who expect the government's commitments to be fulfilled that it makes reform politically unavoidable (Keeler 1993: 437–438).

To explain the influence of crisis, which Keeler defines "as a situation of large-scale public dissatisfaction or even fear stemming from wide-ranging economic problems and/or an unusual degree of social unrest and/or threat to national security" (p. 440), he points to three separate causal mechanisms:

- the *crisis-mandate mechanism,* which empowers and seemingly authorizes a new government to put extensive reform into effect;
- the *urgency mechanism,* predicated on the assumption that already serious problems will be exacerbated by inaction; and
- the *fear mechanism,* predicated on the assumption that inaction may endanger lives and property (pp. 440–441).

It is, of course, only possible to transfer Keeler's thinking with some major modifications to the European level. We suggest the following two modifications. First, because the EU is a multilevel system of governance (Marks, Hooghe, and Blank 1996) we think that it is not possible to concentrate on the mandate of a single European institution (Fligstein and McNichol 1997) or, in the case of treaty negotiations, the influence of the European Council on the policy process is overwhelming (cf. Moravcsik and Nicolaïdis 1999). Second, it is necessary to redefine Keeler's conceptualization of "crisis" so that it fits into the context of the European Union. Therefore, we modify his definition to specify public dissatisfaction as more than a national phenomenon, but one that can only be understood at the European level.

Three new developments in the power configuration of the European Union contributed to a broader mandate for the European Union to take new social policy initiatives during the IGC: First, northern enlargement changed the distribution of power in the European Council in favor of policies conforming to the Nordic traditions of open government, participation of citizens in welfare policy, and the institutional legacies of state feminism (Liebert 1999: 223f). In national position papers presented at the beginning of the IGC, it was only Denmark, Sweden, and Finland—as well as Greece—that urged the introduction of antidiscrimination provisions into the Treaty.[8] Second, the Maastricht Treaty had given the European Parliament (EP) new powers, which it was able to use to act as a sounding board for the public interest group proposals for the IGC (Liebert 1999: 227f). Finally, the victory of the Labour Party in Great Britain removed a major veto that had blocked the European Council in the social policy area during the Thatcher-Major period.

We also perceive a growing sense of "crisis" in the European project, following the debates about the implementation of the Maastricht Treaty (Liebert 1999: 195). This could be seen most clearly in the rejection of the treaty in the public referendum in Denmark in 1992 and in the greater level of disapproval among women than among men for the European Union (Liebert 1999) during the decade of the 1990s. The two factors in combination made the conditions for advances in gender policies more favorable.

Liebert (1999: 225) argues that the European Commission used the information on the gender gap in support of European integration drawn from the Eurobarometer surveys to legitimate its own policy preference for a more aggressive gender-equality stance. By the mid-1990s, a number of different actors saw the revision of the Treaty of the European Union as a chance to increase citizen support for the European project.

The Inter-Governmental Conference (IGC) provided the additional short-term opportunity to make use of this favorable political situation (Mazey and Richardson 1997). The 1996 IGC was the sixth in the European Union's forty-five-year history. To understand why the 1996 IGC was a major opportunity for the EWL, it is enough to recall that one of the major shortcomings of the European gender-equality policy was its limitation to the workplace in Article 119 in the Treaty of Rome. That limitation meant that policy innovation in the area of gender equality was unlikely without a new legal base in the Treaty of the European Union. The 1996 Inter-Governmental Conference was a major chance to achieve such a revision. This window of reform opened the way for serious consideration of changes in the treaty on gender equality. The active campaigning of the EWL was crucial for the extent of the changes.

The final outcome would fall well short of the Lobby's expectation, but it was nevertheless greeted as a success by the organization. While there is no new chapter on gender equality, the new Treaty of Amsterdam integrated gender mainstreaming as a guiding principle for all policies under Articles 2 and 3 of the Treaty. Furthermore it integrated equal opportunities into Articles 137 and 141 and even strengthened the provisions for equal pay by adding a new provision for equal pay for work of equal value. Certain provisions (Article 141) were also reinforced, allowing member-states to take positive actions to ensure more equal participation of women in the labor market. And finally, the new Treaty of Amsterdam added antidiscrimination provisions to Article 13—fighting discrimination on the basis of gender, age, sexual orientation, disability, race, and ethnicity.[9]

BARRIERS TO TRANSNATIONAL COLLECTIVE ACTION

Creating transnational public interest groups is more difficult than one might suppose—even in these times of Internet communication and cheap air travel. The editors of this book are particularly cautious regarding the potential of the Europeanization of contentious politics. "As a result," they write,

> of the difficulties most citizens have in ascribing the sources of their grievance to the EU; of the high transaction costs of coordinating collective action across

> national boundaries; and of the primary role of national governments in the EU, we are likely to see pressure continuing to be exerted domestically to demand their national governments take action on behalf of citizens' groups rather than see a direct replacement of contentious politics from the national to the supranational and transnational level. (Imig and Tarrow 1999: 119)

However, the mere existence of the EWL proves that at least sometimes these constraints do not prevent the creation of transnational public interest groups.

The idea of forming a European interest organization for women dates back to the early 1980s. The EWL's creation can be attributed to the perception on the part of a number of key national women's organizations that policy input at the European level was crucial for the advancement of their national agendas. Needless to say, the national groups that contributed to the founding of the EWL still exist and—as the EWL's Amsterdam campaign shows—can exert pressure on national governments to take action in European policy-making. The EWL is almost exclusively dependent on annual administrative grants provided by the European Parliament—about 85 percent of its total budget—and its survival and effectiveness depend on "friendly individuals" inside the Parliament and the Commission. These strategic alliances speak to the fact that European institutions are not homogeneous—a factor that can be exploited by interest organizations that have learned to navigate in the shifting waters of EU politics. EWL is frequently consulted by the Equal Opportunities Unit of DG Employment (formerly DG V) on a regular basis. Informal friendly contacts have led to formal and more important lobbying interactions, strengthening not only the role of the EWL but that of agencies trying to advance equality as well.

But the mere existence of a transnational interest group does not mean that it can automatically exert influence over European policy-making. On the contrary, certain challenges make it difficult for the group to engage effectively in European politics—challenges such as working in a policy environment in which power is shared by a number of authorities and levels, and overcoming the differences in outlook and interest of its national components. Building on earlier work on the weakness of Euro-interest groups (e.g., McLaughlin and Jordon 1993), we identify two of these aspects and their concomitant challenges—transnational interest formation and multilevel action coordination.

Transnational Interest Formation

Today, the European Union is composed of fifteen member-states with their own distinct histories, political cultures, and levels of socioeconomic development. In this context, interest articulation means not only taking account of different sectoral interests, but also adjusting to different regional differences (i.e., a nongovernmental organization (NGO) in Southern Italy may have different interests than an NGO in Northern Italy). Therefore, EU-wide umbrella organizations are—at least in theory—forums in which EU-wide sectoral interests can be constructed. While the European Commission values the European character of umbrella groups like the EWL (Lahusen 1999: 9), common interest formation presents a major challenge for them. The different outlooks and interests of their affiliates make it difficult to find common ground on positions that will go further than those proposed by the Commission or the member-states. Their political effectiveness depends not only on agreeing on a common policy position on specific issues but on establishing a shared interest. We call this process *transnational interest formation*.

Transnational interest formation is constrained for the EWL, first, by the way women are organized at the national level and, second, by how these organizations relate to their respective governments. In general, the greater the number and diversity of women's organizations at the national level, the easier it is for them to take views at the European level that are independent of their governments. In Germany, for example, only one women's umbrella organization represents the interest of German women in the European Women's Lobby, while in Greece, there is no centralized structure of women's organizations. Competitive relations at the national level are a crucial factor in the formation of a European interest position.

Second, how relations between interest groups and national governments are organized is of utmost importance for transnational interest formation. The Deutsche Frauenrat—the National Council of German Women—receives yearly funding from the German government. This has made it harder for the group to take positions independent of the German government. While the independence of groups like the Greek women's organizations can cause problems of efficiency—including barriers to the wide distribution of information—it offers more space in which to develop independent positions.

Differences in national organizational form and strength are additional causes of difficulty in transnational interest formation. The structures of women's organizations at the national level and European level are very diverse—ranging from individual membership organizations to umbrella organizations, which only accept other associations as their members. Fitting these different organizations into a common structure has caused a lot of debate, in particular in terms of the representation of the different groups. Some affiliated organizations challenged the fact that a small country like Luxembourg could send the same number of representatives to the EWL as a country like Italy or that a European organization with 100,000 individual members had the same number of representatives as another European organization with 300,000 members.

Regardless of these differences, in the course of the 1990s, interaction among national women's organizations allowed them to learn from each other and also to lessen their dependence on national governments. For example, during the EU debate over maternity leave, the Deutsche Frauenrat originally took a position quite close to that of the [conservative] German government at the time; but discussion with its sister groups within the EWL made it impossible for the German women to sustain this position, and they eventually came around to the majority viewpoint.

Given the barriers, the executive bodies of the EWL and its secretariat decided on a triple strategy in order to foster transnational interest formation. This was a conscious strategy, designed by people who had been involved in the organization's creation and who were aware of the fact that success was dependent on a high degree of consensus. Bringing a variety of national organizations of different types together to form a powerful organization with a coherent set of goals and participatory commitment was perceived as the first step in creating a successful transnational social movement organization. The strategy relied on three distinct actions: (1) working on issues that were noncontroversial and shared by all affiliated organizations; (2) providing expertise, funding, and information to member organizations at the national and local level; (3) encouraging dialogue between affiliates and the executive bodies and the secretariat of the EWL.

- With respect to the consensus-building goal, it was recognized that all affiliates shared the frustration over the absence of women in high decision-making positions, a fact that was particularly visible at the European level. Using consultants, the EWL produced a guide for how national and European women's groups could help increase the number of women in decision-making.
- With respect to the goal of service to national and local women's groups, the EWL started to feed information to members on the situation of women in decision-making in all member-states of the European Union, providing them for the first time with a comparative tool for exercising leverage on their own governments. The European elections of 1994 offered an opportunity for testing the utility of the EWL at the national level, first by providing funding for campaigns in each of the then twelve member-states and, second, by ensuring the distribution of information to all affiliates on the status of women's activities in each country.[10]
- With respect to increasing dialogue between national groups and the EWL in Brussels, the organization engaged in a dialogue with affiliates over controversial issues such as wages for housewives, quota legislation, and parental leave provisions.

This takes us to our next point: the organization's attempts to achieve what we call *multilevel action coordination*.

Multilevel Action Coordination

Most public interest groups are not strong enough on their own to have a major influence on European policy-making. This distinguishes them from other interest groups—in particular, business associations such as the European Round Table (ERT) and the EU Committee of the American Chamber of Commerce (Cowles 1995). Therefore, many public interest groups seek political support from the European Commission and the European Parliament (Warleigh 2000). However, even if they are able to mobilize support within these institutions, their influence in EU policy-making is limited compared to the power of the European Council. Therefore—as various authors have pointed out—the national route of lobbying is still of the highest importance (e.g., Mazey and Richardson 1996: 203).

Because of their inherent disadvantages, European public interest groups have to serve as a bridge between the national and the European levels, trying to mobilize their national branches to target their national governments in a kind of vertical "boomerang effect" (see Keck and Sikkink 1998). This interaction between the European and national levels of public interest groups is often problematic. As Lahusen observes:

> Firstly, national branches have different opinions in regard to the European Union and the goals and means to pursue them. Secondly, even in the case that a common position can be formulated there is the problem of committing national staff and local constituency to the activities approved and/or necessary. (1999: 14)

While we have discussed the first challenge in the previous section, we turn to the second one here: namely, that during political campaigns public interest groups must be able to vertically coordinate national and European actions in a process we call *multilevel action coordination*.

Although the EWL operates mainly at the supranational level, the most important lesson learned in its first few years of operation was that influence on European policy-making could only be successful with the support of national lobbying efforts. This implied not only sustained contact with national member groups and attempts at transnational interest formation but greater use of the group's resources to motivate the national organizations to undertake lobbying with their respective governments. The most important decision in this respect was to develop a system for informing members regularly about European policies and politics. This transfer of knowledge to the national level was intended to convince national organizations that European politics are important and that the EWL needed their support to have an impact on European policy-making. Drawing on European project funding, the EWL conducted several consciousness-raising campaigns in the member-states on the importance of European politics. Even today, one of the most important functions of the EWL secretariat is the publication of a regular newsletter that reports on national activities, a bi-weekly newsflash informing members and the general public of the latest developments at the European level and providing member-groups with information on funding opportunities. At the same time, the EWL has invested considerable resources in a Web page and for developing electronic mailing lists.[11]

To sum up, multilevel action coordination requires a learning period and an understanding of the issues at stake. Harmonized action, prepared by the Brussels office, not requiring too much innovative thinking at the national level, can help in developing common action plans. But without a common interest, it is not possible to act in a coordinated manner at different political levels; therefore, we conceive of transnational interest formation as a precondition for multilevel action coordination. We will demonstrate in the next section how the EWL worked to establish the recognition of common interests among its affiliates in relation to the Inter-Governmental Conference (IGC) and conducted a multilevel campaign involving affiliates at the European and national levels.

THE AMSTERDAM CAMPAIGN

In this section we describe and analyze the strategy and activities used by the EWL in the Amsterdam campaign. We structure our discussion in terms of the two major challenges described previously: the EWL's efforts in transnational interest formation and the need for multilevel action coordination.

Transnational Interest Formation

From 1994 onward, affiliated organizations of the EWL became increasingly active in the association—at times challenging the decisions of the relatively independent executive. Successful campaigns, greater recognition of the EWL, and the perception that the body had become an important player at national and international levels led affiliated organizations to demand a greater role in its micro-management. Fundamental policy issues also became more important, coinciding with the revision of the treaty of the European Union. While the EWL had previously shied away from engaging itself fully in a single campaign, affiliated organizations now demanded that it take up the challenging role of trying to shape the equality policies of the European Union.

At first it seemed easy enough to demand the inclusion of equality into the next treaty of the Union, but it took over a year for the Lobby to forge a common position based on a coherent set of principles. For although affiliated organizations at the General Assembly in 1995 decided that the EWL should take up the campaign for the inclusion of equality in the next treaty, the content of this decision needed specification. Meanwhile, the European Union had started to set up a group of experts to advise the member-states on what issues should be taken up by the next treaty revision. This group was, rather unfortunately, called "The Group of Wise Men." The EWL learned quickly that the composition of the group—while sensitive to member-state representation—included not a single woman except for one observer from the European Parliament.

In response to the creation of the group of wise men, the EWL decided to embark on a strategy combining expert advice with the widest possible consultation with affiliated organizations, in order to propose clear textual amendments to the existing treaty of the Union. The executive and the board of the EWL were both aware that successful lobbying depended upon producing a position paper on the treaty revision that not only reflected the vision of the EWL for the future of the European Union but that could be considered a professional and expert contribution to the discussion on the revision. The expertise that was required to produce such a text could not, at that stage, be drawn from the affiliated organizations, as it required extensive knowledge of legal texts and European issues.[12] Therefore, the board decided to appoint a shadow group from the member-states and the three current applicant countries, whose members were at the same time legal experts and active in women's organizations, and to seek funding from the Commission.

This "Wise Women's Group" met several times over the course of a full year. At these meetings, representatives of the secretariat of the EWL and the executive were present. Without much guidance from the political structures of the EWL, mostly because of a lack of knowledge, the group went through rather difficult discussions—in particular, on the scope of the document they were supposed to produce. Two different opinions struggled for predominance: many experts from the northern member-states wanted to limit the amendments to areas of equality issues, while the majority of the experts from the South supported the view that a revision of the treaty from a women's perspective needed to touch on areas outside of what they considered the limited equality field. The southerners believed that the EWL contribution should include amendments on issues such as poverty, education, institutional reform, and the civil dialogue, as well as workers' rights. In the end, a compromise was reached, which included proposing a whole chapter on equality to the treaty, commenting on civil dialogue, promoting the inclusion of the social protocol into the treaty, and calling for affirmative action measures. Comments were also made on poverty and education.

To sum up: between November 1994 and July 1996, the EWL developed its position on the basis of the expert group's document and regularly informed members and interested women on the development of the negotiations around the IGC. Consultation with affiliated organizations on the expert document led to some fundamental revisions of this document. It also showed that there was a growing interest among members to get involved in the overall lobbying campaign of the EWL and an increasing knowledge on their part about the importance of the revision of the European treaty for women. The treaty revision was an opportunity to rally around a single issue—the recognition of women's rights in the construction of Europe.

For the first time, women were being asked to respond substantively to a purely European issue. While there had been attempts before to involve different citizens and citizens' groups in European issues, the parameters had either been procedural (e.g., elections) or financial (e.g., European support for disadvantaged regions). This time around, the treaty revisions were directly related to the differing interests among and between different stakeholders. Moreover, the treaty revisions were to deal with the extent to which the European level could interfere with national politics both within and outside the labor market. This meant that certain issues became Europeanized, not least among them the issue of equal opportunities between women and men. For the EWL, it was a unique opportunity to act at the European level but with the explicit mandate of its affiliated organizations. The fact that the Union was trying to deepen its impact on national policies meant a greater opportunity for legitimization for the EWL.

But had the organization prepared itself sufficiently to take advantage of this "window of opportunity" to influence the process of the negotiations? Much depended on its capacity to articulate its activities with those of its affiliated organizations. There was awareness in the executive that affiliated organizations needed to take ownership of the EWL if the organization was to succeed in influencing the new treaty of the Union. Now was the time to test whether the structures and information channels that had been developed were appropriate to accommodate and instigate their full-fledged involvement in a European campaign.

Multilevel Action Coordination

At the general assembly of the EWL before the start of the campaign, the representatives of affiliated organizations expressed their full support for action at the European level. But it was left to the decision-making structures such as the executive of the EWL to further elaborate the overall strategy. The executive decided to embark on an education and information campaign—an effort that was greatly appreciated by the European Commission and other relevant European institutions, which feared that a lack of information about the IGC would lead to a popular rejection of the next treaty. The campaign was started at a European conference on "Women and the Construction of Europe" held in the European Parliament. It was followed by regular information meetings and discussions at EWL board meetings. The EWL also provided information materials for affiliated organizations, some of which organized information meetings at the national level.[13]

In August 1996, the EWL, interested in evaluating its information campaign and drawing lessons from it, conducted a survey among women on their opinions about the intergovernmental conference.[14] The survey revealed an overall negative attitude of women toward the European Union. Many women said that they regarded the Union as a club where little or nothing was gained, economically or otherwise. The answers to the questionnaire also revealed that women felt uninformed but were eager to receive more information in order to be able to judge better the impact of European integration on their lives. The results of the questionnaire served in no small measure to draw the attention of policy-makers to the needs of women in Europe. In fact, it helped the EWL to argue more forcefully for a gender dimension in the next treaty.

By the end of 1996, the EWL was fully prepared to engage in specific lobbying actions. With the backing of its affiliates, the executive and the secretariat began to develop an overall strategy by identifying relevant actors at the European and national levels, as well as evaluating the needs and possibilities for strategic alliances and interventions. Once its policy position had been amended and accepted by EWL-affiliated organizations, the real lobbying could start. In October 1996 the EWL met with Mervyn Taylor, the Irish minister for equality and law reform and with Bobby McDonagh, the Irish counselor in the Department of Foreign Affairs. In March 1997 it met with the Commissioner's Group on Equality between Women and Men, just to cite two key lobbying meetings that took place.[15]

Responding to a call by the European Parliament to hear the position of civil society on the impending treaty, the EWL was able to intervene there and present its point of view. At that particular hearing, it became clear that the EWL had worked more extensively on the treaty than comparable umbrella groups by providing precise amendments and the views of its affiliates. Important aspects of the EWL positions were thus integrated into the position that the European Parliament developed on the IGC. No small part of this convergence was due to the fact that the attention of many Members of the European Parliament (MEPs) was also captured at the national level where their constituencies were found. Affiliated organizations had had to learn to lobby the European Parliament via its national agents—the MEPs.

For many affiliates of the EWL, this was a new experience. The majority of women who were members of the national women's organizations had never voted or were not interested in the European Parliament, which they considered did not have any power at all. The campaign of the EWL and its affiliates, however, affected this attitude significantly. By providing national organizations with profiles of their MEPs—as well as their phone numbers and an encouragement to "just call them up"—the EWL encouraged, for the first time, contacts between members of the European Parliament and their female constituencies. This led to a dialogue that contributed in no small way to the politicization of women and the attention of the MEPs to women's issues at the European level.

It became more and more clear that the major lobbying work must be done at the national level, rather than at the European level. Therefore, it was decided to use a double strategy: The executive and the secretariat remained responsible for lobbying and information gathering at the European level, while at the same time supporting and encouraging their affiliates to engage in national lobbying efforts. In at least ten member-states, affiliated organizations—using the position paper prepared by the EWL on gender equality—engaged in lobbying their national governments and in efforts to raise public awareness of the importance of the IGC for the future of the gender-equality policy in the European Union.[16] To support these actions, the EWL board held meetings in different member-states for the duration of the campaign. These meetings were coupled with press conferences and meetings with national decision-makers.

The EWL secretariat also assisted national organizations in finding funds to organize national meetings of women's organizations on the issues of the treaty. Regular contacts between Brussels and national levels were intensified, and a large portion of the secretariat's resources was diverted to respond to inquiries about the treaty revision. EWL board members became more visible at the national level, and the programs of affiliated organizations started to emphasize work on the treaty. National organizations created their own publications and dissemination channels in relation to equality and the new treaty, focusing on the impact on women in their particular countries. And the national presses visibly picked up on these national campaigns. Some national parliaments took notice of these activities and organized hearings on this issue.[17]

The permanent contacts between the EWL and negotiating governments, reinforced by lobbying by affiliated national groups, enabled the EWL to go one step further than the other groups working on the treaty revisions.[18] In its consultations with national governments the EWL quickly learned that governments were coming up with different drafts and that—to be relevant—lobbying positions had to be adapted to the current state of negotiations. National government experts were meeting regularly to work on proposals and compromises on different issues. The EWL recognized that it had to get information about the drafts of these proposals and comment on their content. Unfortunately, these documents were not publicly available and governments were reluctant to reveal their contents even after the EWL demanded the documents be released. The EWL eventually got access to draft documents through the Finnish government, which—following a Finnish internal directive—was providing the information on demand. From that time on, the EWL presented its positions in a timely manner and succeeded in having them distributed as information notes during the actual negotiations of the governments' representatives. The information contained in the documents allowed the EWL to inform the national groups about the positions of their governments. The biggest lobbying success of the EWL during that particular time occurred when the Spanish affiliate convinced its government to adopt the EWL position as its own and to present it as such to other negotiation partners.

But the EWL's strategy relied on more than national and European lobbying. It was convinced that for its lobbying efforts to be successful, it would need to attract media attention. Therefore, a Europe-wide petition was initiated. Within six weeks about 40,000 people signed the petition and supported the EWL position on the treaty revisions. On Sunday, the 15th of June, the EWL organized a public march. During this rally, the EWL's president, Gertrud Wartenberg, handed a symbolic petition to a member of the Greek delegation to the IGC negotiations, who accepted it and agreed to bring it to the Dutch presidency.[19] In addition, the EWL worked together with other Europe-wide umbrella organizations—namely, the European Trade Union Confederation, the European Platform of Social NGOs, and other European organizations that all had a stake in influencing the negotiations. In particular, cooperation with the European Trade Union Confederation proved very helpful for the EWL lobbying activities, as the trade unions are part of the social dialogue (see Martin and Ross, chapter 13) and as such were a part of the required process of negotiations.

To sum up, the Amsterdam campaign of the EWL consisted of four central components: (1) the development of a comprehensive position on the IGC based on expert advice; (2) consultation with members of the EWL on the organization's position to provide it with a strong democratic base; (3) an information-awareness campaign on the Inter-Governmental Conference for the revision of the treaty (IGC); and (4) a lobbying campaign at both national and European levels, accompanied by the occasional mobilization of protest.

CONCLUSIONS

While European public interest groups can sometimes have an impact on public policies—as in the case we have just surveyed—they more often fail to do so, as in the case of the pro-migrant groups described by Virginie Guiraudon (see chapter 8). How can we account for this puzzle? Though we must be cautious in generalizing from a single case, we argue that two sequential sets of factors—best captured with the concepts *windows for reform* and *multilevel action coordination*—help to explain why the EWL was able to have an impact in the case of the IGC.

Windows for reform: Our findings about the importance of policy windows for the success of political campaigns correspond to similar findings on the role of periodic crises or cycles of protest in the study of the success and failure of domestic social movements (e.g., Goldstone 1980, Tarrow 1993). The difference in the case of the European Union is that—because it is a governance system of "variable geometry"—such windows open only briefly and at odd angles. We characterized the political context of the Amsterdam campaign as a window of reform created by a combination of factors. These included: (1) The new mandate of the European Union for social policy due to northern enlargement, the expanded powers of the European Parliament, and the victory of New Labour in Great Britain; (2) the legitimacy crisis of the European Union after the conflicts following the signature of the Maastricht Treaty; and (3) the decision to revise the Treaty of the European Union in an IGC. The window was opened at the angle of gender equality by the fact—revealed in Eurobarometer findings and quickly absorbed by the Commission—that the "Euro-skepticism" of the 1990s was affecting women more than men. The conjunction of these factors made for a fluid opportunity structure that could be taken advantage of by groups that were able to capitalize on it, and this takes us to our second—and more dynamic—element.

Multilevel action coordination: Often the strategies of European public interest groups are oriented toward the European Parliament and the European Commission, since both are very open to such contacts (Marks and McAdam 1999). But in the context of important intergovernmental decisions—like the one we have examined here—if a European umbrella organization wants to influence a decision-making process, it is extremely important that the group be able to mobilize its national constituencies, since the influence of both the European Parliament and of the European Commission is limited at that level. Member-states, their European MEPs, and citizen groups within them are potential targets for political arm-twisting.

The most important targets in the case of major treaty revisions are by definition the member-states. As Moravcsik and Nicolaïdis (1999) have shown, neither the European Parliament nor the European Commission had much impact on their outcomes. The EWL was only able to have an impact on the outcome of IGC because it coordinated a multilevel campaign together with its affiliated organizations, coinciding with a crisis of legitimacy for the EU and the entry of sympathetic northern European member-states. We think the EWL was able to do this because it was successful in building a unified transnational interest, but it could not have succeeded without a strenuous effort at multilevel action coordination.

We have used a case of major treaty revision, but we wonder if the need for multilevel action coordination is not just as important for other policy shifts as well. Groups that limit their activities to Brussels can too easily become caught up in the European equivalent of the "Beltway culture," lose touch with their national affiliates, and lack influence on their targets "inside the Ring" precisely because they lack the legitimacy of vibrant contacts with the grass roots. We think these findings and these questions call for a new generation of research on the outcomes of European contentious politics that examines not only the politics of the European Union but the Europeanization of politics as well.

NOTES

We thank Ulrike Liebert, Verena Schmidt, Sven Giegold, Doug Imig, and Sidney Tarrow for helpful comments on earlier versions of this chapter.

1. For an overview of the EWL and its activities, see http://www.women lobby.org.

2. It should be pointed out that the EWL is a nongovernmental organization that does not represent a party-political interest. Yet it does represent the whole ideological spectrum of the women's movement and the way women perceive their interests. There are the purely feminist women's organizations, which perceive women's repression as fundamental to the organization of existing society; and organizations that address women's interests in a more conservative way—even if they call themselves "socialist feminists." These organizations are mainly professional women's organizations, such as business women, or organizations linked to religious interests.

3. The term *Inter-Governmental Conference,* or IGC, refers to the exhaustive negotiations between the member-states of the European Union preceding the formal development of EU treaties, including the Amsterdam Treaty (cf. Mazey and Richardson 1997, Moravcsik and Nicolaïdis 1999).

4. For good overviews of the history of gender-equality policies in the European Union, see Hoskyns 1996 and Liebert 1999.

5. Article 3 of the Treaty adds the principle of "gender mainstreaming" to all policies of the EU; women were also added to the new article on antidiscrimination. At the same time, Article 141 was extended to include equal pay for equal work. In addition, the right and principle of equal treatment was enshrined in the Treaty.

6. We have called the EWL a "public interest group" but intend to draw on social movement theory to explain its outcomes. At first glance this may look problematic. But we agree with Marks and McAdam (1996: 251), who have pointed to the fact that the boundaries and conceptual coherence of traditional categories of interest representation are "historically contingent and, in light of current trends, increasingly problematic." We argue that, in the context of the EU, a rigid distinction between public interest groups and social movements does not mean much, because both stand in much the same relationship to the integration process and share the status of groups that hope to contest and shape the emerging institutions and philosophy of the European Union.

7. Most of the empirical evidence we will provide is based on the first-hand experience of the first-named author, who was the secretary-general of the EWL between 1991 and 1999.

8. European Commission, DG IV: Inter-Governmental Conference; Briefing no. 35, 20 May 1996.

9. It should be underlined that the EWL rejected the inclusion of gender into Article 13, on the grounds that women cannot be considered a group but comprise half of the population.

10. This action not only raised the EWL member groups' visibility—and, incidentally, that of the EWL itself—but convinced the group's members that their actions had contributed to increasing the number of women in the European Parliament from 19 to 25 percent. Needless to say, measuring success in influencing electoral outcomes is difficult, if not impossible; our point here is that many members of the EWL were convinced that their actions contributed to the success of women candidates in the 1994 European elections.

11. But multilevel action coordination also requires that umbrella organizations must be sensitive to the priorities of their affiliates. When European issues arise, such groups must be prepared to offer enough logistical support so as not to strain their scarce resources. European actions must be based on a recognition of the differences of members' resources, their particularistic concerns, and their level of motivation. The organizational structure of the EWL proved helpful for multilevel action coordination. The EWL has a board of administration where all member-states are represented, as well as some ten key European organizations. While its large size of twenty-five members makes decision-making very difficult, it is helpful for reaching agreement about national and European priorities.

12. Expert advice was considered suspicious by a number of affiliates, in particular those closest to the grass roots. Some of these suspicions proved to be well founded; after the expert group had submitted its position, the EWL sent it out to affiliates for consultation. Despite the fact that the experts were aware of their limited remit, some of them presented the expert document to the public as the document of the EWL without awaiting the amendments of the EWL affiliates.

13. There was also a clear divide between northern and southern countries. Interestingly enough, women from the southern countries exhibited more awareness and motivation than women from the north. This can be explained by the fact that the poorer countries depend for their economic development so much more on the funding from the European Union. But that alone is an insufficient explanation. Many women's organizations in the southern countries perceived the EU as a vehicle to improve their national equality legislation. The different degrees of involvement from the south and the north were also reflected in the discussion among the members of the expert group.

14. *European Women's Lobby Newsletter,* Special Edition "The Intergovernmental Conference," April–May 1997, p. 11.

15. *European Women's Lobby Newsletter,* Special Edition "The Intergovernmental Conference," April–May 1997, p. 10.

16. For a summary of these activities, see *European Women's Lobby Newsletter,* Special Edition "The Intergovernmental Conference," April–May 1997, p. 12f.

17. At one point, the EWL was so absorbed in supporting and encouraging work at the national level that it nearly undermined the group's coordination role. However, the EWL was able to pull together information on the activities in the member-states and disseminate it so that organizations that had not been heavily involved

could learn from the "good practice" of others. At the same time, the results of individual campaigns were used to refine the position of the EWL in relation to amendments serving to reinforce the legitimacy of the EWL at meetings at the European level.

18. The following two paragraphs contain material formerly published in Helferich 1998.

19. Newsletter of the EWL, July/August 1997.

8

Weak Weapons of the Weak? Transnational Mobilization around Migration in the European Union

Virginie Guiraudon

PROLOGUE: A TRANSNATIONAL PROTEST AGAINST "FORTRESS EUROPE"

On December 6th, 1998, in Berlin, the German human rights league (Internationale Liga für Menschenrechte) awarded Madjiguène Cissé, a leading figure of the undocumented "Africans of Saint Bernard," the Carl von Ossietzky medal to acknowledge the "civic courage" of the *sans-papiers* movement in France. In his congratulatory speech, *Süddeutsche Zeitung* journalist Heribert Prantl stated: "The *sans-papiers* movement could play the role in the social and political history of the European Union that the Polish trade union Solidarnosc had in Eastern European history." Mixing "fortress Europe" analogies with Cold War imagery, the journalist went on to denounce the "irresponsible European consensus" on asylum and concluded that "the European Union was building a new iron curtain: a wall of computer technology, bureaucracy, and mobile border police units."[1]

A few months later, on March 27th, 1999,[2] a "European demonstration for the rights and freedoms of foreigners" took place in Paris. The French coordination of the *sans-papiers* (undocumented aliens) and allied organizations,[3] along with a dozen social movement organizations from other European countries, signaled a call for an "open Europe" and the end of detention and expulsions of foreigners, as well as the regularization of illegal aliens. Italian left-wing organizations were the most numerous and quickest to respond: the Associazione Ya Basta, the Centri Sociali della Carta di Milano,[4] the Movimento delle tute bianche, and Gli invisibili. The last two movements decided to occupy Italian trains to get to Ventimiglia, the last

Italian town before the French border, and bring with them a delegation of visa-less Albanians from Valona and of asylum-seekers coming from Trieste (on the Slovenian border). The idea was to rally Paris without paying on "the train of free movement."

But the 3,500 Italian, French, and Albanian demonstrators aboard the train from Italy were turned back at the French-Italian border for several hours and, for two days, the French government suspended the implementation of the Schengen agreement that abolishes internal border controls. The protesters had made their point: the supposed Europe of free movement was a sham as long as governments could re-erect barriers when confronted with the risk of social protest. The Italian initiative also gave a new boost to the three-year-old French *sans-papiers* movement that had become plagued with internal strife and rivalries.

These events point to the European dimension of the new social movement that has been calling for the regularization of undocumented aliens in France since three hundred undocumented Africans occupied a church in Paris on March 18, 1996. Is this social movement "transnational" in the sense intended by Imig and Tarrow in their introduction to this book? In other words, can we observe "sustained contentious interactions with opponents—national or non-national—by connected networks of challengers organized across national boundaries" (Tarrow 1998b: 184)? What can certainly be observed are sporadic international political exchanges and instances of cross-border diffusion through press coverage. In the *sans-papiers* movement, we find evidence of several types of transnational activity. The organization has a Web site (http://www.bok.net/pajol)[5] that is frequently updated and has served as a useful means of building an "imagined community" for the movement. By January 1999, over 2,100 people had visited the commemorative multilingual page set up after the death of Sémira Adamu, a twenty-year-old Nigerian asylum-seeker who was killed on September 22, 1998, during a forced expulsion from Belgium.[6] She has become the first "European martyr" of the movement.

Transnational contacts also take place in more direct ways,[7] mainly through young French activists who were *objecteurs de conscience* abroad.[8] Finally, there have been instances of what an activist described as "panic-based transnationalism."[9] When, in the fall of 1998, the "godfathers" of undocumented aliens heard that the Italian government was going to grant legal status to undocumented aliens on their soil, they came to meetings asking activists for the names and fax numbers of associations in Italy that could tell them whether they should take their undocumented protégés across the Alps to obtain papers.

Yet such demonstration effects are nothing new; they have existed since the eighteenth-century revolutions and occurred again in 1848, in 1968, and during numerous movements such as the workers' and the women's rights movements. They are emblematic of the modularity of the repertoire of modern social movements (Tarrow 1998b: 37–41). Moreover, the movement has privileged actions with French natives, other "have-not" movements (the homeless and unemployed movement), and movements with similar repertoires of action such as Act-Up, all of which belong to a new French "cycle of contention."[10] Furthermore, the *sans-papiers* have chosen French-specific frames rather than universal human rights frames. African immigrants recalled their grandfathers and fathers who died for France during the two world wars, arguing that the duties that their ancestors had fulfilled entailed rights for their descendants. *Sans-papiers* were given "Republican godfathers (and godmothers)," French citizens who helped them solve administrative problems. The ceremony emphasized French obsession with the upholding of "Republican values," the same values that the current minister of the interior calls upon to justify why 62,500 undocumented aliens will not be granted a residence permit.

In relation to the EU institutions, instead of grass-roots movements, we will see the emergence of small elite networks of academics, lawyers, and International Nongovernmental Organizations (INGO) activists who use their expertise and present proposals for European action on immigration and asylum.[11] The forms of European-level or Europe-wide contention around migration issues involve these networks with European officials, rather than in transnational social movement activity. More important, there is a missing link between grass-roots, local, or even national-level contention around migration issues and these EU-based NGOs (nongovernmental organizations) or networks.

This chapter asks how and how much the opportunities provided by European Union organizations and rules have fostered cross-border contention and shaped pro-migrant groups' strategies, claims, and capacity to weigh in on policy outcomes. The logic of the analysis is as follows:

- First, I elaborate a matrix of incentives and constraints regarding migrant transnational contention based on theoretical and empirical studies.
- Second, I turn to the transnational "issue networks" and European-based NGOs that focus on migration, citizenship, and antiracism and target EU institutions.[12] Three types emerge: (a) transnational networks stemming from Commission-funded projects that required "transnationality," (b) representative consultative bodies founded and funded by a legitimacy-seeking Commission, and (c) lobby-like initiatives supported and partly funded by an input-seeking Commission. They seem obscure to grass-roots migrant organizations that, by and large, have little knowledge of EU opportunities.
- Third, I analyze EU organizations and institutions to determine the "value added" of mobilizing at the European level. I will ask what resources EU institutions, such as the Commission, have to offer migrants'

groups and whether they provide other incentives for transnational mobilization.

My research indicates that some pockets within the Commission bureaucracy have offered material help and support to pro-migrant European activists. The complex division of labor within the Commission bureaucracy keeps evolving, as immigration-related issues are incorporated within the realm of EU competence. This partitioning and reshuffling might provide "windows of opportunity" for activists seeking entry points into the policy process. However, the EU does not produce a coherent discourse on migrant rights that could frame the claims of transnational pro-migrant organizations, and these organizations have not succeeded in linking collective action at the base to their lobbying efforts in Brussels. What transnationalization occurs is mainly the result of EU incentives from above.

THEORETICAL AND CONTEXTUAL PREMISES

Before turning to migrant groups and their relations to the EU, it may be useful to briefly discuss the various theory-driven *ex ante* expectations that can be derived from the existing scholarship on transnational migrant mobilization.

One set of studies, which examines the *internal resources* of migrants and the specificity of migrant movements, considers that transnational mobilization is a natural phenomenon for migrants. For scholars in this tradition, migrants entertain transnational ties almost by definition as they operate socially, culturally, but also politically in a "transnational space" between their country of origin and the country of settlement. They also have links with fellow migrants in other sending countries—whether these links stem from belonging to the same kin or national, religious, or political group (Cohen 1997). A growing literature on transnational communities illustrated by the work of sociologist Alejandro Portes and his students has insisted that modern communication technologies and cheaper air travel facilitate the maintenance of links across borders—even though such links are not new per se (Portes 1998). Some of them have political ramifications (Levitt 1997). Case studies of Moslem or Turkish migrant social movement organizations in Europe also often point to this phenomenon (Amiraux 1998, Ogelman 1998, Césari 1997).

Yet despite having transnational ties, migrants do not necessarily have the material resources to operate at the European level that other lobbies or interest groups do. Moreover, this generally disenfranchised, socially disadvantaged group is also very divided, not only because it is made up of so many groups—a factor that can impede action coordination at the national level—but also because its members have different agendas, depending on the nation-states where they have settled. As Riva Kastoryano has pointed out, the nation-state has been the main structure or context within which migrant groups have been socialized but also their main interlocutor with which they have sought to "negotiate their identities" as they contested prevailing notions of citizenship or political inclusion (1996). In brief, a predisposition to maintain links across borders with one's community does not solve the "Tower of Babel" problem that emerges when different ethnic groups operating in discrete national institutional contexts seek to coordinate their actions, define a common agenda, and find an Esperanto for collective action.

Nonetheless, a second group of scholars focusing on transnational norms has argued that such a common language is available in contemporary Europe in the form of a human rights discourse. Yasemin Soysal has argued that postwar Europe has seen the emergence of a postnational model of state membership based on residence and "personhood," crafted and diffused through transnational collectivities in Europe (1994). Other studies claim that international human rights norms undermine national policy efforts to control migration flow and curtail migrant rights (Sassen 1996, Jacobson 1996). In Soysal's view, "international governmental and nongovernmental organizations, legal institutions, networks of experts, and scientific communities . . . by advising national governments, enforcing legal categories, crafting models and standards, and producing reports and recommendations, promote and diffuse ideas and norms about universal human rights" (1994: 152).[13]

Soysal's work, along with that of other "institutional" sociologists, belongs to a renewed scholarly interest in the diffusion of norms of conduct through the agency of international organizations, institutions, and transnational activist networks.[14] These "norms"—often defined as collective understandings of appropriate behavior—correspond to a great extent to "framing processes" in social movement studies (McAdam, McCarthy, and Zald, eds. 1996, part 3). According to this view, migrants can draw upon the norms of European Union organizations to claim rights. This view seems plausible since the European Commission and Parliament have tended to support initiatives in favor of migrant rights and integration, and the European Court of Justice has sometimes consolidated the rights of third-country nationals. It should be underlined, however, that EU organizations have supported migrants for reasons that stem from their own institutional modus operandi and *telos:* the furthering of the Treaty of Rome's four freedoms and the internal market, to name the most obvious ones, and the expansion of their own realm of competence.

These claims about the utilization of "postnational" norms in the claims-making strategies of migrants in Europe have not gone unchallenged. A number of recent comparative studies have demonstrated the importance of *national* political contexts in shaping migrant political activism. Patrick Ireland's study of migrant mobilization in France and Switzerland showed that ethnic groups organize along different cleavages, make different claims, and resort to different strategies in the two countries, depending on the participatory channels and citizenship rights available in each nation-state (1994).[15] Similarly, based on event count analysis drawn from a cross-section of British and German newspapers from 1990 to 1995, Ruud Koopmans and Paul Statham found little evidence supporting the "postnational model" (1998). Less than 1 percent of the protest events that they studied targeted EU institutions (.5 percent in Germany and none in Britain). They conclude that the main "territorial frame of reference of minority claims-making on immigration and ethnic relations" remains the nation-state (57.9 percent of the German cases and 86 percent of the British ones).

Still, as several EU states signed the Schengen implementation agreement in 1990, and as the Treaty on European Union of 1992 institutionalized transgovernmental cooperation on justice and home affairs within the "third pillar" of the European Union, there has been a shift in the location of decision-making in the field of migration control to European sites. Perhaps more important, we know from past research on European integration that the EU can regulate areas such as the environment despite the absence of a Treaty basis to do so—even when member-states are opposed to it. Bypassing national institutions to appeal to European institutions whose decisions have a direct effect has generated the desired "boomerang effect" and forced change at the national or subnational level (Keck and Sikkink 1998). These changes could result in a corresponding shift of contention on the part of migrant groups.

Table 8.1 offers a matrix of opportunities and constraints for transnational action around migration in the EU, based on categories drawn from social movement research. As the matrix suggests, in a number of ways we can entertain hypotheses in both directions. Although we are far from possessing the kind of systematic research that Imig and Tarrow call for in their introduction, a qualitative analysis of migrant-based and migrant-supporting contentious politics can help to suggest the kind of EU-driven transnational activity that has already taken place.

EUROPEAN PRO-MIGRANT NETWORKS AND TRANSNATIONALIZATION

Is there currently a Western Europe transnational issue network around migration issues of the kind that Kathryn Sikkink (1993) and Audie Klotz (1995) have discussed in relation to Latin America and South Africa or that Daniel

Table 8.1 **Opportunities and Constraints for Transnational Migrant Contention**

Factors	**. . . enhancing** transnational contention	**. . . hindering** transnational contention
Resources	Transnational migrant communities	Divisions based on the country of origin AND destination among migrant population
Frames	Postnational membership and human rights	National citizenship and incorporation models
Locus of decision making	EU "third pillar" has instituted cooperation on migration and asylum.	National/local government dispenses rights.

Thomas (1995) found in Eastern Europe? Perhaps surprisingly—given the high degree of institutionalization of the European Union and the inherently transnational nature of migration—such networks are much less developed or influential than those of other groups such as the environmental movement or the consumer-rights lobby (Cram 1997).[16] Commission officials never fail to state that they support nongovernmental organizations.[17] But despite the presence of a few NGO projects in Brussels and efforts of the European Commission's Directorate General V (Employment and Social Affairs) to sponsor a Migrants' Forum, there is very little interaction between these European-level groups and migrant organizations that operate domestically in the member-states.

European Activist Networks: Creating or Co-Opting "Input"

In this section, I study the two major migration-related initiatives that involved the creation of a European activist network targeted at EU institutions: the European Union Migrants' Forum (EUMF) and the Starting Line Group (SLG).[18] The EUMF's experience demonstrates the difficulties that migrants face when trying to push for a common European agenda; the SLG initiative in the area of antidiscrimination shows that it is possible, but the group is not made up of migrants and only indirectly serves their interests.

1. *European Union Migrants' Forum.* The Migrants' Forum was founded in 1991 by the European Commission acting upon an initiative of the European Parliament. It speaks for 130 migrant associations that hold an annual general assembly and elect every other year an executive board and executive committee (helped by a six-person staff in Brussels). Since 1995, it has created a "support group" in each member-state, whose elected president

also sits on the board. The Migrants' Forum's charter defines this group as a consultative body of migrant populations designed to ease communication between EU institutions and migrants (Forum des migrants 1995). The Forum is an official channel of interest representation. Its role and functioning are in great part engineered by the Commission (Commission of the European Communities 1985). For instance, the latter succeeded in limiting participation in the Migrants' Forum to third-country nationals or non-EU citizens (Danese 1998). This in effect split the migrant association network that had existed since 1971. Its executive body was called the Conseil des Associations Immigrés d'Europe (CAIE). The main umbrella organizations represented in the CAIE had been composed of associations of European migrants (mostly southern European). They were therefore left out of the Forum, along with the most active organizations and experienced leaders. The Commission's move was perhaps a way of circumscribing the agenda of the Forum according to its own needs for input, as well as a means of resolving some of the problems that the Forum had faced very early on.

Indeed, all studies of the Migrants' Forum point out numerous difficulties in finding common ground among the migrant lobby groups and in defining an agenda (Kastoryano 1994, Geddes 1998). The very word *migrant* was problematic since many people of migrant origin are citizens of one of the member-states. The term was also criticized for suggesting fleetingness. The Migrants' Forum was very divided, as different ethnic groups publicly expressed antagonism. In particular, the Turks and the Moroccans vied for control of the organization, with the Moroccans eventually winning out and giving the organization a francophone cast that sets it apart from the largely anglophone, NGO-lobby world of Brussels.

The Migrants' Forum's problems stem not only from the fact that migrants in Europe are made up of many different groups but also from the different agendas that depend on the nation-states in which they have settled (Kastoryano 1996). In fact, the British Commission for Racial Equality preferred to create a parallel organization (SCORE, Standing Conference on Racial Equality in Europe), rather than join the Migrants' Forum, on the grounds that their system was the best and should not be diluted. Europhobia and a belief in the superiority of their antidiscrimination provisions combined to make the British opt out once again (Favell 1998b). In the Migrants' Forum, there are national groups for each member-state and regional "ethnic" groups grouping migrants of similar origin, but national groups from the EU's largest and most influential countries—the French and the German groups—dominate the discussion.

The "national groups" tend to reproduce the incorporation and citizenship models of their host countries, thereby making dialogue difficult. Migrants from Scandinavia and the Netherlands favor multicultural policies, while those from France have internalized the assimilationist Republican model of integration. In some countries, such as Germany, legal discrimination is still very much an agenda that unites migrant groups, whether they call for an easier access to citizenship, dual nationality, or recognition of minority religions. This is not the case in other northern European countries or in Britain, where the emphasis is on nonlegal discrimination (in housing or hiring). Stemming in part from these differences, the modes of organization of migrants vary as well, from contentious "rainbow coalitions" to federated, ethnic-based interest groups. They therefore have not only different claims but also different cultures of contention (Ruzza 1999).

2. *The Starting Line Group.* Academic and NGO legal experts from six member-states founded the Starting Line Group in 1992 in order to draft an antidiscrimination article for the 1996 Inter-Governmental Conference that led to the Amsterdam Treaty. It now has 130 associated organizations that range from international NGOs to interest groups and associations. Its core group is British and Dutch, and there is a strong "Nordic" bias to its membership. At first, the group received support from well-established national agencies dedicated to antidiscrimination, such as the British CRE (Commission for Racial Equality) and the Dutch LBR (National Bureau against Racism), as well as from the small Brussels-based NGO now called the Migration Policy Group (formerly the Churches Commission for Migrants in Europe). The MPG had local knowledge and provided logistical help. The European Parliament endorsed its proposal for antidiscrimination law in 1993. By now, about three hundred organizations (NGOs, INGOs, and social movement organizations, associations, and interest groups) are associated with the SLG (Starting Line Group 1998).

Unlike the Migrants' Forum, the Starting Line has vigorous leadership and a clear agenda that requires expert knowledge and therefore could gain approval by EU technocratic standards. The antidiscrimination clause project was reminiscent of the Equal Treatment Directive of 1976 and of Article 119 in a very Euro-correct way. Leading up to the 1996 ICG before the revision of the Treaty, EU institutions that had been accused of neglecting the "democratic deficit" were receptive to initiatives that showed a gentler, kinder Europe or in any case had a social component. The timing was therefore ripe for the SLG initiative. In the end, the SLG speaks on behalf of migrants' interests yet is very far removed from their grass-roots organizations. Its relative success suggests that lobbies that propose expertise to EU institutions such as the Commission are more likely to be listened to than those that can only claim legitimacy of origin in migrant communities.

In summary, European-level activist networks in the area of migration are still in their infancy and face a number of hindrances. So far, they resemble more the institutions they are lobbying than the constituencies they are supposed to represent. And as we will now see, the effect of Commission emphasis on transnationalization has been to benefit a few well-placed and savvy groups at the cost of many others whose claims to representativity are equal or greater.

Transnationalization from Above

The Commission funds a number of migrant associations and their initiatives (Commission of the European Communities 1995). Directorate General V—Employment, Industrial Relations and Social Affairs[19] has been the main provider of capital, since it finances projects against racism and xenophobia, actions in favor of migrant workers and their free movement, and initiatives favoring the integration of refugees. In addition, DG-V managed a budget of ECU 4.76 million, allocated to fund local, national, and European activities as part of the European Year Against Racism (EYAR—1997), and the budget has been rising every year since then—up to 7 million in 1999.[20] Finally, after the 1995 Barcelona Euro-Mediterranean conference, DG-I (External Affairs) opened a budget line called "Med-Migrations" that funds migrants' organizations registered in an EU state that have partners in both their sending and receiving countries, so as to foster "co-development."

Securing EU funds would seem to be an incentive for migrant associations and migration-related NGOs to inscribe their action in a European context. In the case of the DG-I "Med-Migrations" budget line, transnational cooperation was made a clear prerequisite for those applying for funds. It has also become a plus when competing for DG-V funding and a requisite for qualifying for funds under the antiracism budget line. It necessitates at the very least a good amount of "Eurosavvy" to write a grant proposal that conforms to the Commission's ideas about (European and migrant) integration and to fit with the categories that the DG-V supports. In brief, European institutions can provide resources to immigrant groups, yet obtaining them requires the mobilization of knowledge and preexisting networks, which is bound to disadvantage some groups. EU capital depends in many ways on social and cultural capital or what Clifford Geertz called "local knowledge" (1980).

Recent research on migrant associations and networks suggests that they operate in a transnational space only under certain conditions and at a price (Ogelman 1998, Amiraux 1998, Danese 1998, Boussetta 1997, and Césari 1997) and that some are far better placed than others to do so. If one takes the example of the Moroccan organizations, interest in their home countries was activated by the creation of associations that focused on cooperative ventures with Morocco (Migrations et Développement in France and Komitet Marokkanske Abeiders Nederland in the Netherlands). They could rely on the Moroccan opposition in Europe, which had maintained networks and contacts both there and in Morocco. When the Commission's Med project took shape, Moroccan associations with ties to the opposition networks were therefore much better placed than other national groups—like the

Malians and the Senegalese—who lacked the European connections or the political knowledge that the Moroccan opposition network had.

Seizing upon European opportunities has proven difficult for many national migrant groups. It seems almost ironic that the Commission in its discourse calls migrants victims of "social exclusion" and yet wants them to organize costly transnational activities. The Brussels-based organizations that speak on their behalf end up benefiting from funds that were intended for grass-roots migrant associations. Churches, trade unions, and NGOs with older and extensive networks throughout Europe have an advantage. A 1995 report assessing 200 of the 560 projects on migrant integration that DG-V funded between 1991 and 1993 demonstrates that only 16 percent of them were migrant-led (Commission of the European Communities 1995: 10). NGOs, churches, trade unions, and organizations involved in housing or education issues made up the rest of the beneficiaries.[21]

Commission funding of projects for the integration of migrants can be divided into two phases. Before 1995-6, division D.4 of the DG-V did not identify funding possibilities, criteria for granting aid, or programmatic goals, aside from "promoting the integration of migrants." As the Commission officials realized in their first evaluation report in 1995, this meant that only a few projects were migrant-led (32 out of 200). Brussels-based NGOs, such as the Churches' Committee for Migrants in Europe (CCME), were overrepresented. Just getting to the information, knowing how to write a budget, and having a contact within the Commission were sufficient to win over the competition.

After 1995, for reasons developed in the next part of this chapter, DG V laid down clearer criteria for support—including that of transnationality. The transnational NGOs that got funded before 1995 because they were in a better position to know about the funding opportunities were now funded because they were able to demonstrate their "transnational" character. With 2.6 percent of the proposals, Brussels-based NGOs got 6.8 percent of total funding, a clear success. Nevertheless, the small local projects that got funded before 1995 could no longer be financed; as a result, Keck and Sikkink's "boomerang effect"—whereby the resource-rich help the resource-poor—disappeared in favor of a "Commission helps those who help themselves" effect. The report on the EYAR (European Year Against Racism) states that 28 percent of the submitted proposals were rejected because they could not satisfy the "transnationality" criterion (Commission of the European Communities 1998).

Operating transnationally is not necessarily a positive sum game.[22] For Brussels-based activists, European skills are not necessarily transferable to the local or national level. The personnel in an NGO such as the Migration Policy Group are typical of the emerging polyglot Euro-elite, conversant in EU jargon, who have mastered the tacit rules that govern the European "political field" (Favell 1998a). Many do not have a local or national "base." Inversely, even local activists living in Brussels have little or no contact with the Migrants' Forum or contacts with Brussels-based NGOs. Other scholars point out that grass-roots migrants' organizations suspect European activists—such as the members of the Commission-sponsored Migrants' Forum—of being controlled by EU institutions, unaccountable, inaccessible, and unaware of local issues (Danese 1998). Even among groups such as the Islamists—who have a European dimension and a transnational agenda—there is still very little knowledge of the EU (Amiraux 1997).

The personal and organizational networks in which an NGO such as the Migration Policy Group evolves include INGOs, UN and Organization for Economic Cooperation and Development (OECD) experts, American liberal think tanks, and foundations such as the Carnegie Endowment for International Peace, as well as legal circles. They produce information for EU institutions and international forums more than they give information to groups from smaller national and local units. These international forums are also the locus where European NGOs find ideas to import to the European context. In this respect, they do not relay ideas or demands from grass-roots organizations to Brussels; in Adrian Favell's terms, Brussels NGOs act as "gatekeepers" for national and local social movement organizations (1998a), if only by choosing whom they help get EU funds or to whom they provide information. As an illustration, the DG-V defines the organizations that qualify for funds within the framework of "actions in favor of migrant workers" as follows: European NGOs, consultants for the Commission, and associations chosen in agreement with local national authorities and the Commission. There are few sustained links between national and subnational activists and Brussels-based NGOs that claim to represent their needs.

EU OPPORTUNITIES AND INCENTIVES FOR TRANSNATIONAL MOBILIZATION

EU institutions and rules favor certain types of nongovernmental activities over others. When considering European Union institutions and their role in guaranteeing the domestic rights of certain groups, such as women, or in certain areas, such as social rights (Pierson 1996, Alter and Vargas 1997), there are reasons to believe that they could constitute a new opportunity structure for third-country nationals, open new spaces for migrant mobilization and new venues for claims-making, and serve as an added source of protection for the rights of foreign minorities. Although states have been circumspect regarding the "Europeanization" of migration-related issues and presently enact restrictive entry and stay policies toward third-country nationals, there is no a priori reason to deny the possibility of a gap between their intentions and EU developments.

To assess whether this is indeed the case, we need to understand the legal openings that allowed migrant interests to become a matter of European "competency" in a particular issue area. We must also study the role that the Commission units have played and analyze their respective outlook, structure, and the instruments at their disposal. Both elements are crucial to understand the strategies of social movement organizations that seek to influence migration policy *through* European institutions or to flourish *thanks to* the support of European institutions.

The Emergence of Commission Funding and Support

Until the 1990s, member-states refused to delegate competence in the area of migration control and immigrant policy to the EU. In 1985, the Commission issued new guidelines on migration (Commission of the European Communities 1985) and argued that integration policy entailed a better access to rights for foreign residents. In July, it adopted a Decision setting up a procedure for prior communication and consultation of new policy toward third-country nationals. Five member-states contested the move successfully, and the European Court of Justice annulled the Decision in 1987.[23] The Commission's competence was confined to the free movement of EU citizens.

The unit (D.4) within the Commission called "Free Movement of Workers, Migrant Integration and Antiracism" was created in 1958 to handle issues related to free movement of labor. It is situated within the DG-V. Over the years, the unit became involved in matters relating to the integration of migrants and refugees and, since 1986, antiracism. The head of the unit, Annette Bosscher, held her post for many years, compensating for the high turnover of her twenty-member staff. European-based activists therefore had a faithful interlocutor, who, as it happens, firmly believed that European integration should go hand in hand with the integration of non-Europeans. DG-V handled many budget lines that sponsored migrant-related projects.[24] As we saw in the last section, the work of DG-V civil servants involves financing and consulting with NGOs, and therefore Brussels-based activists and DG-V civil servants are in constant contact. When, in July 1998, the European Court of Justice ruled that there was no basis for subsidies to antipoverty programs by EU institutions and the Commission blocked all "social budget lines," including support for the integration of migrants, EU civil servants demonstrated side by side with NGO in front of Commission offices.

The unit has faced many challenges, often related to the very thin treaty basis for its actions, and has known many setbacks for the same reason. For its own survival and expansion, it has therefore had to adapt in creative ways. Once the ECJ had ruled that cultural integration of migrants was no business of the EU, other bases of intervention had to be found. One consisted in jumping on the bandwagon of the EU war on "social exclusion"

(Article 137 of the Treaty of Amsterdam) as a justification for its actions. Many of the unit's policy documents insist that migrants and their descendants are prime victims of social exclusion and that nongovernmental organizations know best how to fight it.[25]

Social exclusion encompasses a wide range of issues and programs, and Brussels-based NGOs promptly responded to this signal by linking the question of migrant integration in the 1996 Inter-Governmental Conference to this agenda rather than to the debates on European citizenship (Article 8a of the Treaty on European Union), as had been the case following Maastricht.[26] The way in which DG-V framed the issue has had significant implications. It has found echoes in some member-states, such as Great Britain, where the Giddens-inspired Blairist focus on the need for an "inclusive society" now fit in the Commission's policy frames and was further legitimized by EU institutions. In turn, NGO projects—and academics applying for EU grants—further argued for the relevance of "social exclusion" as a prism to understand the need of migrants.

As member-states became wary of the expansionist attitude of the Delors Commission and of the Commission bureaucracy and Euro-skepticism set in, they jealously guarded the principle of "subsidiarity": what can be best solved at the local or national level should be dealt with at that level. All units managing projects and proposing measures now had to tread softly and explain why they—and not national bureaucracies or local authorities—should intervene. This was also the case among DG-V staff since, in the early 1990s, many of the funds that had been directed to the integration of migrants went to small local projects (Commission of the European Communities 1995). In this hostile atmosphere, where the Commission was also coming under fire for the opaqueness of its funding procedures, the DG-V unit needed to establish clear requirements that also showed the added value of EU funding.[27] Its staff decided to include "transnationality"—defined as projects involving the cooperation of multinational teams—as a criterion for receiving Commission funds. This stemmed from the legal constraints under which it had to operate; for without some underlying "European" justification, member-states could seek to annul programs for nonrespect of the subsidiarity principle before the European Court of Justice.

In summary, the promotion by Commission bureaucrats of nongovernmental actors operating transnationally at the EU level must be understood as their creative way of responding to criticism from other institutions while expanding their realm of allies and their spheres of action. "Transnationality" served the first purpose and "social inclusion" the second one. But the unintended consequence of this strategy has been that the groups most likely to benefit from this situation—rather than grass-roots migrant's associations—were either preexisting transnational networks or Brussels-based NGOs. The latter had the added advantage of being composed of British and Dutch activists who could draw upon their credentials and expertise in the area of antidiscrimination.[28]

Post-1992: Exploiting Divisions within the Commission

Based on the premise that free movement in the European single market presented a security risk that required "compensatory measures," the 1990s have seen increasing cooperation among European Interior and Justice officials on migration control rather than on immigrant integration, and on the retrenchment of rights for asylum-seekers (Lavenex 1999, Hix and Niessen 1996). Title VI of the Maastricht Treaty formally placed discussion of conditions of entry and residence of non-EU nationals under the EU umbrella (articles K 1–9) and created the "third pillar" on Justice and Home Affairs (JHA) with one full subcommittee (GD1) of the intergovernmental negotiating institution (the K 4 committee) dedicated to asylum, visas, and migration. The framework required unanimous decisions by the Council. Moreover, as a separate "pillar," migration policy-making remained outside the community legal order, the Commission did not have the sole right of initiative for proposals, and the Parliament and the European Court of Justice were not involved and were unable to weigh into the Justice and Home Affairs discussions. In brief, while member-states have transferred sovereignty with respect to the migration of EU nationals, they have been reluctant to do so in the "emerging regime" on asylum and migration of non-EU nationals (Koslowski 1998).[29]

From Maastricht to Amsterdam, the Justice and Home Affairs council only agreed on one joint position—on the common definition of a refugee—and on five legally binding joint actions, regarding school travel for third-country national children, airport transit procedures, a common format for resident permits, burden sharing for displaced persons, and human trafficking. Yet although very little has been achieved, there has been an intensive exchange of information, the construction of common terms such as *safe country of transit,* the definition of problems in a supranational context, and common decisions such as the establishment of a list of countries requiring visas. This has been done without input from the aforementioned Commission unit, let alone the NGOs involved in migration-related issues.

The process has also dis-empowered certain pro-immigration national actors. Transgovernmental cooperation in the fields of asylum and immigration is increasingly taking on the characteristics of a multilevel intergovernmental regime, in the sense that the relevant actors in policy-making can be found in Brussels, in certain national ministries and central agencies, and at the subnational level (for instance, German *Länder*). The policy network thus created includes experts, consultants, liaison officers, and non-EU governments but *excludes* a number of actors who had better access in a horizontal negotiating process at the national level: for example, most of the national ministries concerned with aspects of migration do not attend international negotiations and working groups. National parliaments have no input and are not informed: they are faced with the fait accompli when they are given a few weeks to ratify conventions such as the 1990 Schengen Implementation agreement. Certain ministries and agencies have established a quasi-monopoly on international cooperation on migration and asylum and have more autonomy during national ministerial consultations with labor, social affairs, or health ministries. This has led to a new and narrower power distribution.[30]

The other major consequence of the 1992 Maastricht Treaty and the "third pillar" has been the way in which it has divided the Commission. Before 1992, DG-V was the only DG with a unit specialized in migration issues, yet it had no official competence or informal influence when it came to the rights of third-country nationals and asylum. After 1992, some personnel were located in DG-XV ("Internal Market and Financial Services") in a unit dedicated to "Free Movement of Persons and Citizens' Rights" and focused on EU migrants. Concomitantly, a small task force was set up within the General Secretariat of the Commission to liaise with the Council on JHA migration discussions—from two people, its staff has grown to ten. Responsibility was split, personnel scattered, and, more important, divergent points of view emerged within the Commission.

After 1992, European NGOs defending migrant interests therefore had to refocus their agenda on antiracism, antidiscrimination, and questions linked to social exclusion, where a number of Commission divisions could provide funds and lend a sympathetic ear to their proposals. They engaged in venue shopping, building on the various policy linkages that the struggle against racism permitted. The socially conscious units within the Commission have tried to increase their contacts and develop common projects with units in charge of poverty or old age within DG-V. As Luca Pierozzi, working full-time on antiracism in DG-V, pointed out, for procedural reasons alone, it is not easy to work together in this maze-like bureaucratic machinery.[31]

The Treaty of Amsterdam that came into force on May 1, 1999, shifts the whole area of immigration and asylum to the first pillar, while the so-called Schengen *acquis* will be incorporated by protocols into the EU framework. A new directorate general responsible for the application of the Amsterdam Treaty provisions was constituted in the fall of that year. In the new college of commissioners headed by Romano Prodi, for the first time there is a commissioner in charge of justice and home affairs, António Vitorino. Moreover, many lower-level civil servants in the new DG come from other services, including DG-V. Euro-activists have to adapt to this new situation and may have better access than in the previous period to the units in charge of immigration and asylum. This reshuffling within the Commission will provide new opportunities for European activists, and their old Commission friends will get a second chance to make proposals on immigration. EU institutions are reorganizing frequently as new treaties are adopted and European civil servants adapt their strategies to the mood of member-states. The incentives and targets of European activists shift as well, as they seize windows of opportunity (such as an intergovernmental conference or a bureaucratic reorganization). They need to find new access points within the Commission, whose tasks and organization expand by developing new agendas and issue linkages.[32]

In fluid times like these, the nongovernmental actors most likely to read the signs on the wall, to decipher the new organizational grids and lists of personnel, and to anticipate policy priorities will remain the small elite-run, Brussels-based NGOs such as the Migration Policy Group that keep their ear to the ground. They have the know-how and the personal contacts to do so. For local and national-level groups, the effects of these changes are more difficult to grasp; failing to exploit the changes leaves them—if anything—enmeshed in national opportunity structures as the policies that affect their constituents' movements and rights gravitate to Brussels.

CONCLUSIONS

If this story conformed to T. H. Marshall's theory of citizenship (1965), to American social movement theory (Tilly 1995b), and to much of the work of sociological institutionalists (Boli, Meyer, Ramirez, and Thomas 1997), migrants in Europe would mobilize resources on the margins to force their incorporation in the mainstream political system. In this process, they would seize upon the opportunities provided by EU rules and organizations. But so far, grass-roots migrants' associations in the member-states have made little use of this supranational "political opportunity structure." As for migrants' associations at the European level, they have been better able to avail themselves of a discourse of transnationalism than to either forge working ties with their supposed constituencies or positively affect EU policies in their favor.

What explains this "failure" of migrants in Europe to utilize the resources on the margins of the European polity? Three specific reasons and a general, "cultural" one can be suggested:

- First, the EU does not provide incentives or opportunities for pro-migrant groups that do not fit its goal of a deepening of European integration. The unit within the Commission that has been consistently supportive of transnational associative networks and European INGOs, DG-V, has had no clout in the negotiations on the harmonization of migration policy.

- Second, notwithstanding this, one now sees the emergence of transnational ethnic organizations and EU-level lobbying activities seeking to put issues such as racial discrimination and a common status for third-country nationals on the Union's agenda. But these are distinct from the grass-roots migrants groups that organize, for the most part, at the intranational level. The latter lack access to the technical know-how and the Brussels-level connections that the EU-level lobbying groups enjoy.
- Third, officials from regional or national interior and justice ministries have successfully carved out an EU security "policy domain." The forces that seek to further control migration and limit the rights of migrant minorities have been more efficient at building transgovernmental networks than the migrants have in building a transnational movement.
- Finally, migrants face a more subtle challenge: that of being accepted as full members of the polity implicitly forces them to act as natives rather than as cosmopolitans in a way that would not apply, in contrast, to native—regional or ethnic—groups making self-determination claims through international organizations.[33]

For migrants, faced by their inherent dispersion, by the greater resources and expertise of Brussels-based lobbies, by the much greater clout of transgovernmental antimigration forces, and constrained by the felt need to integrate into their host countries, European integration provides them with only weak weapons of the weak.

NOTES

I thank the San Giacomo Charitable Foundation of Turin for support to the workshop on the Europeanization of Contention at Cornell University to which this chapter was first presented. I thank the participants of the workshop; its organizer Sidney Tarrow; the discussant of my paper, Gary Marks; and the Institute for European Studies at Cornell. I am indebted to a number of colleagues for comments on earlier versions of this chapter: Christian Joppke, Adrian Favell, Andrew Geddes, Rainer Bauböck, and Aristide Zolberg. I am grateful to the Social Science Research Council Committee on International Migration, the Mellon Foundation, the Program for the Study of Germany and Europe, and the Program for the Study of Modern France for funding various stages of the research and the writing of this project.

1. The transcript of the speech can be found at: www.bok.net/pajol/international/allemagne/liga/prantl.html.

2. The date was chosen to echo a more global call for a world day of struggle against exclusion launched by the Zapatistas.

3. These included trade unions, the Greens, organizations on the extreme left, and social movement organizations such as Act-Up and the homeless movement Droit Au Logement.

4. They maintain contacts with French Trotskyist groups such as the LCR that have backed the *sans-papiers* from the beginning, hence the large presence of Italian groups.

5. The site's webmaster, Marc Chemillier, the son of law professor Monique Chemillier-Gendrot, who wrote several books on immigration and also supports the *sans-papiers,* participated in the international meeting "The Next Five Minutes" in Amsterdam on March 12–14, 1999, of protest groups that use the Internet. They appeared with the Munich-based "Cross the Border" site that launched the "no man is illegal" network in Germany.

6. See http://active.park.be/expulsions/index_content_htm.

7. Most of the contacts with other movements abroad, especially in Germany, have been made through one man, a left-wing journalist called Mognis H. Abdallah from the Im'média agency.

8. Interview, Cyril Le Roy, responsible for immigration issues, MAN (Mouvement pour une alternative non violente), Paris, March 1999.

9. Interview, Alice de Dehn, member of Les Verts (the French Green party), responsible for security and coordination during *sans-papiers* protests, Paris, March 1999.

10. Many migrant self-help or solidarity groups did not lend any active support to the *sans-papiers*. Some were purposefully kept out of events because of their links to mainstream political parties (e.g., the Socialist-linked SOS Racisme). Institutionalized migrant associations made up of ex-colonial migrants or former guestworkers did not want to be associated with the movement. They had won a secure status and rights and were ready to close the door behind them. African associations, especially *soninke* ones that had been very involved in projects back home, criticized the movement for portraying Mali as "hell on earth" (Costa-Lascoux 1997: 110).

11. The most recent example is that of AGIT (Academic Group on [Im]migration—Tampere). The group's core group is made up of five Dutch and English academics who compiled a document entitled "Efficient, Effective and Encompassing Approaches to a European Immigration and Asylum Policy," published in *International Journal of Refugee Law* (Autumn 1999). Another twenty have been consulted and the document was disseminated through electronic mail and international conferencing. Their stated audience, however, is the policy-making community present at the EU Council and in national and European units involved with migration and asylum.

12. This was a means of generating more cases, and sometimes the issues overlap or one organization or movement addresses both. Of course, the issues are distinct, since different laws and rules govern them and they involve different populations (legal foreigners, naturalized citizens, refugees, illegal migrants).

13. See Checkel (1999) for a critique and corrective of these studies, arguing for process-tracing research design and the need to focus on agency and to study the social learning of norms. See Joppke (1998) for a further critique of the "postnational norms" argument.

14. The latter re-emerged in the early 1990s as a legitimate competitor to interest-based or power-based explanations (Goldstein and Keohane 1993, Sikkink 1993, Finnemore 1993, and Katzenstein, ed., 1996). Earlier, historical institutionalists in comparative politics had explored anew the role of ideas and paradigm shifts to explain policy variations (Hall, ed., 1989).

15. Adrian Favell's longitudinal work on Britain and France (1998b) underlines the ways in which the interactive relationship between national institutions and migrant groups contesting dominant definitions of citizenship and nationhood result in diverging modes of migrant organizations and demands. Other concurring comparative studies include Brubaker (1992), Kastoryano (1996), Guiraudon (1997), and Joppke (1999).

16. About one hundred associative networks have offices in Brussels.

17. See the speech by commissioner Padraig Flynn in the Santer Commission at the conference on "European Approaches to the Socio-Economic Inclusion of Immigrants and Ethnic Minorities" at the European Parliament in Brussels, on 7 July 1998, where he praised Jan Niessen, the head of the think tank Migration Policy Group.

18. This is not a sample but rather an exhaustive list of organizations that claim to represent migrant groups in Brussels.

19. The numbers of the directorate generals are no longer in use, starting in the fall of 1999, and their names and attributions have partly changed—following the implementation of a new treaty, an internal reform of the Commission, and the nomination of a new college of commissioners headed by Romano Prodi. Yet since my research covers the period up to these changes, I use the numbers and names of the Delors and Santer commissions.

20. See Commission of the European Communities (1998) for details on the projects funded.

21. Even fewer migrant organizations were involved in the Year Against Racism: only fifteen associations from all member-states applied for funds that the Commission had explicitly aimed at migrants (*Courrier du Forum,* January–February 1998). In fact, the city forum of migrants' associations in Bologna lodged a complaint with DG V and asked for an extension of the funding into 1998. In Italy, local governments, trade unions, and NGOs had received all the funds (Danese 1998). The same held true in other southern European countries.

22. See Valérie Amiraux's study of Turkish Islamic associations in Germany that demonstrates "the limits of convertibility of transnational resources" (1998).

23. See the 9 July 1987 decision in joint cases 281, 283–5, 287/85, Rec. 1987, 3023.

24. The Unit administers about 10 million ECUs for refugee integration, 6 for migrants, and 5 for antiracism every year. On average, about two full-time members manage each area, the rest of the unit being made up of people handling the legal problems associated with free movement.

25. See, for instance, *Guidelines on Preparatory Measures to Combat Social Exclusion 1998,* which calls for the mobilization of the NGO community and for transnational initiatives (Brussels: CEC, 1998).

26. The gap between EU citizens and so-called "third-country nationals" has widened since the Treaty on European Union granted special rights to EU citizens (local voting rights to EU nationals residing in other member-states).

27. Interview, Joline Wellinghoff, DG-V, European Commission, March 1999.

28. This was not the case of French or German national activists, whose struggles were focused on citizenship issues. Both groups are not present among the personnel of Brussels NGOs focusing on migrants.

29. The only directive adopted by the Council of Ministers that was applied to non-EU citizens regarded the education of migrant children. It dates back to 1977, when

governments were hoping that foreigners would go back to their countries of origin and encouraged pilot programs that taught children their parents' native tongue (Directive of 25 July 1977, *Official Bulletin* no. L199 of 6 August 1977).

30. Actors such as police intelligence and military forces competing for space in their national settings or seeking new functions have welcomed supranational negotiations. Scholars have highlighted their construction of the notion of a "European security space" to legitimize their accrued presence at the supranational level—for example, comparing the single market to a sieve allowing for mass human-smuggling operations and increasing migration flows (Bigo 1996).

31. Interview, DG-V, European Commission, Brussels, March 1999.

32. This should not obscure the fact that the regulatory power of the EU institutions is still limited in the area of immigration, thereby limiting their capacity to impact on policy.

33. On the contrast between migrant and native contention vis-à-vis international law and organizations, see Rainer Bauböck (1998, 2000). I am indebted to the author for pointing out the comparison to me.

4

THE FORMATION OF EUROPEAN ACTORS

9

Media Construction in the Dynamics of Europrotest

Pierre Lefébure and Eric Lagneau

On February 27, 1997, the French car manufacturer Renault announced that it would soon close its Belgian assembly plant at Vilvoorde, laying off some 3,100 employees. In response, a coalition of labor unions, including the combative FGTB (Socialist), the moderate CSC (Christian-Social), and the minority ACLVB union immediately launched a strike. With the support of wide sectors of the Belgian population and external support from unionists and political groups abroad, the strike ultimately lasted seven weeks. Before it ended, the French and Belgian governments, as well as members of the European Parliament and Commission, had become involved. And the media—focusing on the transnational aspects of this collective action—had labeled the campaign against Renault a "Eurostrike." Certainly, the Renault affair revolved around social, political, and legal issues with European dimensions. But how did it come to be framed as European by the media? It was neither the first protest campaign involving European issues, nor was it framed as such by striking workers and their unions. In this chapter we examine the construction of the Renault campaign as a *European* movement action, both in terms of the actions of the threatened workers and also as the result of a series of broader discourses across a wide range of political and media actors (c.f., Lagneau and Lefébure 1999a,b).

To demonstrate the importance of this broader context, we compare the Vilvoorde actions to actions by unemployed workers across the continent. While both protest campaigns revolved around European grievances and targets, they differed markedly in the degree to which they were constructed and portrayed as European by the media. Our explanation of these differences revolves around the internal dynamics of each movement, shifting cultural understandings of the relevance of the EU, the self-definition of participants' claims as European, and the process of consciousness-raising and collective identity construction.[1] We argue that, as these examples demonstrate, the media plays a key role in each of these aspects of the process by which contentious political action comes to be framed as European.

THE MEDIA AND CONTENTIOUS ACTION

At the most basic level, a press report is the product of a set of *interactions* between reporters, their sources, their profession, and the public. Because their work emphasizes coherence and visibility, journalists tend to look at a protest from a simplified perspective, usually drawing heavily upon one or two angles or "frames." Because of time constraints and the effort to maintain a position of neutrality, routine media practice is to seek information from "accredited sources." Through this dynamic, institutions, experts, and public authorities gain precedence over protesters as "primary definers" of public controversies, establishing "the limit for all subsequent discussion by framing problems" (Hall et al. 1987: 59).

Over the last two decades, researchers have emphasized the difficulty that contentious collective actors face in trying to control the ways in which their actions will be framed by the media (Molotch and Lester 1974, Glasgow Media Group 1976, Tuchman 1978, and Fishman 1980). Some observers have gone so far as to suggest that the principal function of the media is to defend the interests of "the ruling class" (Molotch 1979: 78; Olien et al. 1989). Media routines and practices also mean that—in part—protesters will gain more or less favorable coverage, depending on certain "phases of controversy" (e.g., initiatory activity, problem definition, legitimization and mobilization, and "cooling off"). As a result, at certain times "protest groups . . . can succeed in gaining extensive media attention . . . [and] protest group sources were mentioned more frequently during high coverage periods" (Gitlin 1980: 157). Still other researchers differentiate between the quantity and the quality of media coverage, which can be particularly important for movement actors, since getting media attention is one thing, while getting favorable coverage is another (Kielbowicz and Sherer 1986).

We apply two lessons from this research to the campaign against Renault. First, the media collectively are likely to be active in determining the level and type of coverage the protests receive. Second, the ways in which the media interpreted the Vilvoorde actions are likely to have reflected a range of factors beyond any simple evaluation of the "objective" nature of the protests. In short, the relationship between the media and contentious political actors is interactive, with many voices contributing to how protest campaigns are ultimately framed (Snow and Benford 1988; Gamson 1988, 1992; Gamson and Wolfsfeld 1993). As Wolfsfeld (1984, 1991), writes:

> The role of the mass media in political protests is determined by the interaction between the antagonists (e.g., protest group[s] and the political authorities) and the mass media. . . . The transactional approach to this issue views the process as a two-way flow of influence in which it is just as important to study the influence of antagonists on the mass media as it is to look at the more conspicuous influence of the mass media on political actors. (1991: 1)

There is considerable complexity in how social movement activity is presented and understood. To a certain extent, everything seems to hang on interpretive rules that compete with one another at different levels. As Olien et al. write:

> Media reports center on the established rules which are being protested and on whether the protesters are following socially accepted rules for expressing grievances. Which of these two questions of "rules" is emphasized by the dominant institutions will have ramifications for media reporting and, ultimately, for public perceptions of the protest." (Olien et al. 1989: 140)

We think this "interpretive effect" is decisive in determining how a particular protest is represented to and perceived by the public. This, in turn, can condition not only how the protesters behave in subsequent phases of the campaign, but also whether or not the campaign becomes a "founding event" for future interactions. Can we observe this dynamic at work in the Vilvoorde actions?

VILVOORDE

The mobilization against the closing of the Vilvoorde plant provides us with the opportunity of applying this analytical approach to the issue of "Europeanization." A review of media coverage of the actions reveals that during the initial stages of the protest, the Vilvoorde issue received intensive media coverage and elicited numerous statements from central political figures. This stage in the protest campaign also focused on the interactions among a number of major players and a shifting and unstable interpretive logic around the theme of "social Europe."

One of the factors that determined how the actions against Renault were portrayed was the degree of *social conflict* involved in the actions. In addition to their occupation of the Vilvoorde plant, workers also seized an inventory of some 5,000 finished vehicles; there were also ten demonstrations that drew large shares of media coverage, including mass demonstrations in

Paris (10,000 people on 10 March) and in Brussels (70,000 on 16 March). Still other protests brought together several thousand people in Vilvoorde and Brussels and involved cross-border raids on Renault premises. These actions involved transnational coordination among Belgian, French, and Spanish trade unionists. Although such transnational coordination had earlier precedents in Western Europe (Balme, Chabanet, and Wright 2001), it helped considerably to maintain the momentum of the mobilization. Indeed, this coordination was remarkable against an industrial firm whose management had formerly sought to maintain rivalry among its various production sites.

One of the mechanisms by which this transnational coordination occurred was through the recently formed Renault European Works Council (EWC). Originally established by EU authority as a consultative body with no authority for collective bargaining, the EWC became the organizational hub of the transnational mobilization—in part, because 3,000 additional job losses had also been announced for Renault workers in France. This organizational capacity, combined with sensational contentious actions—including the burning of a Renault auto on the steps of the European Union in Brussels—attracted much media attention.

Second, Vilvoorde was a *political issue,* which was quickly linked to national and European institutions and policy-making authority. Initially a matter of intergovernmental relations between Belgium (the "victim") and France (the "aggressor"—since the French State held a 46 percent stake in Renault), the strike turned into a *social Europe* issue when the king of the Belgians expressed his concern about the job losses and the prime minister, government ministers, and Flemish regional and local authorities expressed their outrage (Vilvoorde is in the heavily Flemish-speaking ring around Brussels.) In turn, the French president, prime minister and the government, leaders of the opposition, and the French trade union leadership issued statements for and against the action. European institutions also quickly became involved. The president of the Commission and the Commissioners for Competition and Social Affairs publicly condemned the action by Renault. European Union financial aid for the development of the Spanish plant, where production from Belgium was to be transferred, was canceled, and a left-wing group of members of the European Parliament invited a delegation of Vilvoorde unionists to the Parliament, as a large majority of their colleagues voted a motion supporting the strikers.

The result was an increase in tensions between France and Belgium (at one point, the mayor of Vilvoorde banned the use of French in the public market) and a widening debate in European circles calling for making EU industrial and social policies an axis for economic integration (Vandamme 1997). In France the controversy soon became enmeshed in the developing campaign for the legislative elections in May and June 1997. This political dimension strongly politicized the issue, demonstrated by the presence of a delegation of Vilvoorde workers at French Socialist Lionel Jospin's final electoral rally, just before he was elected prime minister.

Finally, Vilvoorde was a *legal affair* (Moreau 1997). The Versailles Court of Appeals held that the company had failed to inform and consult its workers in an appropriate manner before closing the plant. Should this decision hold, it ultimately will affect all the European workers of any French multinational corporation. In this respect, the legal implications of the Vilvoorde conflict are considerable. Indeed, while the European employers' association (UNICE) was stalling on negotiations with the European Trade Union Confederation (ETUC) under the Social Protocol, the Commission used the conjuncture to put before the member-states a proposed Directive directly based on the Versailles decision.

THE MEDIA

What can we say about the role of the media in the development of the campaign against Renault?

- First, through the media, this conflict spread from being primarily a local and industrial affair until it came to involve the French, Belgian, and European political spheres.
- Second, the interpretation of the Vilvoorde events can be traced through the decisions of journalists on the social affairs desks of the French, Belgian, and European media outlets.
- Third, it was largely through media framing that the Vilvoorde campaign came to be seen as European.

The media's framing of the Vilvoorde issue was structured primarily by the initial positions taken by the principal actors involved in the conflict. Renault's management adopted a twofold media strategy. First, it kept the media at bay, declining requested interviews and, for quite some time, delegating communication responsibilities to a vice president instead of the chairman and CEO. The firm limited its comments about the closure to industrial and financial considerations, attempting to select journalists who would follow the same line. Second, Renault refused to open a dialogue with the unions, thereby prompting them to seek a political outlet beyond the company. As a Confédération Française Démocratique du Travail (CFDT) union leader explained, "The active mobilization of public opinion was required to exert an effective external pressure" on the corporation (Richter 1998: 97).

Concurrently, major public figures began to court the media. The Belgian king's statement to the press, for example, reflected the desire to foster a sense of unity within a country still reeling from the effects of criminal scandals and massive de-industrialization. The prime minister reacted immediately, too, in part because Vilvoorde was in the heart of his own constituency.

In France, meanwhile, the president of the Republic was forced to intervene, both because the left-wing French opposition pointed to the state's responsibilities and because certain right-wing politicians were using the European dimension of the Vilvoorde case to criticize the move toward a single currency. In addition to national political considerations, the issue also brought forth statements from European officials. The commissioner responsible for EU Competition, although known as an ardent supporter of the market, rediscovered that he was a Belgian Socialist and appeared on numerous television talk shows to express his concern with the Renault actions. Likewise, the commissioner for Social Affairs, otherwise a conservative, seized this opportunity to demand that his office be given regulatory and punitive powers over transnational plant closures.

Once politicized in these ways, media coverage escalated as journalists solicited comments from these political actors—further politicizing the issue. This dynamic is evident, for example, in rising levels of media sensitivity to Vilvoorde during the first week of March, just as the issue was becoming politicized in France. This period, particularly between the 3rd and 6th of March, corresponded with the rising political-media spiral. In figure 9.1 we chart levels of attention to Vilvoorde in the dispatches of Agence France-Presse, the major French wire service.

Finally, for their own reasons, some media sources may have had a special interest in Vilvoorde. For example, the center-left Italian daily *La Repub-*

Figure 9.1 Reactivity to Vilvoorde (Number of Dispatches per Day)

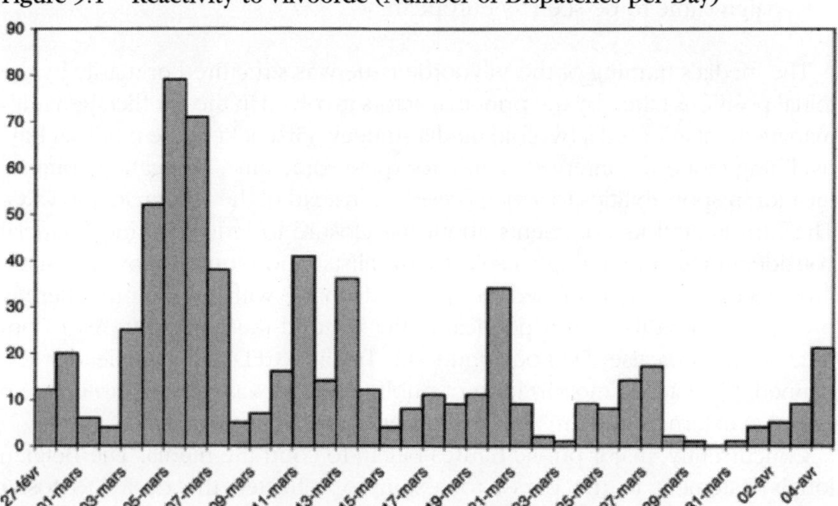

Source: Agence France-Press dispatches, February 27 to April 4, 1997.

blica asked its foreign correspondents to follow the Vilvoorde story and the demonstrations of German miners, both of which showed that other European countries were having economic difficulties at a time when there were doubts about Italy's ability to join the single currency. The conservative and Euro-skeptic *Daily Telegraph,* meanwhile, provided the fullest British coverage, framing it to reveal major shortcomings in the process of European construction. With their penchant for showing spectacular images, television news programs focused on the demonstrations in Paris and Brussels, which provided a visual illustration of European trade union solidarity. The "Social Europe" theme was given unprecedented attention, first in the French media and soon after by the Belgian and other European media. We turn to this point in greater detail in the next section.

The Interpretive Function of the Media

In total, the Vilvoorde events received considerable media attention. We can evaluate the magnitude of coverage of this campaign by comparing it to levels of attention given to other significant political issues, such as the French resumption of nuclear tests in 1995 and to the 1997 French legislative elections. In table 9.1, we present the findings of this comparison. As the table indicates, Vilvoorde emerged as the "top story," generating higher numbers of press dispatches and a higher average number of dispatches per day than did the resumption of atomic testing. But it was the framing and the interpretations applied to the case that contributed most to the media impact.

At the outset of the campaign it was impossible to tell which framings would dominate media coverage. But ultimately, the transnational nature of the strike captured the imagination of a number of journalists, particularly those specializing in social issues. The common multilingual tracts in France and Belgium distributed by the unions, a coordinated strike in all Renault sites in Europe on March 7th, and the involvement of the ETUC,

Table 9.1 Comparison of Media Coverage of Vilvoorde with Two Other Major News Stories in *AFP* during the Period from 1995 to 1997

	Number of Days	*Number of Dispatches*	*Max. No. of Daily Dispatches*	*Average Number of Dispatches/Day*
Atomic Test	99	1,117	73	12
Vilvoorde	37	618	79	17
Elections	34	3,433	151	100

Source: For Vilvoorde (February 27–April 4, 1997): *Agence France-Press* dispatches; for atomic tests: Derville (1997: 605), (June 13 to September 10, 1995) Derville (1997: 605); for elections (April 21–May 24, 1997): Lagneau, Eric, "Couvrir une campagne électorale: les journalistes de l'Agence France Presse et les élections législatives des 25 mai et ler juin 1997" (master's thesis, Institut d'Etudes Politiques de Paris, 1997).

the European Metalworkers' Federation, and several EU Commissioners: together, these helped to frame the issue as "European." In turn, journalists developed an original interpretation of this action—this was a "Eurostrike!" These journalists soon suggested that the emergence of workers' transnational solidarity might well become the standard reaction to multinational plant closures. In particular, the coining on March 5th of the term *euro-grève* by an AFP journalist was repeated extensively the next day, leading to a whole family of related expressions (including *Eurodemonstration* and *Europrotest*) in the French and other European media (including *Le Soir* in Belgium, the *Tageszeitung* and the *Frankfurter Rundschau* in Germany, *The Guardian* and *The Times* in Britain, *El Pais* in Spain, and *La Repubblica* in Italy).

The search for a synthetic frame for the conflict coincided with the journalistic tendency to give emphasis to original aspects of the story. In France, where the Vilvoorde actions were first identified as a Europrotest, most editors gave the story to their social affairs correspondents, who were familiar with the union leaders who had launched the protest. This decision meant that journalists were frequently close to the protesters—reinforced by corporate Renault's withdrawal strategy from the media. One result of this configuration of actors was that even as the level of politicization of the Vilvoorde actions diminished, the events continued to receive high levels of media attention. This is evident, for example, in the coverage of the Eurodemonstrations on March 11th and 16th and the workers' site occupations on March 20th and 21st.

A useful way to assess the importance of the configuration of trade union, corporate, and media actors is in terms of the sources quoted in media coverage of these events. We present the findings of our analysis of the most important sources for AFP coverage of the Vilvoorde events in table 9.2.

As the table indicates, trade union representatives comprised the largest share of identifiable sources for AFP coverage, at times receiving double the sourcing of political actors and institutional sources. Our interviews with trade unionists support these findings. For example:

Table 9.2 Most Important Source of AFP Dispatches (Where a Source Was Named)

Period (No. of Dispatches)	*Management*	*Trade Unions and Reports in the Field*	*Political Actors and Institutions*
1. 27/02–02/03 (31)	29%	45%	25%
2. 03/03–09/03 (203)	13%	39%	48%
3. 10/03–16/03 (98)	3%	56%	43%
4. 17/03–20/03 (43)	0%	86%	14%
TOTAL (375)	10%	50%	40%

Source: *Agence France-Press* dispatches, February 27 to March 20, 1997.

> We are very pleased with the part played by the media. They were supporting us. Especially because of the way the closing was carried out, its brutality. Usually, it is difficult to keep media attention for long and to remain in the news. Most of the time, to end a struggle, it is enough to stop talking about it. But this time it was still going on.

Journalists assigned to the story corroborated this opinion:

> It is rare to find a guy who can speak to journalists, who speaks to them at all, then knows how to speak to them, knows how they work. . . . When you were on the spot . . . you got news from the trade unions.

Furthermore, those social affairs journalists most active in covering the story admitted that they had felt sympathetic toward the workers:

> I do not say that we were too sympathetic in this regard but we never [questioned their] claim to be constructing "the Europe of demonstrators". . . . Because, somehow, we tried to believe in it too.

On the other hand, not all media sources were likely to embrace the image of the Eurostrike. As a reporter for Reuters explained: "This was an issue of little importance for our agency. Traders are not very interested in the closure of a factory."

The journalists' framing of the protests both legitimated them and also placed them within a particular policy narrative. As our collaborators Doug Imig and Sidney Tarrow have noted, "Once protest enters the machinery of the political process, it encounters political games and institutional mechanisms that take it out of the control of its initiators" (Imig and Tarrow 1996: 11). In response, movement actors often employ a division of labor (Gamson and Wolfsfeld 1993: 114). While some engage in protest, others, more presentable to the press, are designated to be interviewed.[2] In the case of Vilvoorde, workers did the protesting, but it was the institutionally based ETUC that came to represent the broader interests of workers laid off by industrial restructuring. As ETUC officials noted after the fact, "The [ETUC] Secretariat's Press and Information Department's hard work with the European media certainly contributed to the impact of the ETUC employment campaign" (ETUC 1999a: 9.4).

Media framing also influenced the actions of the workers themselves; they soon adopted the "European" frame as well. In the words of a Belgian trade unionist:

> We did not get into this action saying: "this is for Europe." That idea only came to us later. But it is true that *once we got it we believed that we would be able to change Europe by ourselves* [emphasis added].

And the journalist who covered the case for *Le Monde* added:

> Speaking of a "eurostrike" is a comment in itself. The media wrote about it first. . . . This European dimension increased the awareness of the audiences,

> the media and the editors . . . and, in fact, tended to support the social movement, at the very least to give it a political importance and not only a social one. . . . By the 5th or 6th of March, as newspapers began to talk about a eurostrike, *trade unionists, purposively or not, saw that there was this European aspect* [emphasis added].

In summary, the media's framing of the Vilvoorde affair—centering on the theme of a "social Europe"—invested these events with a symbolic meaning that lasted long after the protest campaign had ended. Consequently, it is important to look at the ways in which the treatment of the Vilvoorde campaign became a "founding moment" in the politics of social Europe.

Vilvoorde as a "Founding Moment"

William Gamson (1992) has noted that successful social movements need to be able to convey clear messages concerning the injustice, agency, and identity of their participants. In general, media coverage seldom conveys injustice—for example, designating victims of injustice and those responsible for it. Second, the influence of collective action is often ignored. In consequence, media coverage does not help to nurture the collective identity necessary for collective action.

Yet in the Vilvoorde case, we find a different pattern. Striking workers were systematically presented as: (1) exemplary workers who (2) were willing to be flexible and therefore (3) were unjustly victimized by a questionable decision. On the issue of agency—most journalistic accounts commented extensively on the mobilization but also questioned whether it would have its desired effect. The two points can be linked: the social tragedy of job loss (which discourages mobilization) justifies and reinforces indignation (which encourages it).

As for the third dimension of successful framing—identity—the theme of workers' solidarity and the politicization it engendered probably served to alert both the striking workers and a large part of the general public to the transnational aspect of these protest actions. In fact, as it became clear that the workers' material demands would not be met, the unions attached ever-greater significance to the symbolic transnational dimensions of the actions. In this way, the symbolic dimensions of the Vilvoorde protests provided a reference that could be used to frame future protest campaigns.

One of the most visible aspects of the legacy of Vilvoorde is evident in the evolving role of the ETUC. From its position as a lobbying organization, engaged in negotiations with employers' organizations (Abbot 1998, Gobin 1994, Turner 1996), the organization emerged as a representative of transnational labor. At its Ninth Congress in 1999, the ETUC passed a resolution asking that the right to strike be included in the next EU Treaty. The resolution read, in part:

> Above all, bringing the Union closer to its citizens requires that political, civil and social, trade union rights—including cross-border sympathy action, including strikes—be fully recognized by the Union and enshrined in the Treaty. (ETUC 1999b: VII, 57)

Furthermore, the Congress documents pointed to Vilvoorde as having provided a decisive impetus to enriching the repertoire of trade union actions:

> 1997 was marked by a campaign from the ETUC and its national affiliates to support the call for new Community powers and an effective new Community strategy for the fight against unemployment. . . . The starting point was a demonstration in Brussels following the close of Renault Vilvoorde. (ETUC 1999a: 9.4)

A second notable legacy of Vilvoorde is seen in the continuing activism of its former workers. They were to be seen demonstrating again in Brussels (28 May 1997 and 5 October 1998), then in Paris (10 June 1997) on behalf of national ETUC demonstrations for employment in Europe, in the European marches against unemployment in Amsterdam (14 June 1997), and in Cologne (29 May 1999) against factory closures. More broadly, cross-border actions, which used to be exceptional, have become more widespread since Vilvoorde, as protesters seek to gain the level and type of media coverage that was achieved in the Vilvoorde actions. Between 1997 and 2000, there were European actions by truck drivers and railway workers within the Federation of Transport Workers' Unions, pensioners, workers in the energy sector, Alcatel workers, Unilever workers, ABB-Alsthom workers, and a cross-sectoral strike by ETUC affiliates. In this respect, Vilvoorde may have constituted a "founding moment" for the development of a transnational repertoire of collective action in Europe.

EUROPEANIZATION AND MEDIATIZATION

Can we evaluate the impact of the Vilvoorde episode on the media and on the capacity of social actors like the Vilvoorde workers to promote European actions? In an effort to do so, we compared media attention to Vilvoorde to several other protest campaigns that were launched in Western Europe between 1997 and 1999 (actions by the unemployed, road blockages by truck drivers and railway workers, and Eurodemonstrations by farmers). We found no definitive and unidirectional growth of media recognition of Europrotests in these campaigns. This should come as no surprise—especially given the continued importance of what Imig and Tarrow call the "domestication" of European protests (chapter 2, this volume). Here we briefly examine the unemployed workers' protests of 1997 and 1999, as a point of comparison with Vilvoorde. Sampling from fourteen major newspapers in six European countries,[3] we analyzed the interpretive framings given to these actions of the unemployed and then compared them to the trends we identified in the coverage of the Vilvoorde strike.

EUROPEANIZATION WITHOUT MEDIATIZATION: THE UNEMPLOYED WORKERS

Since the early 1980s, the unemployed have engaged in organizing across Europe. The European Network of the Unemployed, created in 1996—principally through the initiative of several French associations—organized two marches against "unemployment, precariousness and exclusion," one in 1997 and the second in 1999. The marches themselves were fairly similar, but the coverage given to them by the media was very different.

Why these differences? As we have seen in the Vilvoorde case, context matters a great deal, as does the identity of the groups involved and the type of action planned. In addition, in the interval between the two marches, national campaigns were organized by the unemployed in France (1997, 1998) and in Germany (1998) that demonstrated the impact—sometimes quite strong—that the unemployed can have in their own country. The first march against unemployment lasted for several weeks, starting with peaceful marches in each country and converging on Amsterdam on June 14th 1997 to coincide with the official meeting of the EU Heads of State and Government. The planning for these marches began long before the Vilvoorde affair, but Vilvoorde had a major impact on the campaign in several ways.

First, several dozen Vilvoorde workers took part in the final demonstration. Second, following its support of the Vilvoorde campaign, the new French left-wing government seized the opportunity of the EU Summit to propose a European employment policy. In response, a first European Summit on employment was held in Luxembourg in November 1997, where 30,000 demonstrators called for a reduction in working hours and the coordination of policies against unemployment. Though the Luxembourg meeting produced only modest gains (the Pact for Employment that emerged from the Cologne Summit in June 1999 and the Lisbon Summit in March 2000), the strategy of challenging national and European politicians through a transnational protest campaign was reminiscent of Vilvoorde.

Turning to the Amsterdam march, we find a high level of media coverage of the campaign: each of the fourteen newspapers we analyzed covered the event at least briefly and intensely. During the central two-day period, for example, there were thirty-five articles focusing on the event. The demands and the identity of the protest actors also were well represented in media coverage. In twelve articles (35 percent of the total) the exact identity of the unemployed network was mentioned. As in the Vilvoorde case, the European TV channels (TF1, France2, ARD, TVE) revealed the diverse origins of the demonstrators, through the languages used on their slogans and the posters along the route. Both print and television media also mentioned the European nature of the protest.

In comparison, however, the second march drew little positive coverage from the press. Only five of the fourteen newspapers we studied even mentioned the event, which brought together 30,000 demonstrators in Cologne on May 29th, 1999. In total, there were twelve articles, all published in France and Germany, of which half were in the French Communist paper *L'Humanité*. Among these, only three gave the exact name of the protest organization. This relative lack of coverage is all the more surprising because the second march might have built upon, and amplified, the first, especially as the national movements in France and Germany had intervened, generating high levels of media attention.

This relative failure can be explained by several factors. First, the dynamics of the mobilization were weak. A year previously, at the meeting of three hundred representatives of organizations against unemployment from twelve EU countries (18–19 April 1998), the representative of the French unemployed network AC!, Christophe Aguiton, who was very much in favor of Europeanization and media strategies, nevertheless felt that "the organization of a second march against unemployment and exclusion . . . is not on the agenda." Second, at the final demonstration, despite efforts to "discipline" them, German extremist groups and anarchist unions from France (CNT), Spain (CGT), and Sweden (SAV) competed with the unemployed organizations for media attention. The demands that were to have been made regarding employment were diluted with declarations of opposition to the military intervention in Kosovo and of support for the Kurdish leader Ocalan, who had recently been arrested in Turkey. In these respects, the demonstration lacked the focus of the earlier march on Amsterdam.

Finally, the context was different. By the time of the Cologne march, Vilvoorde was well in the past and there was no event comparable to it that could create favorable conditions for the political and media reception of demands to fight unemployment. Likewise, ETUC, which had been central in the organization of the Luxembourg demonstration, took no initiative in Cologne. For all these reasons, and especially because of the lack of linkage between the protest dimension and the political dimension, the countersummit formula turned out to be counterproductive for its organizers.

MEDIATIZATION AS A RESOURCE FOR EUROPEANIZATION

What can we conclude from the comparison of the Vilvoorde case with the two marches against unemployment? First, the connection between the

Europeanization of protest and media framing of protest as European is not automatic. Consider the European farmers' demonstration in December 1999 in Brussels. This action, organized as a protest against the reform of the Common Agricultural Policy (CAP), had a clear European policy goal—affecting the largest item in the EU budget. The action was also unquestionably transnational, with sizable French, German, Italian, and Belgian contingents taking part. But the purpose of Committee of Agricultural Organizations in the European Economic Community (COPA), the European farm organization that mounted the demonstration, was *neither* to create a transnational identity *nor* to promote unitary demands. COPA was primarily lobbying in defense of European Community assistance to farmers and attempting to smooth over national differences on the subsidy issue. In response, the media treated the farmers' protest as a manifestation of COPA's efforts to target the EU, rather than framing the campaign as another example of transnational social movement mobilization. Our analysis of this media coverage, for example, reveals that the media concentrated on the violence of the protesting farmers (emphasized in 41 percent of the 58 headlines we analyzed and in 43 percent of the 37 photos), and on the economic issues at stake. The transnational dimension of the protest failed to attract particular attention.

For the farmers, the lack of positive attention to their protest posed no great problem; their goal was indeed to advance their policy goals and to complement COPA's negotiations with the demonstration of their power to disrupt. But for a group like the unemployed, establishing the European dimension of their protest was a major goal—because they were seeking Europe-wide policy responses. While the unemployment theme lent itself fairly well to the task of generalizing the actors' claims, it failed to gain significant media attention for the movement. On this point, we identify a number of differences between Vilvoorde and the European marches against unemployment.

At the outset, the Vilvoorde unions did not define themselves as European actors. The opposite was the case for the unemployed. Second, although the first actions of the Vilvoorde unions were relatively large for such a local conflict (4,000 demonstrators in Brussels on March 3rd), they were much smaller than the number that turned out for the marches in Amsterdam and Cologne. The European dimension of the Vilvoorde protests, however, was established well before the two large demonstrations of March 11th and 16th. In contrast to the unemployed marchers, in other words, the Vilvoorde unionists did not need to construct a European spectacle in order to have their actions framed in European terms by the press.

These observations underscore the importance of the *interpretation effect* of the media. Independent of the number and the status of the mobilized actors, it is the meaning given to their action that constitutes their most effective symbolic resource. The media's interpretation of collective action events provides incentives for political elites to become involved. Their involvement, in turn, fuels the intensity of the media's coverage. While this dynamic was in place for Vilvoorde, it was much less evident in the case of the unemployed.

Diffusion as a Mechanism for Europeanization

But the explicit recognition of a protest as "European" may not be the only way the press advances the construction of European social actors. In the concluding chapter of this volume, Sidney Tarrow discusses four forms of the transnationalization of contention: political exchange, diffusion, transnational advocacy networks, and transnational social movements. In his typology, the diffusion of forms and frames of contention is classified as "traditional" and short term, compared to the more robust forms that help to create transnational actors. Yet when forms and frames of action are transmitted across borders, and when the cross-border nature of this diffusion is recognized and represented by the media, it can have a more lasting impact. The very act of the media's representation of contention in different countries as emerging through a unified process may itself advance the process of Europeanization.

To assess this thesis, we analyzed media attention to the unemployed workers' protests within Germany and France to see if we could detect signs of the recognition of diffusion in the media.[4] Since the French protests occurred first, we searched for references in the press to the *importation of a French model of protest* and for explicit references to the *emergence of European protest networks* from the diffusion of the French forms into Germany. Many of the articles and dispatches that covered the German protests made references to the protests across the Rhine (35 from 14 sources). For example:

> France took pride of place on this cold, gray morning of Thursday 5 February. In the town of Bielefeld, in the north of Westphalia, several demonstrators brandished tricolor flags. It was a tribute to the French unemployed. (*Le Monde*)

And again,

> Organizers of the street protests which have swept France and won large concessions from the Socialist government now see Germany as the crucial battleground in their struggle. (*The Daily Telegraph*)

As these examples suggest, the media did allude to the European character of the mobilizations through references to diffusion processes from one country to another.

Moreover, those newspapers that drew their information from direct sources were more likely to orient their comments toward the European dimension of the protests than those that limited themselves to official sources. This was particularly true of newspapers ideologically closest to the protesters, like the French Communist journal *L'Humanité* or the German left-wing newspaper *Die Tageszeitung*. Media accounts also contained many quotes from unemployed workers who mentioned the French example (AFP, Reuters, *Le Monde, Libération, Le Soir, The Independent, The Irish Times, Birmingham Evening Mail, Frankfurter Rundschau, Berliner Morgenpost,* and *Frankfurter Allgemeine Zeitung*). For example:

> When I saw the protests of the French unemployed [on TV news], I felt like . . . something was happening at last. (*The Irish Times*)

And again:

> When I saw the demonstrations of the French unemployed on the television, I said to myself: we must do the same thing. We are too quiet. (*Le Soir*)

And finally:

> We saw what the French were doing, and it gave us ideas. (*Reuters*)

Many press observers made the inferential leap from French-German diffusion of collective action to a more general process of Europeanization. One applauded the organization of protest on a European scale:

> The French protest leaders have sought out solidarity action from elsewhere in the name of creating a European identity. And they are getting it. The German protests are expected to materialize in at least 30 cities. (*The Irish Times*)

Another hoped for the further diffusion of protest:

> It is high time the German unemployed made their voices heard. The wave of protests that first hit France, and now Germany, will spread to other countries. (*Die Presse*)

And finally, one journalist in the progressive Berlin *Tageszeitung*) already saw a "social Europe" present in these protests:

> Something new is emerging that goes further than the protest run by the unemployed in previous years—the idea of a Europe from below where 20 million affected people rise against governments' projects towards a rigid economy which lacks democratic legitimacy.

CONCLUSIONS

What can these brief comparisons of the European marches and of French/German diffusion processes among the unemployed tell us about the role of the media in the construction of European protest movements?

The European marches suggest, first of all, that Vilvoorde was a hard act to follow. It is not enough for social actors to identify themselves as "European" (something that the Vilvoorde protesters only did after the media so identified them) for the media to define their actions as such. In contrast, the German protests against unemployment tell us that how the media covers even a *national* protest can give it more of a "European" meaning than an explicitly transnational event that the media fails to frame in European terms.

In more general terms, we see several variables working together to lead to an event's framing as "European": *the collective identity of the actors, their interpretation by the media, and their capacity to establish a political theme.* In the Vilvoorde case, the first factor was not at all present in the protesters' self-identification, the second appeared in the media coverage of the events, and the events themselves were constructed as both European and political. In the German unemployed workers' protests, the second and third factors were also present—but less strongly than in Vilvoorde. In the example of the protests by the unemployed, though the marchers sought to be identified as "European," they lacked the political and rhetorical resources to gain this status in the press. Table 9.3 summarizes these hypotheses.

As the table suggests, the degree to which collective actors claim a European identity may be independent of the degree to which they will gain this status in the press. Recall that at the beginning of their mobilization, the Vilvoorde workers did not even consider themselves to be European actors. Conversely, the organizers of the marches against unemployment—who consciously defined their actions in European terms—were never framed as European political actors. In these cases, media representation appears to have been decisive.

Our analysis also suggests, however, that even when actors gain European framing from the media, there is no assurance that they will succeed. Lacking participation in a policy community (Le Galès and Thatcher 1995), media support is at best a fulcrum for trying to influence the decision-making arena. Thus, even the strongly mediatized and politicized Vilvoorde protest might have been no more than a marginal episode in Europe's march toward a single market. The strikers' actions may only have gained a response that was late, diffuse, and uncertain.

Table 9.3 Hypothetical Elements in the Europeanization of Protest

	European Identity	*Media Framing*	*Political/ Rhetorical Resources*	*Degree of Europeanization of Protest*
Vilvoorde	–	+++	+++	++
German Unemployed	–	++	++	+
European Unemployed	+++	+	–	–

In sum, the events surrounding Vilvoorde demonstrated a volatile mix of interactions—both national and supranational, horizontal and vertical, and involving industrial, political, and juridical conflicts. In such a complex opportunity structure—which is becoming more and more common in Europe (c.f., chapter 10 on the struggle over genetically modified foods)—the media increasingly plays a key role. As the process of integration develops, Europeans may look back at Vilvoorde as a founding moment in the formation of a European public sphere to which more institutional actors will need to become accustomed.

NOTES

We thank Christopher Thiéry, with the collaboration of Susan Tarrow, for the translation of this chapter.

1. These elements have recently been analyzed in depth by Snow and Benford 1988, Johnston and Klandermans 1995, and McAdam, McCarthy, and Zald, eds. 1996.

2. For example, in the case of protests against the nuclear site of Seabrook, journalists turned toward experts (Union of Concerned Scientists, UCS) rather than seeking the views of the activists involved in the occupation: "when demonstrators are arrested in Seabrook, phones ring at UCS" (Gamson 1988: 235).

3. *L'Humanité, Libération, Le Monde, Le Figaro, Le Parisien (France), The Guardian, The Times, The Daily Telegraph* (United Kingdom), *Frankfurter Rundschau, Frankfurter Allgemeine Zeitung* (Germany), *La Repubblica* (Italy), *El Païs* (Spain), *Le Soir* (Belgium), *The Financial Times* (international).

4. Our corpus includes the AFP and Reuters' long dispatches (i.e., more than 200 words), 2 international newspapers (*Financial Times, International Herald Tribune*) and 26 newspapers from 9 European countries (6 French, 4 British, 4 German, 4 Italian, 3 Austrian, 2 Spanish, 1 Belgian, 1 Swiss, and 1 Irish)

10

The European Conflict over Genetically Engineered Crops, 1995–1997

Vera Kettnaker

INTRODUCTION

Since the mid-1990s, there has been considerable grass-roots resistance in Europe to the cultivation of genetically modified plants and their use in food products. Before the first half of 1996, the protest was mostly confined to sporadic local campaigns against experimental fields of genetically modified crops. Yet in November 1996, when the first crop of genetically modified corn and soybeans was to arrive in Europe, many Europeans—still shaken by the BSE[1] crisis—protested in fear of yet another food safety scandal. Activists fervently pressured the European Union to avoid this seemingly unnecessary danger or at least to uphold the freedom of choice for consumers by imposing labeling requirements for genetically modified food. Concurrently, consumer campaigns were launched to pressure food producers and retailers into making promises not to produce or sell products that contained genetically modified material.

Although European legislators moved closer to the position of the consumer and environmental NGOs (nongovernmental organizations) over time, the slow and complicated European legislative process proved unsatisfactory for the activists. It took the European Union nearly two more years to agree on labeling requirements because it was difficult to reach a compromise that would prevent a trade war with the United States, satisfy the economic wish of the EU to promote biotechnology, and yet take into account the concerns of the population. Since the continuously changing position the EU legislators kept the authorization and labeling requirements of genetically modified organisms (GMOs) in constant uncertainty, national solutions were sought and implemented at all stages of the process,[2] although the tendency to seek national solutions became stronger in 1997. This situation provides us with the unusual opportunity to compare protest behavior against governments at both the national and the European levels within the same campaign and time period. Since public protest targeted companies even more frequently than governments, we will also be able to investigate actions against businesses.

THE CONTROVERSY

A plant is genetically modified by splicing into its DNA a DNA segment of another plant, of an animal, or of a microbe in order to change its properties as a plant or the properties of the plant product.[3] Most commercially cultivated GMOs to date are modified to either have the plant produce a pesticide to protect it against infestation by insects or to make the plant resistant to a particular herbicide so that only the crop plant will survive when the field is sprayed. According to the biotechnology corporations, these plants give higher yields than conventional crops, while requiring fewer herbicides and pesticides.[4] They also argue that biotechnology techniques could lead to the development of more nutritious crops that can grow in fewer favorable climates and thus contribute to feeding the ever-growing population of this planet.

Yet crops with actual benefits for the consumer have yet to appear on the market, and many spokespeople of developing countries not only reject the use of the poverty argument but, on the contrary, believe that genetic engineering is likely to exacerbate world hunger.[5] The main concern of the European critics is that unintended health and environmental side effects of genetically engineered plants are likely to occur but are hard to predict and have not been researched sufficiently. They argue that increased business profits do not justify exposing the population and the environment to the risks of poorly understood long-term effects. Environmental activists and consumer advocates have successfully invoked the precautionary principle that was adopted in the EU with the Maastricht Treaty to legally justify more caution regarding the introduction of these plants.

One concern for human health is that randomly inserted genes can lead to unintended production of toxins and allergens or to a reduction of nutritional value.[6] For technical reasons, many of the genetically modified plants also contain a gene for antibiotic-resistance that could be transferred to bacteria that are harmful for humans (Eckelkamp et al. 1998). This could make many illnesses harder to combat and has alarmed many doctors and health officials.[7] One environmental danger is unintended harm to beneficial insects, soil organisms (Saxena et al. 1999), and nontarget animals that feed on the plants. A few studies have already shown such harmful effects in laboratory settings for lacewings, ladybugs, and monarch butterflies (Poldervaart 1997, Gledhill and McGrath 1997, Crabb 1997, Losey et al. 1999). Many environmentalists also oppose the broad-spectrum herbicides for which the genetically modified crops are engineered, because they will reduce field-margin habitats that are essential for wildlife in the highly cultivated landscapes of Europe. Finally, if wild relatives of the crops grow close by, the genes introduced by genetic engineering also have been shown to spread through cross-pollination (Joergensen and Anderson 1994, Chèvre 1997). This means that weeds could become herbicide-resistant ("super-weeds"). Engineered genes can also spread to other organisms such as fungi and microbes (Gebhard and Smalla 1998, Hoffman et al. 1994, de Vries and Wackernagel 1998). Worrisome in this respect is that once released, genes from engineered plants cannot be recalled from the environment if later research should find that they have negative side effects.

Such unintended side effects could occur because current technology inserts the genes at random positions, which can disrupt original genes. However, since our knowledge of the full interplay of all chemical processes and pathways is still limited, the effects of such disruptions may not always be detected before a product reaches the market; even the effects of the intended changes on the plant are difficult to predict.

Concerns about insufficient knowledge are increased by the fact that research about side effects of genetic modifications is largely left to the biotechnology corporations. The U.S. Food and Drug Administration (FDA) decided in 1992 to treat all genetically modified plants like the unmodified original plant and thus does not require human testing. The U.S. Environmental Protection Agency (EPA) and the U.S. Department of Agriculture (USDA) seem to base their decisions primarily on the summaries of corporate research reports.[8] However, as long as the biotechnology corporations are not liable for the harmful side effects of their products,[9] there is no real incentive for them to thoroughly investigate unintended side effects. In the early years, European authorization agencies were often satisfied with the U.S. approval and did not perform independent tests.

Economic factors reinforce health and environmental risks. Some farmers are concerned that the new seed-and-pesticide packages will make them captive to a single producer in an already oligopolistic sector (Vidal 1997, Vidal and Milner 1997). Organic farmers oppose genetically engineered crops because they will quickly render the Bt bacteria used in organic farming useless.[10] They are also worried about pollution of organic fields by engineered genes through cross-pollination, which would threaten certification of their crops as organic and GE-free. For some activists, the struggle around genetically modified food is also a struggle against the increasing power of multinational corporations and against corporate influence on politics. Others oppose genetic engineering on religious or ethical grounds, but these arguments were not used very frequently during this time period.

European governments in general promote and support the biotechnology industry because it promises to be one of the future big business sectors and could create new jobs—an important argument in Europe—although even the most optimistic estimates are rather low and do not necessarily predict *net* increases in jobs.[11] The United States exercised a considerable external influence on the European debate because the biotechnology industry is most developed in the United States and most of the world's genetically engineered crops are grown there. Therefore, the U.S. government vigorously fought European attempts to limit the import of such crops and also opposed labeling requirements. The United States claims that there is "no scientific evidence" that genetically modified foods are less safe than others, and it maintains that labeling requirements are simply unfair trade barriers. Aside from economic interests, this is also a conflict over the role of scientific research in trade regulations. The United States wants to put the burden of proof (e.g., of harmfulness) on the EU regulators, whereas the EU wants to put the burden of proof (of safety) on the producers. The EU also claims the right to proceed with caution as long as neither safety nor lack of safety are proven and scientific doubts of safety exist.[12] As one activist put it, "Absence of proof is not proof of absence."

THE DEVELOPMENT OF THE CONFLICT AROUND GMOS

During the period covered by this study, the BSE crisis was still reverberating and is widely acknowledged to have had a strong impact on the conflict around GMOs. The BSE crisis left the public in distrust about premature official and scientific pronouncements of food safety, especially since this was only one in a series of food scandals (Jasanoff 1997). A Eurobarometer poll in February 1996 showed that 35 percent of European citizens thought that food is not safe, and only 11 percent believed that EU information about food safety reflects reality (Commission of the European Communities 1997). In a UK public opinion study, the information that British authorities granted safety approval to a GM food actually *reduced* public support for these products (Greenberg 1998a). In general, the European public is strongly in favor of labeling requirements: 74 percent of all respondents in a Eurobarometer poll (Europe Information Service 1997b) and 94 percent of respondents in a separate German poll (GfK 1996) insisted on clear and accurate labels. Another illustrative case is Austria, where, in a public petition in April 1997, more than 1.2 million voters (over 20 percent of the electorate) asked for a five-year moratorium on the import, use, and cultivation of GMOs (Europe Information Service 1997a). This was the second highest turnout in the history of Austrian national petitions and the highest ever for a grass-roots initiative. Public opinion was probably also influenced by discussions of several related issues in the EU around that time, like the directive on biotechnology patents, the Bioethics convention, and the ban on cloning.

The BSE crisis also left politicians wary of another trade war, this time threatened by the U.S. government on behalf of its farmers and agrobusiness firms (*Nature* 1997). In the same period of time, Europe was already involved in trade-related conflicts with the United States over hormone-treated beef and the Helms-Burton laws. In the United States, the introduction of genetically engineered crops had gone largely unnoticed by the public, and neither the cultivation nor the use of genetically modified plants in food products raised much opposition in the years prior to the Seattle WTO meeting.[13] In Europe, however, genetic engineering has been a subject of passionate discussion for over a decade. One example is the European directive on biotechnology patents, which was finally passed in May 1998 after more than ten years of deadlocked negotiations. Genetic research was severely regulated and restricted in Europe throughout most of the 1990s, and commercial cultivation of genetically modified plants was illegal until recently. This restraint was mainly due to strong ethical concerns and to a more cautious approach toward technology, as expressed in the "precautionary principle" adopted with the Maastricht Treaty. When imports from the United States started to contain genetically modified corn and soybeans, legislators were forced to decide upon the commercial cultivation and usage of genetically modified crops on European soil.

Against this backdrop, the process of the GMO legislation followed a long and complicated course. In 1995 and the first half of 1996, the EU institutions discussed several drafts of the "Novel Food" directive that would regulate which food products have to be labeled and how the labels are to be worded and positioned. Since the European Parliament, the Commission, and the Council could not develop a common position, a conciliation committee passed a labeling directive on November 26, 1996, that in practice would have excluded about 80 percent of the products that contain ingredients from genetically modified plants. Although the proposed wording was considered confusing for consumers, the European Parliament accepted this proposal in January 1997 to avoid a legal vacuum. The directive came into effect in May 1997, but since specific labeling rules had not been decided upon, implementation was postponed until November 1997. Due to strong public protest and in light of new scientific studies, various labeling regulations proposed in the following months would have controlled labeling more strictly. Yet by the end of 1997, new rules still had to be agreed upon. Labeling rules for a disappointingly narrow scope of products were finally adopted in May 1998, but activists continued to press for amendments of the directive.

Parallel to the debate on the novel food directive, the EU also had to decide on the authorization for cultivation of genetically modified corn developed in Europe by Ciba-Geigy.[14] After a regulatory committee of the EU voted against approval in late April 1996, the Council of Environmental Ministers could neither vote unanimously in favor nor unanimously against the approval because only France favored approval. The environment ministers therefore asked the Commission to withdraw the authorization proposal. Instead, the Commission established three scientific committees in July 1996, which, after a long period of uncertainty and despite a wave of public protests, decided on December 18, 1996, in favor of authorization. The European parliamentarians were incensed about the undemocratic process, especially when minutes of the commission debate were leaked and revealed that the fear of a U.S. trade war was involved in the decision. In April 1997, the European Parliament therefore passed with near unanimity an unusually strong-worded resolution that requested renegotiation of the authorization and a change in the decision-making process (The European Parliament 1997). By then, Austria, Italy, and Luxembourg had already imposed national bans or labeling requirements on the corn, although the legal status of these national regulations was ambiguous.[15]

It is important to stress that although some countries adopted a more tentative position than others, even the most cautious governments, like Austria, tried to strike a balance between safety considerations and economic interests in the development of biotechnology. Likewise, although it was France that had proposed the authorization of Bt corn and alone voted for its authorization, France, under its new Socialist-led government, imposed a ban on Bt corn when it was finally approved by the EU. Rather than an intergovernmental struggle, the legislation process around this issue seems to be best viewed as a heavily contested process of norm generation, where stronger divisions often existed between the different ministries of each national government than between the different national governments as unitary actors. The slow development of the directives toward stricter and safer regulation was strongly influenced by the activism of social movement organizations and consumer groups. Let us turn now to their activities.

DEVELOPMENT OF THE PROTEST CAMPAIGN AGAINST GMOS

It is important to note that protest intensity against GMOs peaked at different times in different countries of the EU. The first wave of protest (1996–1997), which is the topic of this chapter, developed mainly in Central Europe. Switzerland introduced relatively strict GE legislation early on but was put under heavy pressure by its chemical industry. In June 1998, a public referendum to limit research and cultivation of genetically modified plants failed drastically there. In Austria, on the other hand, a referendum in April 1997 calling for a five-year moratorium on genetically modified plants had a resounding success, and the Austrian government imposed a national ban on

GE plants, a move followed by Luxembourg and Italy shortly thereafter. Many Scandinavian countries also seemed to show strong public opposition during these first two years. In Germany, gene technology research had long been severely restricted due to historically rooted ethical concerns. The government, however, considered genetic engineering a lucrative technology of the future and pursued its pro-GE course even times of strongest public protest.[16] Protest activity and public opposition in Germany peaked in 1996 and—although still among the strongest in Europe—has since lost steam. A new public opinion study conducted on behalf of Monsanto (Greenberg 1998b) attributes this to a growing sense of inevitability and a feeling of powerlessness.

In 1998, a second wave of protest gained momentum in Britain as well as in France. During the years of the first wave, a diverse set of smaller social movement organizations had campaigned against genetically modified plants in Britain, and Prince Charles had voiced his opposition to genetic engineering. Although some UK supermarket chains had already gone GE-free in 1997, most British consumers were still unconcerned and even claimed to prefer genetically modified tomato paste. In 1998, however, Monsanto launched a $1.6 million advertising campaign and several influential British newspapers ran critical articles on genetic engineering, resulting in broadened public awareness. In 1999, Dr. Pusztai, a researcher in Scotland, was fired for releasing to the public experimental results on modified potatoes before peer reviews had taken place. It also became public that many of the members of Britain's regulatory committees had private interests in the biotechnology industry. These events strongly reminded Britons of the government cover-up of the BSE scandal and triggered a broad public backlash against genetically modified food. A public acceptance study performed for Monsanto in September 1998 diagnosed an "on-going collapse of public support for biotechnology and GM foods" in England (Greenberg 1998a). By 1999, most of Britain's supermarket chains, food producers, public institutions, and restaurants had gone GM-free.[17]

France performed a similar turn-around: In the summer of 1996, the French government had been the sole proponent of an authorization of Novartis GE corn. After the change in government in the spring of 1997, however, the cultivation and processing of genetically modified plants was restricted step by step and moratoria for several types of plants went into force. France now even faces legal action by the European Commission for dragging its feet over several GMO approvals (Friends of the Earth Europe 1999b).

Event Data Analysis

In order to analyze the numerous protests against GMOs that occurred between 1995 and 1997, I collected and coded data from a variety of newspaper archives, following in the tradition of protest-event analysis (Tilly et al. 1975, Tarrow 1989, Kriesi et al. 1995). The database that I compiled was based on the collection of press clippings contained in the archives of the Campaign to Ban Genetically Engineered Foods, as well as from queries to the Lexis-Nexis collection. The activists' archive contained 222 articles from the German press (covering the period from May 1996 through December 1997), as well as 232 articles in English (from August 1996 through December 1997) from various international news sources. I also located an additional 1,500 media reports of European protests against GMOs (in both English and German) indexed by Lexis-Nexis for the two-year period 1995–1997.[18] The resulting article collection is biased toward detailed coverage of the German- and English-speaking countries and contains superficial coverage of the other European nations.[19]

These articles were coded for all actions by nongovernmental actors that were opposed to genetically modified plants. In order to limit the scope of the study, protests concerning genetic engineering of animals, cloning, and the patenting of genetic information were deliberately excluded from the analysis. Actions by political parties or party members were included when they were not related to institutional politics; for example, when the small Dutch Natural Law Party sued the Ahold supermarket chain for claiming in pamphlets that genetically modified products were identical to unmodified ones. Bans of genetically modified products and similar actions by food retailers or producers were included when these bans were proclaimed by a *group* of supermarket chains or by an *association* of food retailers, food producers, or farmers.[20] Following Kriesi et al.,[21] all the events described in the articles were coded for date, location of event, actor, target, type, and geographical affiliation of actor and target, as well as type of event. All duplicate reports were then removed, resulting in a collection of 296 contentious political events.

For this analysis, each event may consist of several incidents; for example, the action could be directed against multiple targets, could use multiple types of action, or could occur concurrently in several countries. It will be noted separately how such actions within events were handled. In order to perform a qualitative characterization of the actions, we categorized all events by intensity of pressure according to the schema presented in table 10.1. In the following section, I first discuss the campaign as a whole, before turning to an analysis of protests against each type of target.

The Campaign as a Whole

Inspection of the time series of event counts[22] in figure 10.1 shows that the first wave of public protest peaked in the period between October 1996 and January 1997, around the time when the first shiploads of genetically modified corn and soybeans were arriving in Europe. In this time series, "biotech"

Table 10.1 Coding Schema for the Intensity of Contentious Actions

Intensity Level	*Sample Actions*
0	Press release with no target mentioned; educational actions.
1	Lobbying, petitions, small peaceful or symbolic demonstrations.
2	Confrontational but legal actions.
3	Confrontational, illegal actions such as occupations and blockades.
4	Actions of light violence (limited property damage).
5	Actions of heavy violence (e.g., destruction of experimental fields).

also contains protests against the companies' experimental fields. The category "vehicles and other" contains actions against transports carrying genetically modified crops, as well as actions without a clear target.[23] Protest directly targeting biotechnology corporations (e.g., corporations that develop modified seeds) was infrequent, but other companies (mostly food producers, supermarkets, and food transports) were targeted quite often. Protest against food producers and retailers started only in the fall of 1996, shortly before the first modified crops were scheduled to arrive.

Aside from the overall peak of protest in December 1996, there were also smaller peaks in April 1997 and October 1997. These can be attributed to actions that were part of the "Global Days of Action" campaigns against genetic engineering that were mounted for two weeks each in April and October 1997 and were initiated by American activists (including Jeremy Rifkin's Foundation on Economic Trends and the Pure Food Campaign). The relatively low level of events in February and March can be partly explained by the fact that in February 1997, cloning of the sheep Dolly made news, and many activists concerned about biotechnology were busy demanding a cloning ban. Actions against cloning were, however, excluded from this study. Similarly, European decisions on the biotechnology patent directive might have artificially depressed the event counts in the summer of 1997,

Figure 10.1 Event Frequency by Target Type

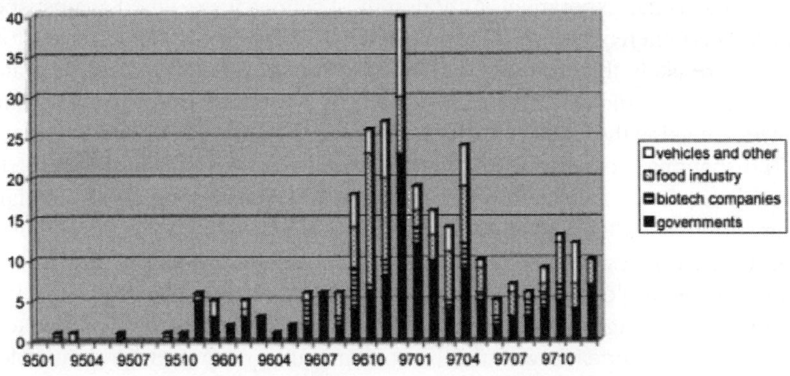

since actions concerning the patent-on-life directive were not part of this study either. The parliamentary summer recess probably also contributed to low event counts during that time.

Greenpeace and other environmental movement organizations accounted for the largest share of protest activities. A smaller number of mostly verbal protests came from consumer and farmer's organizations, especially from their European umbrella organizations. Protests of the Natural Law Party and a few members of other parties made up another smaller portion of the reported activities. Initiatives for public referenda or for the establishment of "GM-free" certificates were usually brought forward by broad coalitions of movement organizations, parties, and churches. There were also a few new social movements that specialized in the opposition to genetic engineering. A few professional associations, notably physicians and chefs, entered the debate as well.

The analysis here will only distinguish between predominantly national and predominantly transnational actors. Such a categorization is often not as clear-cut as it may seem at first. For example, although Friends of the Earth is technically a transnational organization, it is in fact an umbrella organization made up of almost totally independent national branches (Smith et al. 1994) with little crossnational consistency of actions. Though Greenpeace is more centralized, its national branches also choose and plan particular actions on their own (Smith et al. 1994); but across nations, Greenpeace actions are very similar and appear overall more coordinated.[24] A comparison of the overall frequency of protest of national and transnational actors against the five main target types is shown in table 10.2. (The numbers do not add up across the rows because some events were directed against multiple targets.)

As the table suggests, there was a strong presence on the part of transnational actors in the anti-GMO protest campaign. National actors targeted governments most frequently, and food retailers and producers almost as often. The events by national actors listed in the biotech category also contain local protests against experimental fields, which are not necessarily aimed at the company that conducts the experiment. Although most actions were aimed against specific targets—there were very few purely "expressive" protests—national actors were more likely than transnational ones to mount actions or to make statements that were directed against no specific target. These events were usually aimed at making the public at large more aware of the genetic foods issue.

Transnational actors invested much of their efforts in pressuring governmental targets—at any level, which probably also goes a long way to explain their strong overall involvement in the issue: they were well positioned to influence EU politics. In only a few cases did transnational actors directly target the biotechnology corporations, but the food industry was pressured frequently. Actions against food transports were only mounted by Greenpeace. In general, Greenpeace was the most dominant group and accounted for

Table 10.2 Frequency of Actions, by Actor Affiliation and Target Type

	Governments	*Biotech*	*Food*	*Vehicles*	*No Target*	*All Targets*
National actors	40.7%	17.0%	30.4%	0.0%	16.3%	
	(55)	(23)	(41)	(0)	(22)	N = 135
Transnational	52.7%	3.6%	26.3%	9.6%	9.6%	
Actors	(88)	(6)	(44)	(16)	(16)	N = 167

roughly *half* of all the actions by transnational groups, with 44 actions against governments, 3 against biotechnology companies, 30 against food companies, 16 against vehicles, and 10 with no specific target. In the following section, protest against governments and against companies will be analyzed separately and in more detail.

Activism Targeting Governments

In order to investigate how the existence of an additional supranational level of legislation in Europe influences protest, the following two sections will explore if and in what respect protest against the EU differed in frequency or intensity from protest against the national governments. Imig and Tarrow (1997) have put forward three hypotheses relating protest to the level of its targets in the EU: the first hypothesis (*transnationalization*) postulates that —as the EU gains policy competencies—domestic actors will increasingly shift the focus of their demands and their targets to the EU. The second (*polarization*) suggests that domestic actors are divided into two camps, those with privileged access to transnational institutions (e.g., industry) and those that remain trapped in national opportunity structures (e.g., labor). Finally, their third hypothesis (*domestication*)—the one they emphasize in chapter 2 in this volume—proposes that domestic actors target the nation-state as an intermediary in supranational decision-making. Each of these hypotheses will in turn be investigated for its support by the event data of this particular campaign. In the following discussions, the term *supranational* will be used to refer to the EU level of decision-making, in full awareness that only some aspects of the EU are truly supranational.

Transnationalization of Protest

Table 10.3 shows the percent distribution of anti-GMO protests targeting the subnational, the national, the European, or the international level (e.g., protests at international conferences or UN meetings), as well as three categories of indirect targeting. The percentages are computed separately for direct and indirect targets and add up to more than 100 percent, due to events that targeted multiple levels of government.[25]

Table 10.3 Frequency of Events Targeting Different Levels of Government

Target	*Percentage*	*Frequency*
Direct Targets	**102.4**	***N* = 129**
Subnational government	3.1	4
National government	48.1	62
U.S. government	2.3	3
EU	47.3	61
International	1.6	2
Indirect Targets	**105.6**	***N* = 18**
National government, indirectly EU	77.8	14
National, indirectly international	16.7	3
EU, indirectly international	11.1	2

Note: Figures total over 100% because of multiple targets for some events.

As the table demonstrates, protesters were equally likely to target national governments and European institutions. This finding lends impressionistic support to the hypothesis that there has been a shift in focus of protest in general toward the EU, since the ratio of protest targeting the EU on *this* issue is quite high—nearly three times as high as the 17 percent that Imig and Tarrow report for general EU targeting (c.f., chapter 2). Of course, we cannot draw any firm conclusions on the basis of a single campaign, but more of the events of 1999 around the issue of genetic modification suggest that these findings may turn out to be robust—at least in the area of health and consumer issues.

Polarization

Imig and Tarrow's second hypothesis, "polarization," cannot be directly investigated with this data, since only actions favoring stricter regulation were coded and not the actions of the biotechnology industry. However, the industry lobby in general is very well organized at the European level. Furthermore, the European Union as well as all the national governments sponsor research programs for biotechnology, so that one can safely assume that the biotechnology industry in fact had excellent access to European decision-makers. However, the newspaper data show that the activist organizations also lobbied the EU to a considerable degree, which may be due to the favorable opportunity structures of the EU for environmental issues (Marks and McAdam 1996), although the EU Commission proved not very receptive to activists' concerns in this case.

The data in table 10.4 distinguish those actions that were organized by a transnational actor from those that were nationally organized.[26] The table reveals an interesting division of labor: most of the transnationally organized actions were aimed at agents at the supranational level, while most of the nationally organized actions were aimed at authorities within the nation-state. The division of labor in the newspaper data is also supported by the statement of the Austrian group Global2000 that their organization was the only national group with an office in Brussels for three years, at which point they joined Friends of the Earth (Global2000 1999).

The data presented in the table suggest that national protest movements are indeed more likely to be confined to the national arena, but that the presence of professional transnational movement organizations alleviates this confinement, enabling domestic activists to be heard at the supranational level. It is possible that the division of labor was so pronounced in this campaign because the combination of technical and moral appeals strongly favored the kind of transnational advocacy organizations that can organize effectively beyond borders (Keck and Sikkink 1998).[27] However, the example of Global2000 also shows that one should probably make a distinction between inherently international movements like Greenpeace and the cooperation of multiple national groups that choose to pool resources to maintain a common European "outpost." Apart from the advantage of pooling resources, such transnational cooperation can also offer the political advantages of increased clout and easier coordination. An example of the latter is ECOBP (European Campaign on Biotechnology Patents), a network of over forty European groups opposed to biotechnology patents that was founded in early 1998 in order to establish a common political platform. In the future, it will be possible to examine whether protest not facilitated by transnational movement organizations and umbrella organizations is less likely to target the EU. If so, it would be interesting to find out whether this is due to a lack of European identity and perspective, or if the legislative process in the EU is so intricate and impenetrable that professional activists and lobbyists in Brussels are an absolute necessity. If the latter were true, it would constitute a systemic bias toward consolidated, well-organized, and well-financed movements and a trend toward the polarization of collective action.

Table 10.4 Level of Government Targeted by Nationally Based and Transnational Actors

	National Target	*National (Indirect Supranational) Target*	*Supranational Target*	*US*	*Total*
National actors	81.8%	10.9%	14.5%	0%	
	(45)	(6)	(8)	(0)	(55)
Transnational actors	23.9%	12.5%	64.8%	3.4%	
	(21)	(11)	(57)	(3)	(88)

Domestication

Finally, Imig and Tarrow's third thesis, the pattern of the government-as-intermediary, is much less prevalent in the GMO campaign. Looking at table 10.3, only 14 of a total of 142 government-oriented protest events targeted the national state in order to indirectly reach the EU; 5 of these protests targeted other levels as well. However, in reality, indirect protest probably occurs more frequently, since many politicians have functions on several levels of government, and newspaper articles and protesters may not always mention each function explicitly.

In conclusion, the hypothesis of a general trend toward the transnationalization of protest in Europe seems to be supported most strongly by the data of this campaign, but an analysis of the development of the target-proportions over time, as shown in figure 10.2,[28] suggests a more specific version of this hypothesis.

As figure 10.2 indicates, the relative proportions of protest targeting the EU versus the national level fluctuated considerably over time. Such strong fluctuations would not be expected if we were witnessing a secular shift of protest direction from the national to the supranational level. Rather, it suggests that demands and criticisms are selectively directed against those legislative bodies that are about to decide on a certain issue or are blamed for a decision just made.

A qualitative comparison[29] of a detailed timeline of events of the legislative process with the targets of protest events supports this interpretation. Targeting behavior seems to be quite specific, especially for the actions of transnational NGOs. However, the specificity decreased in the second half of 1997 (as well as the frequency of activities against the EU in general), pre-

Figure 10.2 Number and Target Level of Government-Targeting Events

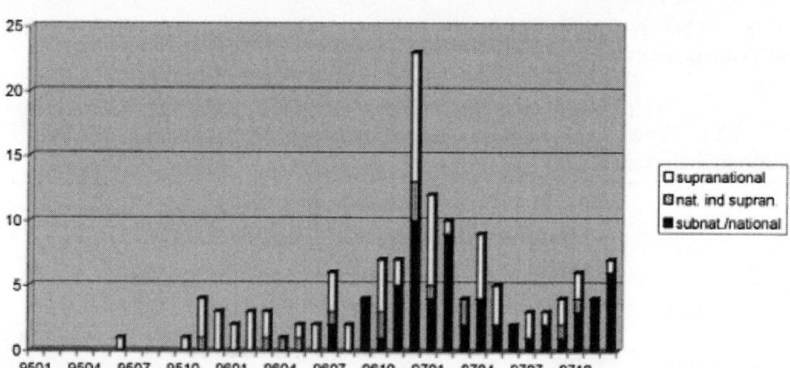

sumably because activists were becoming increasingly disillusioned with the EU legislative process. There is yet another piece of evidence that underscores the deliberate, rational choice of targets of opportunity: only an insignificant portion of protest activity was directed toward the subnational level (e.g., Germany's *Länder* or Switzerland's *cantons*), which have no legal competence in this issue area.[30]

But a word of caution is in order: although this deliberate choice of targets has an opportunistic flavor, it does not fit the traditional dimensions of a political opportunity structure such as openness of the system, elite alignments, elite allies, or state repression (McAdam 1996). However, one can interpret this behavior as the dynamic reflection of a structural argument put forward by Risse-Kappen, ed. (1995), who argued that a fragmented institutional state structure presents many points of access to nongovernmental actors. Protest actors in the GMO campaign indeed use multiple access points, but they also focus their activity on those access points that have the most influence on the decision process at any given point of time.[31] This means that arguments about institutional opportunity structures may have an additional, dynamic dimension. If transnational social movement organizations in general employ such dynamic, selective targeting of protest, then it might be that the hypothesized trend toward a transnationalization of protest targets is merely a reflection of the degree to which the legislative process in the different issue areas has moved to the EU level, mediated by the degree to which transnational activist groups dominate that area.[32]

Qualitative Differences in Protest

The dependency of the forms of protest on the target level of protest has been very little theorized, as theories for national protests mostly consider factors such as state repression or state openness to predict it. Although the openness of the European Union to societal actors in general is debatable, European institutions are quite favorably disposed and open toward environmental NGOs (Marks and McAdam 1996). In a recent article, however, Marks and McAdam argue that the structure of political opportunity in the EU is decidedly more open to conventional than to unconventional activity (1999). They also argue that mass mobilization in Brussels is expensive in time and money; that geography constrains such activities to activists from nearby countries; and that mass protest targeting the EU is unlikely because open public discourse seldom takes place at the European level. Their article suggests two further hypotheses to test in this analysis:

> *Hypothesis 1* (Remoteness and Political Opportunity Structure): The European Union does not provide a likely target for violent protest due to its complexity, abstractness, and distance, and structurally favors polite, low-intensity forms of

protest such as petitions, lobbying, and proclamations rather than violent mass demonstrations that are often used against national governments.

Hypothesis 2 (Protest Repertoires): Activists protest against the European Union in a similar way as they do against their national governments, using those forms of protest with which they are most familiar (Tilly 1995a).

Although extensive data are not available on specific protest repertoires, we are able to construct a proxy measure of levels of protest intensity.

As table 10.5 demonstrates, discursive, low-pressure action forms were the predominant form of contention employed against *both* levels of government.[33] To a degree, this finding supports the second hypothesis—the modularity of the repertoire of contention. Knowing whether groups that operated at both levels used similar methods of protest will require an analysis of each country or each group separately. The actions against the EU were predominantly institutional and polite, as predicted by hypothesis 1, and seem to be more so than the actions directed against national governments. However, the low numbers of events here make these findings speculative at best. It will take analysis of campaigns that are both domestically and supranationally organized by the same groupings to detect whether EU-directed activism is more or less conventional.

Confrontational actions, in turn, garnered much press attention. Examples included the dumping of several tons of modified corn in front of the U.S. embassy in Vienna—to the tune of Elvis's "Return to Sender"—and an occupation of the office of the Austrian health minister, who incensed protesters by favoring labeling rules rather than an outright ban on GMOs. The curious fact that both of these more confrontational actions occurred in Austria hints at the possibility that the action repertoires may be most strongly influenced by societal or organizational culture and tradition, and that the target level is quite irrele-

Table 10.5 Intensity of Protest Pressure against Governments

Intensity Level of Protests	*National Governments (N = 71)*		*Supranational Institutions (N = 78)*	
0	16.9%	(12)	16.7%	(13)
1	73.2%	(52)	83.3%	(65)
1a	53.5%	(38)	76.9%	(60)
1b	9.9%	(7)	0.0%	(0)
1c	9.9%	(7)	6.4%	(5)
2	12.7%	(9)	2.6%	(2)
3	1.4%	(1)	0.0%	(0)

Legend: Pressure categories 0, 1, 2, and 3 were defined in table 10.1. Subcategory 1a contains actions that could be broadly described as lobbying. Subcategory 1b contains actions that require broad mobilization, such as citizen initiatives and campaigns. Subcategory 1c contains small demonstrations and "flashy" actions.

vant for the choice of protest methods. Other tentative evidence for this hypothesis would be the observation that British groups have a tendency for spectacular and comic direct-action methods, and that Greenpeace has a traditional, crossnationally applied action repertoire. Yet protesting against the EU with methods similar to those traditionally used against national governments is clearly made difficult by the fact that few proximate targets could be protested against in lieu of the institutions in Brussels. The EU neither has national embassies, nor does it provide other obvious symbolic targets, such as Disney World Europe or McDonalds do in the case of protests against the United States.

ACTIVISM TARGETING COMPANIES

On the whole, activism targeting corporations was characterized by much higher intensity of pressure than that against governments (c.f., a comparison of figure 10.3[34] and table 10.5). A direct comparison of protests targeting national versus transnational companies, however, proved unfeasible on the basis of newspaper articles. On the one hand, protest rarely targeted biotechnology corporations directly. Food retailers and food producers, on the other hand, were pressured frequently, but company names were seldom mentioned in the articles. However, the different types of companies targeted show different patterns of geographical affiliation and different degrees of vulnerability to protest, depending on their customer base. An analysis organized by industry sector therefore allowed the clearest distinctions between protest patterns.

Biotechnology Corporations

Biotechnology companies (i.e., corporations that develop engineered plants) usually own seed retailers or work closely with them, so that farmers

Figure 10.3 Number and Intensity of Events Targeting Companies

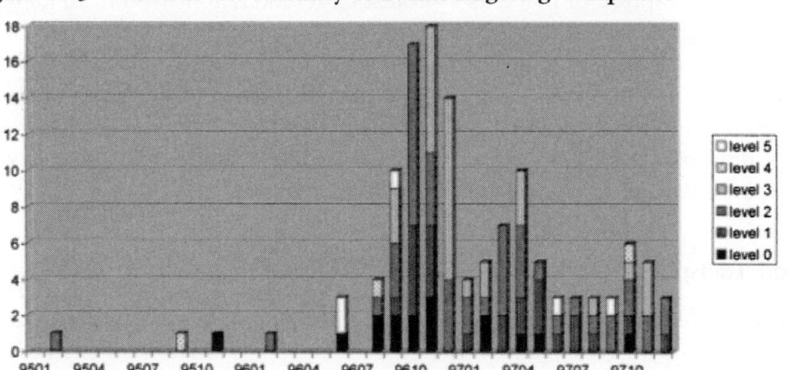

can be considered their main direct customer base. However, since commercial cultivation of GMOs was illegal in the EU during the time period analyzed, the biotechnology companies did not have a customer base in Europe[35] at that time that could have pressured them or that could have been pressured by other societal groups. During the period of this study, biotechnology companies were mainly affected by events involving protest against, destruction of, or occupation of their experimental fields, which usually incurred considerable financial damage.[36]

The low number of actions against experimental fields reported in the press did not allow for statistical analysis; however, the activist group ArcheGenoah maintains a list of all experimental fields in Germany and lists the company or institute conducting the experiment, the time period of the experiment (usually several years), and the opposition launched against the experimental field by activists.[37] In addition, all biotechnology companies that conducted field trials in Germany operate multinationally.

Employing this database, I conducted an analysis of the relationship between the number of actions that were against a company's fields and the number of countries in which that company operated, in order to assess whether multinational corporations were more likely to be targeted. This analysis did not show a direct correlation between multinational status and propensity to be targeted.

Monsanto's experiments were opposed at a somewhat higher frequency than warranted by the number of trials or their duration, but the sample sizes are small and other factors might be more influential.[38] For example, activists have noted that experimental fields are most likely to be targeted by local residents, so that the variations in protest may be mainly due to differences in protest inclination or the resources of local populations (Hissting 1999).

This suggestion is also supported by media accounts of actions against manufacturing plants and biotechnology corporations. Local and national groups performed about 80 percent of those actions. This is markedly different from protest against other types of targets, where transnational targets were most likely to be targeted by transnational groups.

Monsanto's pride of place as a protest target likely followed from its high name-recognition in Europe and a broad perception that the corporation is "singularly unscrupulous—a real symbol of corporate greed and power" (Greenberg 1998a, 1998b). In turn, the recent tumble in the stock price of Monsanto and its decision in 1999 to step back from its plan to force farmers to purchase only seeds that could not be reproduced suggest that the protest campaign has had an effect.

Food-Transport Protests

During the period of this study, no genetically modified crops were grown in the EU, and all genetically modified corn and soy from abroad entered the

European market by ship and then were transported inland by train, truck, and ship. All these vehicles proved to be easy targets for blockades by anti-GMO activists.

The first shiploads of genetically modified soybeans and corn arrived in Europe when their import was still illegal, which put Greenpeace and other groups into the curious position of conducting illegal blockades against imports that were in violation of European law. These actions highlighted the failure of national governments to enforce the import ban. This led the EU commission to admonish all member-states to crack down on illegal imports, an action that, in turn, brought the EU to the brink of a trade war with the United States.

However, the EU commission quickly backed down, declaring the imports legal after the fact and thereby sanctioning the aggressive behavior of the biotechnology companies. Often, it proved difficult to identify the indirect targets of actions against vehicles transporting corn or soybeans from the United States (possible targets included American farmers, biotech corporations, the transportation business, or receiving food processors).

Food Retailers and Producers

The primary corporate target of the anti-GMO campaign proved to be food producers and food retailers. Boycotts were employed against grocers who sold products containing genetically modified ingredients and indirectly hurt grain mills, farmers of GMOs, and, ultimately, the biotechnology corporations that developed the seeds (Cott and Ilman 1999, Mitsch and Mitchell 1999). In this section, I describe the activism launched against food retailers and food producers, before turning to an analysis of the differences between protests against national and transnational companies.

By September 1996, NGOs had started to pressure food retailers and producers for guarantees that they would not produce or sell products containing genetically modified ingredients.[39] In Austria, Germany, and Switzerland (and to a varying degree in other countries) major food retailers agreed quickly to such pledges. However, since soybean products are contained in about 40 to 60 percent of supermarket food, these guarantees were not easy to implement. This difficulty caused some retailers and producers to back out of their promises and others to fight attempts to introduce clear labels. Avoiding genetically modified ingredients was particularly difficult for producers because of obstruction by U.S. grain providers, who mixed modified with traditionally grown soybeans. Therefore, the campaign's success required that activists find alternative sources of traditionally grown soybeans. EuroCommerce, representing the retail and wholesale sector in twenty European countries, became a spokesperson for the wishes of European consumers and extensively lobbied the U.S. agricultural and trade industry for crop segregation. Greenpeace also distributed leaflets in the Chicago Board of Trade, promising a huge European market for traditional soybeans. In the end, only a very few soybean shipments from the United States were GE-free. Therefore, Greenpeace collaborated with an Austrian broker to guarantee a supply of one million tons of Brazilian GE-free soybeans for Europe, to which they directed the attention of food producers and retailers. By 1999, a long list of alternative suppliers existed, and many organizations such as Global2000 were working closely with food producers and retailers in order to provide consumers with GE-free food products.

Protest against small or national food producers often appeared in the newspapers only indirectly—for example, in an announcement that a single food producer had become GE-free or blanket announcements by Greenpeace that "fifty food processors in Germany" were GE-free. This suggests that small food producers were put under pressure but that these protests did not necessarily surface in the media. Intense brand-name protest campaigns were directed at the four largest food producers with headquarters in Europe: Nestlé, Unilever, Danone, and Kraft Jacobs Suchard. Kraft Suchard quickly agreed not to use genetically modified products, but Nestlé, Unilever, and Danone proved formidable targets. At the beginning, Nestlé and Unilever only agreed to abstain from using genetically modified products in their German branches, since consumer protest had been strongest there. Much later, they selectively made similar concessions to other countries with high consumer pressure.[40]

If we look at the affiliations of activist organizations targeting food-related organizations, we see a roughly equal distribution of national and transnational groups (refer to table 10.2). However, around 75 percent of the actions by transnational actors against food targets were mounted by Greenpeace. This number may even understate its involvement, since Greenpeace repeatedly organized actions against Nestlé and Unilever in many countries on the same day. These multicountry actions are counted as single actions in this analysis. Greenpeace's actions against the multinational food producers also were highly visible, whereas actions against food retailers were often simply requests of various groups that modified foods be taken off the shelves. A notable exception is seen in the United Kingdom, where supermarket chains were routinely targets of picketing and other direct-action methods.

In their actions against food producers and food retailers, NGOs have asserted a consumer's right to choose between modified and traditional foods. NGOs located alternative crop suppliers in order to make norm implementation feasible and attempted to enforce compliance by organizing consumer boycotts. In this respect, in the absence of a legislative solution, NGOs established a regime of their own. This is an interesting example of what Wapner has described as "governance structures" in economic systems (1997). Through these efforts, NGOs were able to demonstrate both that it was feasible to implement bans and labeling requirements and that consumers cared about the issue.

In addition, this campaign indicated the susceptibility of nationally organized food retailers and smaller food producers to consumer pressure. Across Europe, food retailers joined with concerned customers in demanding an alternative to GMOs. Although it is easy to be cynical about such moves, support by retail chains in the form of complete bans or product labeling was more effective than slow-moving and hesitant EU legislation in maintaining freedom of choice for consumers in the early years of the conflict. As Debora Spar has recently noted in the case of human rights campaigns, companies can become "important instruments" of movements if they can be convinced by consumer pressure that it is in their financial interest to behave in a certain way (Spar 1998). This was exemplified by the retail umbrella organization EuroCommerce, which actively lobbied both U.S. farmers and European politicians. Interestingly, it is possible to view the retail industry in a pivot position similar to that which Imig and Tarrow hypothesize may increasingly characterize the nation-state (chapter 1, this volume). In this campaign, consumers pressured supermarkets to pressure the food producers on their behalf. The main difference seems to be that the pivot is located in a hierarchy of consumer and producer relations instead of a hierarchy of political institutions.

In contrast to the more cooperative, nationally organized parts of the food industry, the transnational food corporations Unilever, Nestlé, and Danone faced frequent and intense protest. Greenpeace singled out these targets because of their dominant market presence and headquarters in Europe. The European headquarters of these biotechnology firms provided ready targets for media-worthy actions and demonstrations. In addition, the intransigence of these companies served to intensify the protests, this was similar to Monsanto's original strategy of brute force.[41] Interestingly, these food corporations did not respond to the protests as a unitary, transnational actor—as the protesters had certainly hoped—but made concessions separately for each of their national branches.

The frequency of industry-oriented protest was also a likely response to the apparent disjunction of the political elites from their constituents. The attitudes of politicians in the UK and Germany toward genetically modified foods, for example, differed markedly from popular opinion (Greenberg 1998a, b). Especially in Germany, the regulatory process appeared closed to public scrutiny and input, and both major parties were strong advocates of biotechnology despite strong public opposition (Dreyer and Gill N.D.). The gap between public opinion and elite action also spurred on the anti-GMO campaign. A British member of Parliament noted:

> As we debate the relationship between Britain, Europe, the USA, and the World Trade Organization, we must understand that people have given up waiting for

> a parliamentary lead. . . . Rulings may go in their favor, but if Monsanto and the USA win the right to dump unsafe foods in United Kingdom markets, we can overrule that right with a civic right to dump those products in the sea or leave them stockpiled at supermarket check-outs. (Simpson 1999)

As European governments align closely with business interests, consumer action is likely to increase. This is suggested by a recent poll of over 25,000 citizens worldwide, in which over one in five respondents reported having avoided a company's products or speaking to others against the company for "not behaving responsibly." A similar number report they are likely to do so (*Food Issues Monitor* 1999). In the campaign against genetically modified foods in Europe in the late 1990s, we may be witnessing both Europe turning the tables on the United States by initiating an international wave of protest and the twentieth century's high point of activism beyond borders (Keck and Sikkink 1998).

CONCLUSIONS

In summary, the activists of the European campaigns against GMOs targeted the EU and their national governments, as well as the food industry. In this campaign, protests against national governments and the EU were strikingly similar in frequency and intensity. However, the data suggest that the high frequency of protest targeting the EU might have been due to the strong involvement of transnational movement organizations in the campaign, which were much more likely to target transnational organizations. In contrast, domestic protests were predominantly organized by national groups and directed against national governments. This might hint at a bias of the EU system toward well-organized movements, placing fledgling movements or movements with few financial resources at a disadvantage.

Experimental fields and vehicles transporting genetically modified crops were subject to violent attacks. In the food industry, transnational corporations were a main focus of actions by transnational NGOs because of their strategic importance and intransigence. In contrast, food retailers and smaller food producers were more cooperative and—with the exception of the UK—faced little direct action. With the EU as a hesitant intermediary, the consumer campaign that began in the mid-1990s seems to have deterred food producers and retailers from the mass marketing of genetically modified food in Europe.

What lessons might this case suggest for the future? First, the combination of moral and technical issues that combined in the anti-GMF campaign offered an ideal opportunity structure for transnational coalitions of activists, which are particularly suited to transnational contentious action. Second, the shift of protest to the supranational level appears to correlate with the growing policy competency of the EU (corroborating the findings of Bush and Simi in chapter 5). Third, it is when the EU's legislative process progresses too slowly or deviates markedly from public preference that consumer campaigns are most likely to emerge and to have an effect. That this effect seems to have been greatest on national corporations is one of the complexities of the emerging European polity.

NOTES

I thank Sidney Tarrow for his support and advice, and all participants of the Workshop on the European Union and Transnational Contention for stimulating discussions. In particular, I thank Matthew Evangelista, Ron Herring, Liesbet Hooghe, Doug Imig, Margaret Keck, and David Meyer for their comments on earlier versions of this chapter.

1. BSE (Bovine Spongiform Encephalopathy) is also known as mad cow disease.

2. In the words of *The Economist* (19 June 1999): "The European system for approving such foods for sale on the shelves or for planting in the fields is a mishmash of national and supranational authorities."

3. This description is drawn from Anderson (1999) and Donaldson and May (1999).

4. The empirical data on these claims shows high variability and seems inconclusive. See Lappé and Bailey (1998: 81–84) for statistical evidence of a reduction in yields. See also Benbrook (1998) and Watts (1999).

5. Chapter 3 of Anderson's 1999 book discusses and refutes in detail the argument that genetically modified crops are necessary to feed the world's growing population.

6. In one experiment, a soybean that had been modified to produce a protein from Brazil nuts also inherited the Brazil nut allergene (Nordlee et al. 1996).

7. There are scientific studies that show how bacteria can pick up genes from DNA in the environment (Neilson et al. 1994). Previously, it was thought that bacteria in human intestines would not be able to pick up the antibiotic-resistance gene from food DNA because DNA is broken down very rapidly in the stomach. New research shows, however, that DNA survives longer than anticipated (MacKenzie 1999) and that pieces of foreign DNA were found in tissue cells of mice fed with free DNA (Schubbert et al. 1994). It is currently an open question whether DNA from *food* can be transferred to bacteria in human intestines.

8. The *New York Times* recently printed a detailed case study of a particularly lax USDA approval (Yoon 1999). Mr. Glickman, U.S. secretary of agriculture, responded to these shortcomings:

Glickman: "The government is not going to be able to do all this testing. It's impossible. We have to rely on the private sector to do it." [. . .]

Question: "Is your department adequately staffed to handle this research? Has downsizing gone too far?"

Glickman: "The answer is no. I think we are not adequately staffed . . . "

(From the question-and-answer part of the speech of Mr. Glickman at the National Press Club on 13 June 1999.)

9. On 23 February 1999, the European Commission rejected several amendments of the directive 90/220/EEC that the European Parliament had proposed. One of these rejected amendments demanded a liability regime compensating damage caused by genetically modified organisms to human health or the environment. The Commission has promised a white paper on environmental liability that is expected to appear in 2000 (Friends of the Earth Europe 1999a).

10. Several U.S. NGOs have charged the EPA with gross negligence for its approval of Bt crops. For an account, see Natural Law Party Canada (1997).

11. The previous German government proclaimed that biotechnology will create 100,000 jobs by 2000, although the study on which they based their estimate claimed only 40,000 jobs and a spokesperson of the institute that did the study remarked that in all likelihood, the net gain in jobs would be close to zero (Keeler 1993).

12. Levidow, Carr, and Wield (1999) have also pointed out that risk assessment implicitly rests upon normative judgments and technology assessments and is therefore not a question that can be answered by value-free science.

13. In two October 1999 U.S. polls, only 38 percent of the public knew that genetically modified foods were currently sold in supermarkets. A majority of respondents regarded biotechnology as positive, and only 27 percent believed it posed a health hazard to consumers (IFIC 1999, Gallup 1999). However, the U.S. organic farming movement protested successfully in 1998 against plans to allow genetically modified plants in food products labeled as organic. In the run-up to the WTO meeting in Seattle in December 1999, both media coverage and activists' pressure seemed to increase. A handful of U.S. food producers had gone GE-free as of late 1999.

14. In January 1997, Ciba Crop Protection merged with Sandoz Agro to form a new agrochemical corporation named Novartis.

15. National regulations are only allowed to restrict access of a product allowed in any other European country for reasons of public health safety. However, since the question of whether GMOs pose a danger to public health is so highly contested, the decision on the legality of these national regulations has been tossed back and forth.

16. Dreyer and Gill (N.D.) describe the biotechnology controversy in Germany in more detail.

17. Levidow (1999) gives a detailed account of the GMO debate in the United Kingdom.

18. Indexed news sources include *Reuters, Agence France Presse,* and various official EU news services, alongside a number of national newspapers. Although the time periods covered by the two news archives are slightly different, the archivist for the activist's collection confirmed that little European protest activity occurred over this issue prior to June 1996.

19. For example, the collection contains very few events from countries like Luxembourg and Italy, where the governments imposed national bans, or from Sweden, where supermarket chains went GE-free relatively early. It seems therefore reasonable to assume that there was more grass-roots pressure in these countries than surfaced in the international news sources indexed by Lexis-Nexis.

20. Marks and McAdam have recently argued that in the EU, rigid distinctions between interest groups and social movements "do not mean much" (Marks and McAdam 1996).

21. See Koopmans (1995) for a discussion of their coding method.

22. In the few events with multiple equivalent targets I selected and coded one at random.

23. This category also contains a single action by Greenpeace pressuring the churches to take a stand.

24. I coded all Greenpeace actions as transnational. In contrast, I coded actions of national organizations that are affiliated with FOE as national protest and only as transnational in cases where the action was attributed to the umbrella organization itself.

25. In this table, each event with multiple different targets was listed once for each target type.

26. In this table, subnational targets were classified as national, and all events targeting the EU or the UN were classified as supranational. Events aimed at several target types were counted once per target type.

27. Margaret Keck has brought this argument to my attention.

28. In this time series, events with multiple target levels were assigned to one target level, chosen at random.

29. Technical considerations prevented construction of a formal time series analysis.

30. In comparison, on average 11.8 percent of all protests of new social movements targeted the subnational level in the time period of 1975–1989.

31. Clearly, the expected power to effect change is only one of many considerations influencing the choice of target. Shifting the target of protest or lobbying activities is also known as *venue shopping*.

32. Interestingly, it might not only be the case that transnational organizations often target supranational targets, but the reverse may also be true. Time will show if all national organizations engaging in EU-directed activism will sooner or later form supranational alliances with other national organizations.

33. In this table, events with multiple types of protest and with different intensity levels were listed once for each intensity level and once for each action type employed in that event.

34. In this time series, events with multiple types of action with different degrees of intensity were only listed once for the most intense level employed.

35. Most of the genetically modified crop is still grown in the United States.

36. Financial damage of around 100,000 DM per destroyed field has been claimed in newspaper reports.

37. This listing is based on the records of the institute that authorizes experimental releases, and the listing of protest is based on newspaper reports.

38. Monsanto's share of protested experiments (18.18 percent, 54 percent, and 55.55 percent) is also much higher than its share of all experiments (7.5 percent, 23.85 percent, and 23.07 percent) in the years 1996–1998. However, Monsanto started experimental plantings in Germany only recently. The higher protest frequency may be due to a higher share of new fields.

39. An example of such a campaign is the "EinkaufsNetz" network, organized by Greenpeace Germany (Greenpeace N.D.).

40. For example, in mid-1999, both companies agreed not to use genetically modified ingredients in products sold in the UK.

41. Initially, Monsanto pursued a very aggressive stance regarding the introduction of GE crops into Europe. In 1998, the company changed its strategy, apologized for the way it introduced genetically modified soybeans into the European market, and launched a $1.6 million advertising campaign that may have led to heightened public suspicion (Harris 1998, Greenberg 1998a,b).

5

COMPARISONS AND CONCLUSIONS

11

Contentious Politics in a Composite Polity

Sidney Tarrow

When the editors of this volume first began to examine contentious politics in the European Union in the mid-1990s, few scholars saw the point of what we were trying to do. "European contention?" some would ask. "What do you mean by that—'Euro-skepticism'?" We would explain that although opposition *to* European integration was an important phenomenon, we were more interested in something else: in contentious politics *within* Europe, on the part of citizens who might support an integrated Europe, oppose it, or have no opinion about its desirability, but whose interests and values led them to focus on Europe as the source of their grievances and to make claims intended to affect its policies or its institutions. In the absence of robust representative institutions, ordinary citizens would be likely to make Brussels the object of their contentious claims. Just as the focus of protest in the early nineteenth century shifted to the consolidating national state, contention, we reasoned, would follow the shift of policy competencies to Brussels in the late twentieth century. We were also interested in seeing whether this will lead to the formation of *transnational* forms of mobilization in Western Europe; if we found such evidence, we thought it would indicate a trend toward a unified polity.

It is a significant marker of how far studies of the European Union have moved toward such a perspective that, a half-decade later, few students still ask what we mean by "European contention." Some, at least in the UK, still identify it largely with *Euro-skepticism*—but at least in the Euro-zone, this term has taken on a faintly antique air. Others see it as limited to the protests of farmers, since these actors continue to make the most vociferous claims on Europe's resources; but our data show that many other actors—like the Vilvoorde workers analyzed in chapter 9, the antigenetic food activists in chapter 10, and the migrant groups who organized a European protest against exclusion described in chapter 8—increasingly aim their protests at the European Union. In one form or another, contentious politics is becoming a European practice.

Since we began our study, more and more scholars have tried to understand the impact of European integration on domestic politics. Some focus on political parties and domestic cleavages; others on the effect of integration on national and subnational institutions; others on the fusion of European and national administrators; still others on the impact of monetary union on national social and economic policies. But particularly given the growing interest in transnational politics both in Europe and elsewhere (see the fourth section of this chapter), interest in European collective action has been growing, too. Our work should be seen as a contribution to this literature—one that takes as its subject not the institutions of Europe or even their interaction with economic elites, but contentious interactions among international and national elites, institutions, and ordinary people (Keck and Sikkink 1998; see the review in Tarrow 2001).

Uncertainty still reigns about the nature, the extent, and the dynamics of European contention. Do French farmers who dump potatoes before a prefecture, Italian milk producers who block Milan's airport, or Vilvoorde workers burning a Renault auto on the steps of the European Commission only provide an entertaining sideshow that pales next to decision-making that takes place within and around elite networks and institutions? Or are such protests part of a broader conflict system—an "actor constellation," in Fritz Scharpf's words (1997: chap. 4)—that extends from grass-roots social actors and their organizations through national governments and European interest representatives to European institutions? Finally, what—if anything—do our studies tell us about the "democratic deficit," a topic that has received much intelligent speculation but little empirical analysis?

In this chapter I first summarize our findings and explore their meaning and limitations, then reflect on the system of conflicts and alignments our work shows emerging in Europe, draw some parallels between European contention and the "new" transnational politics, and close with the question of how contentious politics relates to the problem of European representation. For this is surely the Big Question that lies behind European claims-making: Will it find its way into routine institutional processes or—given the continued weakness of these processes—will it coagulate in transnational contention?

SUMMARY OF FINDINGS

The contributions to our study can be easily summarized—though they will be less easy to interpret.

In part 1 we presented a set of findings from our protest event analysis that showed a growth in Europrotest in the 1990s, revealed few significant differences between the forms of contention that Europeans employ in domestic and European arenas, and identified a larger number of occupational- than nonoccupational-based protests against EU policies. With respect to the scope of organization of protest activity, we identified a predominantly "domesticated" mode of reaction to European grievances and found little evidence of a major shift from national to transnationally based contention—though this may be changing as Europe enters the new century.

Putting these findings together, we came to the not-very-surprising inference that the social groups that protest against European policies are those hurt most by Europe's increasingly integrated market. But they protest on native ground because that is where their political resources and opportunities are the greatest and where they play at the least disadvantage against the powerful actors who wheel and deal in Brussels. With a few notable exceptions that I will mention, Europeans have not learned to cooperate contentiously across Europe's internal boundaries. Indeed, much of the Europrotest our collaborators found was overtly *competitive,* supporting the view that the European single market has created more incentives for competition than for cooperation.

In part 2 our co-authors focused on two of the main occupational groups whose interests are closely bound up with Europe's economic integration—farmers and workers. Farmers remain the major contenders against EU policy and are beginning to reach out to cooperate with one another beyond their borders. Workers' representatives are increasingly aware of Europe's challenge to their members' interests, but despite the presence of a well-organized and well-funded transnational organization—the European Trade Union Confederation—they have been unable to use their institutional strength effectively at the European level.

In both cases, though coordinated national protests appear in our data, sectoral and national conflicts of interest inhibit the possibility of utilizing capacities for collective action transnationally. If this is true of such well-organized occupational groups as farmers and workers, it is probably even more true of a third population group we didn't study, welfare clients and pensioners, who are poorly organized, lack transnational ties, and are widely dispersed—not to mention immigrant workers, minority ethnic groups, and the unemployed. The Vilvoorde and other worker mobilizations suggest changes in this direction, but—as Lefébure and Lagneau's chapter suggests—its context and its "European" construction will not be easy to reproduce.

Part 3 of the study turned from occupational groups to three nonoccupational sectors that are organized as "public interest" lobbies in Brussels: environmentalists, women, and migrants. With some differences, all three have chosen a strategy that we call "virtual representation"—that is, representing the interests of their chosen constituent groups at the center of the European Union rather than attempting to mobilize them transnationally.

Our term *virtual* will be contested by many of these dedicated people, who see their work in Brussels on behalf of these groups as the vanguard of a transnational civil society. They may be correct with respect to the future, and we do not mean to impugn either their motives or their devotion to their causes. However, lacking the "punch" that comes from being able to mobilize mass organizations within the member-states behind their proposals, we see public interest lobbies in Brussels occupying a weak position vis-à-vis both member-states and European institutions and depending for their influence on special ties with sectors of the Commission or the European Parliament. For the most part, they array only "weak weapons for the weak"—in Virginie Guiraudon's apt phrase.

It is instructive that in the most successful campaign we studied—the European Women's Lobby's attempt to gain inclusion for the goal of gender equality in the Amsterdam Treaty—the Lobby gained its success by breaking out of Brussels and developing what Helfferich and Kolb in chapter 7 call "multilevel action coordination." The least successful group—the European Union Migrant's Forum—not only suffers from the gaps between different national groups of immigrants but finds itself cut off from contentious politics at the base (see chapter 8). The environmental groups analyzed by Dieter Rucht in chapter 6 are more effective both nationally and internationally, but they, too, have problems mobilizing European citizens at the European level. We agree with earlier work by Rucht (1997) and Turner (1996) that without a mass mobilizing capacity in the member-states, supranationally based lobbies can have little effect on the outcomes of policy-making in Brussels.

Our most tantalizing, but fragmentary, findings relate to the formation of European political actors. We do not see European collective identities or Euro-citizens developing in short order, but in part 4, our co-authors proposed two mechanisms that may one day lead to the formation of European political actors: the social construction of contention as "European" by the media—as in the Vilvoorde case studied in chapter 9—and the formation of transnational and national coalitions, as in the campaign against genetically modified foods described in chapter 10.

A sidelight on methodology: many other scholars of European integration are interested in the issue of "European" actor formation, too. The problem with most of these studies is that they measure the distance Europeans have traveled toward the goalpost of European citizenship without positing robust mechanisms through which such a process may be occurring. Our studies suggest that such mechanisms may be in the process of formation but can only be observed in the interactions among ordinary Europeans and their interlocutors—and not through answers to survey questions about whether or not people "feel" European. We think it is more likely that European identities will develop—as national identities did in the age of nation-state formation—through repeated interactions of conflict and coalition formation. I will speculate about some of these mechanisms in the third section of this chapter. But first let me turn to the interpretation of our findings.

INTERPRETING THE FINDINGS

In the still emerging world of European contention, we see tendencies and possibilities, rather than certainties and probabilities. Scholars who study EU treaties, directives, Euro rates, or decisions of the European Court of Justice may be disappointed by the cautious tone and the approximate nature of the generalizations we offer. For this we make no apology; we think there have been far too many off-the-shelf generalizations and prefabricated general models concerning the nature of the emerging European policy and think that the identification of mechanisms of integration will take us further along the road to understanding the future of Europe than general deductive models.

Caution is particularly appropriate with regard to the statistical analysis by Imig and Tarrow of the European protest data in chapter 2. As we have more than once reminded ourselves, our quantitative data are based on untried methods, uncertain sources, and a combination of computer-assisted and manual coding; no one who does this kind of work can afford to strike a bold pose or claim to have uncovered robust processes. Moreover, the time period we studied—though long in terms of the brief history of the European Union—is still too short for a reliable statistical time-series analysis to be carried out; nor do we yet feel comfortable using it for cross-national comparative analysis (see the appendix).

Nevertheless, we feel reasonably confident that our central findings will turn out to be robust: Europeans *are* beginning to recognize more and more that the sources of many of their claims—especially occupational ones—are increasingly found in Europe's integrated market and institutions. And in some cases, they are beginning to organize themselves transnationally. But while business associations have found it relatively easy to influence European decision-making in Brussels, weaker social actors continue to face imposing transaction costs when they attempt to organize across borders. Thus they continue to rely on mainly domestic resources and opportunities to target national decision-makers when they seek redress for their claims against European policies.

Is the inevitable result, as Philippe Schmitter provocatively put it, that the "Euro-Bourgeoisie has at long last found in the EC the 'Executive Committee' for managing its common affairs" (1993), while labor, farmers, immigrants, and other social actors are condemned to protest fruitlessly at a lower level?

We find intuitive evidence for Schmitter's speculation in our findings, but we put forward three cautions:

- First, since basic European decisions are largely made through bargaining among national governments, it is not at all clear that the national political level accessed by weaker social actors is a "lower" level—though it is certainly a *dispersed* one when it comes to influencing the outcomes of intergovernmental decisions. So-called "lower" levels often get more out of their "penetration" by central powers than the central powers themselves, as the history of state-making in nineteenth-century Europe showed (Tarrow in preparation).
- Nor does organized business, seen from close up, exhibit the unity in approaching the EU that would be needed to justify the appellation of the European Union as its "executive committee." In many sectors, firms prefer to defend their own interests, rather than unite with their competitors, and in others, individual sectoral organizations are far more powerful than the peak business associations that claim to aggregate their interests.
- Third, in some areas—for example, the environment and women's issues—determined public protest, technically informed lobbying, and use of the European Court of Justice and cooperation with friendly governments or European officials on the part of the "losers" in European integration have succeeded in effecting important changes in European decision-making.
- Finally, protesters and public interest groups have shown a capacity to *learn* how to use Europe's dispersed and competitive institutions. This will never provide them with the clout of the business groups that ride the wave of Europe's preference for opening markets, but it does give them the opportunity to exploit the partial autonomy of—and the competition between—European institutions and policy makers (Heritier 1999).

Criticizing Schmitter's peremptory dictum is one thing; interpreting the implications of our findings and the tendencies we discern in them is another matter. Consider the process of "domestication" of protest that we found most frequently in our protest data: does it signify a neat two-stage process—conflict-as-usual in national politics; the representation of national interests by national states at the European level—as the advocates of intergovernmental models of European integration would likely maintain? Or does it mean that internal politics is being Europeanized, as constructivists would probably argue? The implications for the nature of the emerging European polity would be exactly the opposite, according to which of these interpretations is given to our findings.

Or consider the calibration of transnational with national protest campaigns that Vera Kettnaker found in the conflict over the approval of genetically modified food. Is this a preview of future transnational social movements or an exception to the norm of "domestication," produced by the European valence of food-related issues after the Mad Cow crisis and the fact that the main producer of Genetically Modified Organisms (GMOs) is the superpower across the sea? Both the European visibility of the issue and its inherently transnational and transatlantic nature produced a high degree of media attention, a great deal of uncertainty, and concern on the part of national governments at outraging a frightened public (Lezaun 1999b). We can only know if this pattern of transnational/national interaction is robust if the same patterns are observed for other—and perhaps less unusual—protest campaigns.

Next, consider the Marks and McAdam thesis that European groups use lobbying strategies at the European level while they employ protest at home (1999). Is this evidence of the effect of the lobbying culture that surrounds the European Commission on the repertoire of collective action—as Marks and McAdam hypothesize—or is it a specific instance of the more general trend that we find throughout the advanced industrial democracies for confrontational forms of protest to give way to more routine forms of activity (Dalton 1996; Meyer and Tarrow, eds., 1998)? The meaning of our findings would be considerably different, depending on which of these two interpretations they fit. European interest groups that engage in lobbying in Brussels may simply be projecting onto the European scene the conventional forms of collective action that have come to serve them well in their domestic contexts. If that turns out to be true, rather than telling us there is a "European Union effect" on contention, rendering it more like lobbying and less like protest, it would be one more piece of evidence for Tilly's (1986, 1995a) established theorem that people tend to use the forms of collective action with which they are familiar.

Finally, consider the media "construction" of the Vilvoorde strike as Lefébure and Lagneau describe it. Their chapter makes clear that "European" contention is as much a matter of how a conflict is constructed as of any "essential" character it may have. But some events are constructed in a particular way for years without having a transformative effect on people's future actions: think of how Yugoslavia was constructed as a nation-state under Tito, only to disintegrate and give way to "ancestral ethnic hatreds" after 1989. We will only know whether there is a progressive and an irreversible tendency to construct crossnational conflict or any other kind of transaction as "European" in the light of evidence on whether Europeans "enact" these constructions in their future behavior.

More broadly, we have studied European contention during a transitional stage in Europe's institutional development. What is likely to be the future of contentious European politics if—as seems likely—the European

Parliament wrests more power from the Council and comes to exercise more control over the Commission, as seemed likely with the fall of the Santer Commission in 1999? Some scholars see a strengthened Parliament filling the democratic deficit and thereby providing an institutional channel for claims that currently find an outlet in contentious behavior. Others see Brussels' neocorporatist forms of interest representation as too deeply entrenched to be uprooted by the EU's part-time roving Parliament. These are questions I can only speculate about but will return to in my conclusion.

I put forward these questions and qualifications not to undermine our and our collaborators' findings but to underscore how open-ended the question of European polity-building becomes when we look beyond the transactional politics that reigns in the European quarter of Brussels. Some of our uncertainties will surely be clarified as more EU scholars venture outside Brussels and try to either verify or invalidate our findings; we offer this volume in part to provoke them to do so. Other questions may be answered as the processes we have sketched are better specified and operationalized; we welcome that process, too. But we think part of the problem results from the narrow way in which the European system has been conceptualized by its students. At this stage, we turn to this broader issue—how the integration between domestic actors and the emerging European polity is best conceived.

COMPOSITE STATE POLITICS

In chapter 1 we expressed dissatisfaction with several general models of European integration on the grounds that they leave the relations between elite and mass levels of participation unspecified. I do not think these models are mistaken with respect to the issues their authors deal with, but I worry that they are extremely elite-centered. In looking for a broader and more inclusive approach, we borrowed a perspective from historical work on Europe that we found illuminating: Wayne te Brake's model of "the composite polity." In this section, I return to and modify it, suggesting four forms of alliance and conflict formation that it points to.

"At the beginning of the early modern period," writes te Brake, "most Europeans lived within composite states that had been variously cobbled together from preexisting political units by a variety of aggressive 'princes' employing a standard repertoire of techniques" (1998: 14). Some territories, like England or Wales or the mosaic of *pays d'election* and *pays d'etat in France,* were made up of continuous territories; others, like the checkerboard of units in the Hapsburg Empire, were physically dispersed and boasted strong local rulers making competing claims on loyalties and resources—like Catalonia and Portugal (pp. 14–15). Still others lived in city-states or Cathedral cities. For centuries, most people lived under the sway of local elites, bishops, merchant aristocrats, dukes, and rival princes. Te Brake writes,

> Since the dynastic "prince" promised to respect the political customs and guaranteed the chartered privileges of these constituent political units, ordinary political subjects within composite states acted in the context of overlapping, intersecting, and changing political spaces defined by often competitive claimants to sovereign authority over them. (p. 14)

European state-building was not simply a process of insistent nationalizing pressure from above and ultimately futile resistance from local rulers and ordinary people. Out of this triangular structure of relations among nationalizing princes, local rulers, and ordinary people, a variety of alignments and conflict structures developed among actors whose strategies and successes varied with the context and the strength of the pressure from their opponents:

- *Nationalizing princes* could either try to co-opt local rulers or form coalitions with merchants, bankers, or the ordinary people living under their direct rule to subvert their power.
- Under pressure from these nationalizing princes, *local rulers* could attempt to fight them off or join them. If they chose to fight, one strategy was to oppose the creation of large, national states through coalitions with the merchants, religious groups, and even the ordinary people living in their territories.
- Although they lacked the power and discretion of their betters, these *ordinary people*—oppressed by either local rulers or nationalizing claimants—did not simply "resist" superior power. As opportunistic as their betters, they sometimes made common cause with local rulers against intrusive nationalizers and sometimes reached out to the latter against the former. On occasion, but more rarely, they made common cause with people like themselves from other territorial jurisdictions in cross-territorial social movements.

"It was often in the interstices and on the margins of these composite early modern state formations that ordinary people enjoyed their greatest political opportunities," concludes te Brake (p. 15).

These alternative alignments growing out of different patterns of opposition suggest three paths of polity building to te Brake:

- *Local consolidation:* alliance structures between local rulers and ordinary people, which produced either sovereign city-states, as in Italy, or confederated provinces, as in the low countries and Switzerland;

- *Elite consolidation:* alliances between nationalizing claimants and local rulers, creating layered sovereignties, as in Catalonia or the Empire; and
- *Territorial consolidation:* the erosion of the power of local rulers leading to unitary states, as in Britain or France.

Possibly because the period he studied offered less evidence of it than the centuries before or since, te Brake elides what we see as a fourth form of alignment:

- *Cross-territorial alliances:* leagues of cities or religious groups against either nationalizing princes or local rulers (Spruyt 1994: chap. 5).

For a longer period than is often realized, political contention in Europe was fought out not only between or within territories but also among a triad of players with unequal resources whose playing field was both intra- and extraterritorial. In figure 11.1, I present an amended version of te Brake's three forms of alignment with the addition of "cross-territorial alliances."

I do not rehearse Wayne te Brake's argument here to suggest twenty-first-century Europe is subsiding into a pre-Westphalian jumble of jurisdictions, but because his model has strong analogies with what is happening in Europe today—but at a different level and with different actors and alignments.

- First, it underscores the idea that—even in a period of history more dominated by elites than ours is today—ordinary people could occasionally gain the resources and opportunities to exercise influence over their fate. Te Brake's work emphasizes the relative instability of political alignments within the polity, the availability to popular movements of influential allies, and the high degree of political division among established elites in a period of uncertainty and shift in territorial powers. These features sound remarkably like the current stage of European integration.
- Second, early modern Europe possessed an overlapping checkerboard of political jurisdictions that is analogous to the "variable geometry" of today's Europe. As in early modern Europe, this produces what te Brake calls "multiple and overlapping structures of opportunity" (p. 14). In social movement terms, we would say that while ordinary people possess weaker internal resources than the social actors whose interests cohere with the Union's market logic, they can avail themselves of the "external resource" of a political opportunity structure in which there are a number of potential levels at which they can make their claims and exploitable conflicts among the elite actors they face.

- Third, te Brake's perspective suggests a coalitional approach to European integration that has seldom been explored by theorists of European integration or of territorial consolidation. In the mix between supranational, intergovernmental and governmental decision-making and regulation, the map of European politics today offers the potential for coalition-building among social actors across states, sectors, and levels of decision-making.
- Fourth, as amended by the addition of translocal coalitions, te Brake's model underscores the fact that polity building has a horizontal axis as well as a vertical one. Though leagues of cities are unlikely to become governments today, regional governments, political parties, and even social movements are reaching across territories to increase their leverage against both national states and supranational authorities.

Let us take as an example of these processes the recent (1999–2000) tug of war over the labeling and importation of genetically modified foods[1]—at least temporarily resolved through a compromise in April 2000. The issue brought together a loosely coupled coalition consisting of elements within the Commission (mainly within DG-Environment), the European Parliament's Environmental Commission, a Brussels-based environmental and consumer coalition, several key states that—for reasons of their own—were suspicious of the approval of genetically modified foods, with a transnational social movement coalition that had been meeting and planning its strategy since the mid-1990s (see chapter 10). Opposed to them were other elements in the Commission, governments with an interest in genetic engineering, large grain producers and food distributors, and pharmaceutical companies with a heavy investment in agricultural biotechnology.

The campaign was notable for the interlarding of its cross-sectoral *and* crossterritorial nature—with environmental and consumer groups at both the European and the national levels cohering around a common platform from their respective ideological positions—and for the divisions among member-states, within the Commission, and between sectors of the pharmaceutical industry (Lezaun 1999b, Rhinard 2000). The bargaining and negotiation that produced the April 2000 compromise (which will probably not be the end of the dispute) included elements of all four of the alignment structures pictured in figure 11.1.

We do not yet have many examples of such broad transnational and transsectoral coalitions in the politics of the European Union (but see Warleigh 2000), and the relative success of the anti-GMO coalition may have been due to an unusual confluence of political and international factors following the BSE affair, as we have said. But the GMO case illustrates the fact that the European Union is developing as more than a "multilevel" polity; it is at the same time crossterritorial, intergovernmental, and multilevel, which opens opportunities

Figure 11.1 Hypothetical Forms of Polity Coalition Formation (after te Brake 1998)

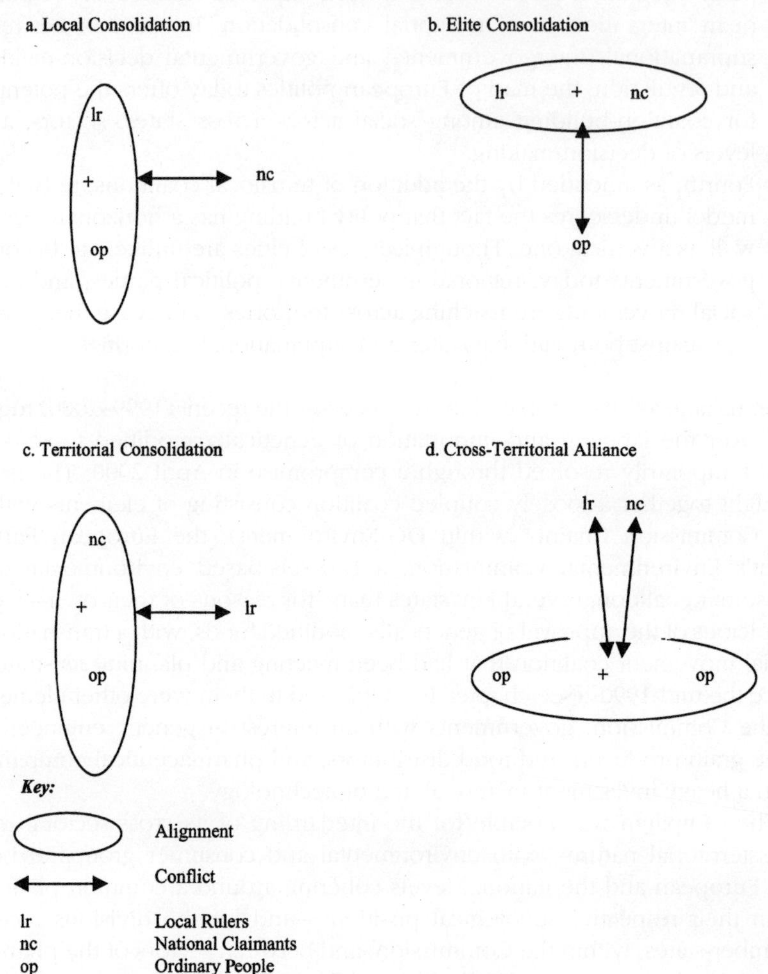

for coalitions of actors and states to formulate common positions and overcome their diversity and dispersion to exploit its political opportunities.

What forms are these coalitions likely to take? And what theoretical reasons do we have for predicting their appearance in the face of the largely "domesticated" protest patterns that we saw earlier in this volume? Although there is very little theory from the European experience to help us, a new area of research offers a suggestive hypothesis: that *transnational advocacy coalitions—including actors within both national states and international institutions—may be the constitutive agents of a new transnational politics.* Let us turn to these now.

THE NEW TRANSNATIONALISM

In recent years a group of scholars in both Europe and the United States have begun to examine transnational politics on a global scale.[2] With few exceptions, they work mainly on non-European parts of the globe. Yet these "transnational" scholars are examining many of the same processes we see emerging in Europe today and have much to teach students of European integration. In this section I will survey one strand in this literature—the analysis of transnational advocacy networks—and draw from it some mechanisms that I see as analogies to the relations among nonstate actors, states, and European institutions.

Consider first what we can learn from the pathbreaking work of Margaret Keck and Kathryn Sikkink on "activists beyond borders" (1998). Keck and Sikkink show that in several parts of Latin America and Southeast Asia, transnational advocacy networks linking grass-roots movements, internationally active Non-Governmental Organizations, international institutions, and governmental representatives have brought about changes in human rights, environmental policy, and women's rights. Keck and Sikkink posit a "boomerang effect" through which weak domestic actors can use alliances with external allies, mediated through other states and international institutions, to advance their claims against their own governments.

Other scholars have not been far behind: Taking Keck and Sikkink's book as their starting point, Risse-Kappen, Ropp, and Sikkink, eds., find cases in the human rights area in which transnational activism has had positive effects on the oppressive policies of authoritarian governments (1999). In his work on the former Soviet Union, Matthew Evangelista has shown how a transnational network of scientists penetrated that authoritarian government to bring about "new thinking" on nuclear disarmament (1999). Studying the emergence of North American free trade, both Jeffrey Ayres (1998) and Jonathan Fox (2000) have shown how transnational alliances emerged among opponents to an integrated North American market.

I do not claim that the transnational processes uncovered by these authors can be transferred unchanged to Western Europe, or that North American Free Trade Agreement, the United Nations, the World Trade Organization, or the World Bank are similar to Europe's institutions. What we do see are potentially revealing analogies between the systems of conflict and cooperation that have grown up around these institutions and the European Union:

- Like these other international institutions, the EU was created by states for the pursuit of their collective interests;
- Also like them, they created permanent secretariats—admittedly, with much less power than the European Commission—to administer their affairs;
- Like the European Commission, these central administrations have been delegated different degrees of authority to resolve disputes

between their members and to deal autonomously with third-party states;

- Also like the Commission, with its doctrine of "information, communication and transparency" (Mak 2000), they have expanded this autonomy to deal with nonstate actors. For legitimization's sake, they cultivate these ties, subsidize many of these groups, and provide them with a venue;
- Finally—and this is the most fertile analogy—nonstate actors gravitate around these institutions and have developed relations with their officials outside of, though not necessarily against, the states whose interests the institutions were created to serve. Not only that: encountering one another in the arena of international institutions may help them to frame their claims in transnational terms and—on occasion—to form true transnational coalitions.

Consider the World Bank's "Inspection Panel" with Jonathan Fox (1999). "In 1993," writes Fox, "the World Bank's board of directors responded to international environmental and human rights critics by creating a precedent-setting public accountability mechanism." Created in response to sustained advocacy campaigns by North-South NGO/grass-roots coalitions, "the World Bank board of directors recognized the legitimacy of the normative principle that international organizations should be publicly accountable" (1999: 1–2). When it comes to the actual impact of the panel on World Bank decisions, Fox finds that "nation-states retain powerful levers to block accountability politics most of the time" (p. 3). But in the meantime, the Bank has created powerful incentives that draw nongovernmental organizations into an orbit in which lobbying and information politics count more for them than domestic mobilization and in which they encounter other groups like themselves from other countries and can form at least temporary transnational coalitions.

Much evidence is accumulating to suggest that European institutions not only are the subjects of pressure by interested groups of citizens but that—like the World Bank's Accountability Panel—they actively encourage such groups to organize and interact with one another. In some cases, the Commission even seems to "deliberately build up coalitions and networks as an opportunity to enhance its own position and influence" (Mak 2000: 9). For example, British environmental groups were able to bypass their own government in the implementation of the biodiversity policy, write Jenny Fairbrass and Andrew Jordan, through the "(not entirely) independent activities of supranational agents such as the European Court of Justice and the Commission" (2000: 3–4). In other words, not only are European institutions a source of funding for groups of European citizens that seek to influence them; like other international institutions, they serve as a kind of "coral reef": encouraging the formation of such groups and bringing them into proximity with others, with whom they may form coalitions to exert common pressure on both Brussels and their national states (Tarrow 2001).

Let us put this point somewhat more formally. Research on domestic social movements has shown that three kinds of processes must occur for mobilization to take place: the construction of collective identities; the formation of social networks; and the opening up of political opportunities (McAdam, McCarthy, and Zald, eds., 1996). The obstacles to this triad of processes are formidable in any setting—which is why most social movements are ephemeral and are apparently obsessed with identity construction. Particularly when prospective participants live in different countries, speak different languages, and are accustomed to working within different sets of political opportunities and constraints, the formation of transnational social movements is extremely problematic.

Under what conditions can the obstacles to transnational mobilization be lowered? Global communication and cheap international transportation have, of course, made a difference; so has economic internationalization, which, in some cases, has created overlapping interests and produced common aims among social actors in different countries. But the main fulcrum around which transnational groups organize are international *institutions,* which serve as sources of group claims, as targets for their protests, and as sites that can bring parallel groups together internationally.

International institutions do not do this because they or their state sponsors wish to encourage transnational contention: they do so, in part, because they are instruments of a *liberal* order in which group representation is seen as a legitimate activity; in part, because they seek information and legitimization from the societies they wish to regulate; and in part, because they are natural and highly visible targets—even for groups whose claims arise primarily in opposition to the policies of their national states. This was clear in both the highly publicized insurrection of the Ejercito Zapatista de Liberacion Nacional (EZLN) in Chiapas against the Mexican government—which carried the banner of opposition to globalization—and in the Seattle WTO meeting, much of which was animated by North American activists whose main claims were against the United States government.

There results from this situation an ambivalent relationship between international institutions and the nonstate actors that surround them, in which certain kinds of groups with limited aims are encouraged to organize while others are either ignored or discouraged. But as officials of the WTO discovered in Seattle, it is not easy to deal differentially with "acceptable" and "unacceptable" civil society groups. This is not only because—in a liberal international order—allowing some groups access to an international institution opens opportunities for others; it is also because such groups watch one another, learn from each other's norms and tactics, and coalesce around common or proximate goals. Transnational contacts around international institutions help to create longer-lasting ties among them and legitimate the "global" framing of their claims. It is only a rallying cry that "globalization" is the ultimate source of many groups' grievances today, but the important point is that contacts around international institutions provide a glue that can ultimately lead to transnational mobilization.

Scholars have only just begun to chart the various forms and structures that are emerging from these encounters in different sectors of transnational activism. There is evidence that the process has advanced more rapidly and meets less resistance in some sectors (for example, human rights) than in others (for example, labor transnationalism). There are also hints that these networks are not nearly as independent of the power of states as their advocates claim. Nor are their representative quality or their long-term effects on grass-roots populations without contradictions (Anner 1999). They are frequently "virtual representatives" and their global reach often extends well beyond their grasp—leaving weak domestic allies in the lurch when they depart to campaign elsewhere or on other issues. We do not claim that these experiences can be translated wholesale to Western Europe. But they can help us observe the kinds of mechanisms that may eventually lead to the formation of robust transnational networks in Europe as well.

Four mechanisms in particular seem to be operating in the formation of transnational networks of activists around international institutions: *brokerage, certification, modeling,* and *institutional appropriation*. These terms need some elementary definition:

- By *brokerage* I mean making connections between otherwise unconnected domestic actors in a way that produces at least a temporary political identity that did not exist before. The role of the European Metalworkers' Federation in the Vilvoorde strike reflects such a temporary mechanism; in the future, the European Works Councils may do this on a more continual basis;
- by *certification,* I mean the recognition of the identities and legitimate public activity of either new actors or actors new to a particular site of activity. The recognition of the identities of indigenous populations by the European Union contributed to legitimating these groups' representatives and to providing a common site for their activities;
- by *modeling,* I mean the adoption of norms, forms of collective action, or organization in one venue or campaign that have been demonstrated in another. The tactics of French farm organizations protesting against the import of farm products from other EU countries has served as a model for European farmers to organize against the Common Agricultural Policy; and
- by *institutional appropriation,* I mean the use of an institution's resources or reputation to serve the purposes of affiliated groups. The close relationship between DG-V (Employment) and the European

Women's Lobby has helped the latter to gain support in the European Parliament and in the member-states.

We could find many examples of such mechanisms operating in the case of many of the social movements, public interest groups, and lobbies that have been discussed in this book. But at this stage of the development of Europe's contentious politics, such anecdotal evidence will not get us very far. Instead, we need more systematic empirical work on the links among grassroots activists, those they hold responsible for their claims in Brussels, the Euro-lobbies that attempt to represent their interests there, and the national states they usually target in Europe's composite polity. We think this actor configuration may be particularly important in helping us understand the role of political contention in the future representative politics of the European Union. Let us conclude on this note.

A CONCLUDING CONUNDRUM

Earlier in this volume, the editors cautioned our readers that we and our collaborators have studied European contention during a transitional and possibly an unstable stage of European development. As ordinary people and the organizations that represent them increasingly target Europe with their claims, old institutions are changing and new ones are developing. How these trends will intersect in the future is the most important question in the so-called "democratic deficit": Will Europe's institutions begin to fill the representative gap that some believe has given rise to a more contentious European politics? Or will they reinforce and diversify the institutional channels that Europeans have available to provide incentives to act collectively?

Ordinary people seeking representation for their interests at the European level have traditionally had two strongly constrained pathways open to them:

- *indirect representation* through their own governments in intergovernmental forums, in which state interests, European collective goals, and interstate coalitions constrain the capacity of any intranational group to gain representation for its claims; and
- *functional representation* through quasi-corporate or interest group channels, in which the big and the powerful possess natural advantages over the small and dispersed interests of ordinary people.

The imperfections and inequalities of access in these processes have led both to the desire to broaden the web of organized interests in Brussels to so-called "civil society groups" and to growing pressure for more direct territorial representation by increasing the power of the European Parliament.

How are these trends likely to affect the magnitude and direction of contentious politics? Will strengthened European civil society lobbies and greater power for a directly elected Parliament still the voices of protest that we have heard both within and across the EU's member-states or will they increase them?

With respect to European-level public interest groups, our findings suggest that they have great difficulty creating and maintaining representative links with their claimed constituencies in the member-states. And without such ties, it would be surprising if such groups gained much political clout either in Brussels or with respect to national governments. They prosper in Brussels largely because it is in the interest of the Commission that they do so, for they provide both information for policy-making and legitimization for the European project. Even the European Trade Union Confederation, based more than any other such group on a well-articulated grass-roots structure, has been unable to convince its national constituent confederations of the importance of European social policy for their members' interests. ETUC's conundrum is that to the extent that it has adopted the logic of lobbying that links it to EU officialdom, it is unable to draw upon the tactic of mobilization that is the most familiar and powerful weapon its constituents possess on the national level.

This takes us to the argument that increasing the power of the European Parliament will lower the incentives for national social actors to employ the forms of contentious politics that we have examined here. The argument has a certain superficial logic to it: after all, why go to the trouble of protesting against European policies if effective MEPs are available to carry your claims to Strasbourg? But it should be recalled that, historically, the strengthening of parliamentary government did *not* lead to a decline of contentious politics; on the contrary, as Charles Tilly has shown in Britain's contentious history, it led to a greater focus of contention on central governmental institutions (1995a). Instead of a substitute for protest, a strengthened European Parliament may provide more channels for European contention and greater incentives for taking protests to a higher (in this case, *supra*national) level.

Responding to frustration at the delays and contradictions in the construction of a democratic Europe, some theorists have looked to the prospect of postnational citizenship—and therefore to postnational representation—developing in Western Europe in short order (Habermas 1992). I leave it to other scholars to examine the formation of European identities.[3] For the record, I think a more plausible scenario is that different forms of representation—direct and indirect, territorial and functional—will coexist and develop in intricate national, international, and transnational venues.[4] Democracy, if it evolves at the European level, will grow out of the capacity of social movements, public interest groups, and other nonstate actors to make alliances with combinations of national governmental actors (the analogy to te Brake's "local rulers"), supranational institutions (analogous to his "nationalizing claimants), and with each other in Europe's increasingly composite polity.

NOTES

1. I am grateful to Javier Lezaun for his advice on an earlier version of this section, based on his current research on the GMO controversy. See Lezaun 1999b.

2. For recent reviews, see Risse-Kappen, in preparation, and Tarrow 2001. For a bibliography of transnational contention, see Tarrow and Acostavalle 1999.

3. See the proposal by Thomas Risse-Kappen and his colleagues to the 5th Framework Program of the European Commission, "Improving the Socio-Economic Knowledge Base" for the project on "European-Ization, Collective Identities, and Public Discourses (IDNET)."

4. For a not-dissimilar view based on a constructivist perspective, see Cederman 2000

Methodological Appendix: Building a Transnational Archive of Contentious Events

Doug Imig

An empirical study of the Europeanization of contentious politics required that we develop a specialized source of data. Our tasks were multiple: We needed to be able to track the evolving pattern of collective political action across the member-states of the European Union over the recent history of European integration; compare protest against European policy with the forms of contention that people use domestically; and detect whether out of these processes, transnational social actors are emerging. The data set needed to answer these questions would have to be cross-national and longitudinal, and it would need both to cover a significant period of the EU's development and at the same time provide us with comparable information across a range of different countries. It would also need to be specific enough to identify the major social actors engaging in both European and national social protest.

National newspapers—the usual source of protest event analysis—would be our first choice for solving these problems for individual countries but would be problematic for comparative purposes because of their bias toward coverage of their own country's news, because they are written for different audiences in different countries, and because of the enormous effort and investment that would be required for anything more than a superficial survey. As a point of comparison, Charles Tilly estimates that his study of British contention during the seven-year period from 1828 to 1834 required a year-per-year collection and coding effort from his team of researchers (Tilly 1995a). Sidney Tarrow's research on Italian contention from 1965 to 1974 required three years of coding on the part of a somewhat smaller team (Tarrow 1989).

For this project, we optimistically—and no doubt brashly—were proposing to discuss all forms of contentious political action undertaken across the entire European Union, for as much of the recent period of European integration as possible. Even after excluding all noncontentious forms of political action, our ambitions were still grand. Our initial optimism was founded on two recent technological developments. The first was the growing accessibility of electronic archives of media data such as the *Reuters* international news wire; the second was the construction by a small group of talented researchers of methods of computer-assisted parsing and coding of machine-readable electronic text sources.

With respect to the first advance, the online version of *Reuters* appeared to offer a number of advantages for a study such as this:

- It was available in electronic format that could be accessed online (originally through the Lexis-Nexis service, and more recently, directly from the Reuters Web site) from January 1st, 1984, forward.
- It has an explicitly international perspective.
- It is fairly consistent in style and coverage.
- It does not take a partisan position.
- It is much less subject to the seasonal variation in levels of news coverage that characterize print sources.

By collecting and coding articles and press releases drawn from the *Reuters World News Service* and *Reuters Textline,* we felt it was theoretically possible to compile a data set containing a complete record of the shifting forms of contention in Western Europe over the recent history of European integration, to the extent that these were reported in this media source. But we should not minimize the work that such an undertaking would require. Even limiting our investigation to the range of articles found in *Reuters* would mean sifting through more than 100,000 articles on political interaction in Western Europe for each year to be studied.

But in addition to the availability of electronic media archives, a second technological innovation had appeared during the period when we began this study. It offered the possibility for researchers without massive resources or personnel to analyze an extensive amount of information drawn from a range of national contexts and across an extended period of time. This technological innovation was the development of automatic coding systems designed to "read" and assign basic events-data codes to media-generated political event reports. The first publicly available versions of these systems, such as the Kansas Events Data System (KEDS), developed by Phil Schrodt and his colleagues at the University of Kansas, and the closely related Protocol for the Analysis of Nonviolent Direct Action (PANDA), developed by Doug Bond and his colleagues at Harvard University, relied on a sparse parsing technology that drew from a basic syntactical understanding of the English language and extensive dictionaries that could be tailored to individual research questions.[1] We also learned much about this technology from the work of Robert Franzosi (1987, 1989) and Robert Francisco (1996, 1999). Drawing extensively upon the pathbreaking work of these researchers, we employed the PANDA coding protocol to code the location, source, event type, and target of every political event reported in our *Reuters* sources for Western Europe for the period from 1984 through 1997.

Automated coding appeared to hold two keys to crossnational and longitudinal events data collection: First, it offered the promise of a parsimonious way to collect and code media reports relatively rapidly on a large number of contentious events taking place in various countries and over an extended period of time from electronic media sources. Second, automated coding held the promise of approaching the full set of European press releases without imposing a priori an overlay of what counted as contentious politics. Because we had access to everything that *Reuters* collected and posted, we attempted to let the automated system assign each event an "action code" and only then to build our data set on contentious political action by looking at the configuration of these coded events, the actors who launched them, and the targets of their actions.

In practice, we soon discovered that the utility of our findings was limited, first, by the modest amount of information that it was possible to collect and code from each event report.[2] Second, it proved difficult to define our collection criteria to minimize both "false positives" (i.e., events that fit our coding criteria although they were not instances of contentious action) and "false negatives" (i.e., events that were excluded because they did not fit our criteria, although they actually were instances of contentious action). The problems of false-positives and false-negatives often are the result of variations in journalistic style. It would be difficult, for example, to program an automated coding system to attribute an account of European Greens hurling insults at their parliamentary foes to institutional politics. This left us in the position of needing to make sure that we were keeping everything we wanted and removing everything that didn't belong in the data set.

Moreover, the problem of false positives and false negatives was, in turn, bound up with the difficulty of constructing a data set that would not simply draw from a list of well-known and understood forms of contentious action. For example, in one of our most pungent cases of Europrotest, a group of French farmers threw cow dung at police trying to restrain their demonstration. No elegant set of inclusion criteria would allow our system to make sense of this event, since "dung-throwing" is not a standard form of protest in anybody's lexicon. Yet as the context told us, a protest it was! To deal with that, and with many other exotic or symbolic forms of protest, we would need to know more about their contexts than the simple acts they entailed.

On its own, automated event coding could not easily provide that kind of detailed contextual information.

Our first solution to this problem was to establish a rough, though reasonable, set of general criteria for the inclusion of events in our data set. We specified that, in order to be included in our data set, a specific political event had to have occurred in one of the twelve states that were members of the EU through the entire period of our study; be initiated by a private group or actor; and be contentious in nature rather than an instance of routine political interaction. Though crude, this set of criteria allowed us to draw a sample of 33,727 coded events from our *Reuters* sources. Working from this set of events, we were able to sketch the basic trajectory of contentious action in Europe over the fourteen years of our study, to describe its ebb and flow across the member-states, and to create a basic taxonomy of the sources, processes, and targets of contention.

At this early stage of our analysis, we were struck by the tantalizing trends suggested by our data about the developing processes of contention in Europe. At the same time, we were chastened by its limitations. First—against the inclusive data set that our method seemed to promise—we found that a disturbing number of other types of events still had slipped into the resulting data. Second—despite the massive amount of data we had thus far collected and coded, we were still unable to comment with any certainty on our central questions, which concerned the European features of these contentious events. Resolving these issues required that we develop a deeper understanding of each of the events uncovered than our rudimentary event codes allowed.

For these reasons, we began to look past the still developing technologies of automated data coding. In doing so, we returned to the set of 33,727 event reports that fit our original inclusion criteria. Using keyword searches, we combed through this data set to clean the data, to gain a clearer sense of the range of actions that were included, and to begin to collect a greater level of detail about each of these events. The keywords we used identified 104 groups of social actors engaged in contention in Europe and 65 forms of contentious political action that we had encountered in our preliminary work, including forms of protests and demonstrations, strikes and boycotts, blockades and property occupations, and riots, violent clashes, and destruction of property or attacks on people.

Through this process, we developed a data set that contained 9,872 examples of contentious political action that had occurred in Western Europe during our period of investigation. Within this data there is a wealth of empirical information concerning the range of actors involved in contentious politics, the forms of protest in which they engaged, and the location and targets of their claims. At the same time, this data set was much more modest than our original aims. (For example, especially for some of the smaller European countries, the number of cases our method uncovered for particular years was often too small to permit comparative crossnational analysis.) Moreover, in taking the step of drawing a sample of contentious political action using keyword searches, we had shifted the direction of our data collection effort and, in so doing, had limited our analysis to an even smaller sample of the contentious action in Europe reported in our sources.

But even this much-refined data set was largely unable to provide insight into our central questions concerning the processes of Europeanization. Principally, its limitations were of two types:

- For each of the events in this sample, we had at our disposal only extremely rudimentary coded data, including the date, the place, source, event type, and target for each action. In order to discuss the relationship between contentious politics and the European Union, a great deal more information would be needed. Furthermore, the majority of the events in our sample occurred at some level of remove from the EU itself. For most issues, the EU proved to be the source of the grievance to which social actors responded, but these actors often chose more proximate and domestic targets for their claims. In order to conduct an empirical analysis of the Europeanization of protest, we needed far more information than our rudimentary event codes provided, including some insight into the issues motivating contentious action and the ability to distinguish between—and catalogue—both its direct and indirect targets.
- Second, the difficulty of tracking European contention involved much more than a lack of detailed data. At heart, there appeared to be a fundamental conceptual difficulty in neatly differentiating between domestic and European contentious politics. Principally, the problem is that there is a complex, ambivalent, and evolving relationship between national and European policies. (Our analysis of this complexity led to the development of the four-fold typology of European protest that we present in chapter 1 and that we employ in beginning our analysis of the data presented in chapter 2 of this volume.) While some claimants affected by EU decisions are likely to frame their grievances in terms of European institutions and policies, others—at a greater remove from the source of their grievances—are more likely to continue to frame their grievances in national and domestic terms. For example, when German coal miners responded to the Kohl government's threat to remove subsidies to mines that were eating into Germany's budget in order to qualify for entry into the Economic and Monetary Union in 1997, German miners protested against Bonn—and not Brussels. Was this a "European" protest or a German one? Close students of Germany would have no trouble answering the question in individual cases, but

> we found hundreds like it. It proved difficult to gather the contextual information to make accurate coding decisions and still carry out the kind of systematic time-series study we needed to support our hypotheses.

In light of these empirical and conceptual concerns we sought a more satisfying way to plumb our data in search of insight into a number of unanswered questions: What share of the contentious political events that we found were launched in response to European issues—either directly or indirectly? What is the relationship between European contention, on the one hand, and the larger set of domestic contentious events, on the other hand? And how have these relationships evolved as integration has proceeded?

The methodological innovations we adopted to address these questions took two forms: we both undertook to bore more deeply into a still-smaller sample of our data and also attempted to recruit other investigators to augment our longitudinal and cross-sectional data by triangulating our findings with their work.

On the first dimension—conducting a deeper and more satisfying analysis of the insights concerning Europeanization available within our data set—we began by isolating the much smaller subset of events in which a clear and explicit link to the institutions and policies of the EU was established. That filtering process occurred in two steps: First, we sought any mention of EU issues, institutions, treaties, or personnel in the first sentence of our news reports. This search produced a much slimmer sample of some 1,400 contentious events. We then sat down with a group of trained coders and reviewed, sifted, and hand-coded every one of these events across a more complete set of dimensions, weeding out those events only ambiguously tied to EU action. Through this distillation process we created a subset of 490 European contentious events that serve as the empirical foundation for the discussion of Europrotests in chapter 2.

Each of the operational decisions in this data development process forced us to recognize the ambiguity that characterizes the relationship between contentious claims-making in Western Europe and the policies and institutions of the European Union. At the same time, this same process of data development allowed us to make what we believe to be a significant gain: a measure of confidence that we have developed an accurate—though incomplete—sample of European-directed protests within twelve of the member nations of the EU, over the fourteen years we investigated. In analyzing this sample, in turn, we hoped to gain the ability to apply a crossnational and longitudinal perspective to our understanding of the developing place of contentious politics in Europe—resolving in a small way the "grasp" versus "reach" problem that has plagued the systematic study of contentious politics from the beginning. We hope that our efforts have made a contribution to this new, ongoing, and exciting adventure.

NOTES

1. We extend our sincere thanks to Phil Schrodt at the University of Kansas and to Doug Bond at Harvard University for generously sharing with us both their expertise in automated data development and the automated coding systems and protocols that they have developed. Since our research project began, both of these research teams have continued to develop more sophisticated coding and analysis systems for media-generated events data, which hold tremendous promise for researchers. For information on the most recent iterations of both projects, please visit the KEDS homepage at: http://raven.cc.ukans.edu/~keds/ and the PANDA homepage at: http://data.fas.harvard.edu/cfia/pnscs/panda.htm.

2. The PANDA automated coding system used the first sentence from each media article as its data source. Collecting information from deeper within news articles presents several difficulties for automated systems. Attributing actions to actors identified by pronouns presents a particular difficulty, for example. More recent versions of a number of automated coding systems have made tremendous advances on such problems (c.f., the work of Virtual Research Associates under the direction of Doug Bond).

Bibliography

Abbot, Keith. "The ETUC and Its Role in Advancing the Cause of European Worker Participation Rights." *Economic and Industrial Democracy* 19, no. 4 (November 1998): 605–631.

Aguiton, Christophe. "Le réseau des marches européennes contre le chômage, la précarité et les exclusions." In *Vers une société civile européenne?*, ed. Jean-Claude Boual. La Tour d'Aigues: Editions de l'Aube, 1999, 83–87.

Allum, Percy. *State and Society in Western Europe.* Cambridge, UK: Polity Press, 1995.

Alter, Karen, and Jeannette Vargas. "Shifting the Domestic Balance of Power in Europe: European Law and UK Social Policy." Paper presented at the 93rd American Political Science Association Annual Meeting, Washington, D.C., September 1997.

Amiraux, Valérie. "Turkish Islamic Associations in Germany and the Issue of European Citizenship." In *Islam in Europe: The Politics of Religion and Community,* ed. Steven Vertovec and Ceri Peach. London: Macmillan, 1997.

———."Transnationalism as a Resource for Turkish Islamic Associations in Germany." Paper presented at the European Forum seminar series, European University, Florence, 1998.

Anderson, Benedict. *Imagined Communities.* London: Verso, 1991.

Anderson, L. *Genetic Engineering, Food, and Our Environment.* White River Junction, Vt.: Chelsea Green, 1999.

Anderson, Svein S., and Kjell A. Eliassen. "EU-Lobbying: between Representativity and Effectiveness." In *The European Union: How Democratic Is It?* ed. Sven S. Anderson and Kjell A. Eliassen. London: Sage, 1996.

Anner, Mark. "Transnational Campaigns to Defend Labor's Rights in Central America's Export Processing Plants," unpublished paper, Cornell University Department of Government, 1999.

Arcq, E. "L'UNICE et la politique sociale communitaire." In *Quelle union sociale Europenée?,* ed. M. Telo. Bruxelles: Editions de l'Université de Bruxelles, 1994.

Ayres, Jeffrey. *Defying Conventional Wisdom: Political Movements and Popular Contention against North American Free Trade*. Toronto: University of Toronto Press, 1998.

Balme, Richard, Didier Chabanet, and Vincent Wright, eds. *L'action collective en Europe*. Paris: Presses de Sciences-Po, forthcoming 2001.

Banaszak, Lee Ann. *Why Movements Succeed or Fail: Opportunity, Culture, and the Struggle for Women's Suffrage*. Princeton: Princeton University Press, 1996.

Bartolini, Stafano, Thomas Risse-Kappen, and Bo Strath. "Between Europe and the Nation State: The Reshaping of Interests, Identities and Political Representation." Robert Schuman Centre for Advanced Studies, European University Institute, 1999.

Bauböck, Rainer. "Sharing History and Future? Time Horizons of Democratic Membership in an Age of Migration." *Constellations* 4, no. 3 (January 1998): 320–345.

———. "Liberal Justifications for Ethnic Group Rights." In *Multicultural Question,* ed. Christian Joppke and Steven Lukes. Oxford and New York: Oxford University Press, 2000, chapter 7.

Benbrook, C. "Evidence of the Magnitude and Consequences of the Roundup Ready Soybean Yield Drag from University-Based Varietal Trials in 1998." Ag Biotech Infonet Technical Paper 1, 13 July 1999. http://www.biotech-info.net_/RR_yield_drag_98.pdf

Bigo, Didier. *Polices en réseaux. L'expérience européenne*. Paris: Presses de la Fondation de Sciences Politiques, 1996.

Boli, John, John Meyer, Francesco Ramirez, and George Thomas. "World Society and the Nation State." *American Journal of Sociology* 103, no. 1 (1997): 144–182.

Boli, John, and George M. Thomas. *Constructing World Culture: International Nongovernmental Organizations since 1875*. Stanford: Stanford University Press, 1999.

Bond, Doug, Craig Jenkins, Kurt Schock, and Charles Taylor. "Contours of Political Contention: Issues and Prospects for the Automated Development of Events Data," *Journal of Conflict Resolution* 41, no. 4 (1997): 553–579.

Bond, Joe, and Doug Bond. "The Protocol for the Assessment of Nonviolent Direct Action (PANDA): Codebook for the P24 Data Set," Program on Nonviolent Sanctions and Cultural Survival, Weatherhead Center for International Affairs, Harvard University, 1998.

Bonnell, Victoria. *Roots of Rebellion: Workers' Politics and Organization in St. Petersburg and Moscow, 1900–1914*. Berkeley: University of California, 1983.

Boussetta, Hassan. "Le nouveau partenariat euro-méditerranéen. Enjeux et perspectives pour les sociétés civiles et pour les communautés immigrés." *Nouvelle tribune* 16 (1997).

Brand, Karl-Werner, Klaus Eder, and Angelika Poferl. *Ökologische Kommunikation in Deutschland*. Opladen: Westdeutscher Verlag, 1997.

Brewer, Marilynn B. "The Social Self: On Being the Same and Different at the Same Time." *Personality and Social Psychology Bulletin* 17 (1991): 475–482.

Brubaker, Rogers. *Citizenship and Nationhood in France and Germany*. Cambridge: Harvard University Press, 1992.

Brysk, Alison. *From Tribal Village to Global Village: Indian Rights and International Relations in Latin America*. Unpublished ms., University of California, Irvine, 1998.

Busch, K. "Le danger de dumping social et salarial." In *Union économique et monétaire et négociations collectives,* ed. O. Jacobi and P. Pochet. Brussels: Observatoire Social Européen, 1996.

Bush, Evelyn, and Pete Simi. "Harvesting Contention: European Integration, Supranational Institutions, and Farmers' Protests, 1992–97," *San Giacomo Charitable Foundation Working Paper 99-5,* Cornell University Institute for European Studies, 1999.

Cameron, D. R. "The 1992 Initiative: Causes and Consequences." In *Euro-Politics: Institutions and Policymaking in the "New" European Community,* ed. Alberta M. Sbriagia. Washington D.C.: Brookings Institution, 1992.

"Campaign to Ban Genetically Engineered Foods." Newspaper archive at www.netlink.de/gen/zeitung/home.html (1 December 1999).

Caporaso, James, and Joseph Jupille. "The Europeanization of Gender Equality Policy and Domestic Structural Change." In *Transforming Europe: Europeanization and Domestic Change,* ed. Maria Green Cowles, James Caporaso, and Thomas Risse-Kappen. Ithaca and London: Cornell University Press, 2000.

Cederman, Lars-Erik. "Nationalism and Bounded Integration: What it Would Take to Construct a European Demos," Robert Schuman Centre for Advanced Studies, European Forum Project, Seminar Paper EUR/48, 2000.

Cederman, Lars-Erik, and Christopher Daase. "Endogenizing Corporate Identities: A Sociational Research Program." Paper presented to the Third Pan-European International Relations Meeting of the ECPR/ISA, Vienna, September 16–19, 1999.

Césari, Jocelyne. *Réseaux transnationaux entre l'Europe et le Maghreb.* Research report for DG-I. Brussels: European Commission, 1997.

Champagne, Patrick. "La manifestation comme action symbolique." In *La manifestation,* ed. Pierre Favre. Paris: Presses de la FNSP, 1990, 329–356.

Charron, Jean. "Les pseudo-événements de contestation: la cas du regroupement autonome des jeunes (RAJ)." In *Les médias, les journalistes et leurs sources,* ed. Jean Charron, Jacques Lemieux, and Florian Sauvageau. Québec: Gaétan Morin, 1991, 101–133.

Checkel, Jeff. "Norms, Institutions and National Identity in Contemporary Europe." *International Studies Quarterly* 43 (March 1999): 84–114.

Chèvre, A. M. "Gene Flow from Transgenic Crops." *Nature* 924 (October 1997): 389.

Chilton, Patricia. "Mechanics of Change: Social Movements, Transnational Coalitions, and the Transformation Processes in Eastern Europe." In *Bringing Transnational Relations Back In: Non-State Actors, Domestic Structures, and International Institutions,* ed. Thomas Risse-Kappen. Cambridge and New York: Cambridge University Press, 1995.

Cohen, Robin. *Global Diasporas.* Seattle: University of Washington Press, 1997.

Coldrick, Peter. "Employment and the IGC." In *The Future of the European Union,* edited by the European Trade Union Institute. Brussels: ETUI, 1996.

Commission of the European Communities. *Orientations pour une politique communautaire des migrations.* COM (85) 48 def. Brussels: CEC, 1985.

———. *Assistance Given to Migrant Associations.* Brussels: DG-V, 1995.

———. "Consumer Policy: European Citizens Support the Action of the Union and Ask for More." Press Release, IP: 97/445, RAPID, 27 May 1997.

———. *European Year against Racism Directory of Projects.* Brussels: DG-V, 1998.

Costa-Lascoux, Jacqueline. "Les sans-papiers de Saint-Bernard." *Revue française des affaires sociales* 51, no. 2 (1997): 101–115.

Cott, S., and K. Ilman. "Midwest Farmers Lose Faith They Had in Biotech Crops." *Wall*

Street Journal, 19 November 1999.

Cowles, Maria Green. "Setting the Agenda for a New Europe: The ERT and 1992." *Journal of Common Market Studies* 33, no. 4 (1995): 501–26.

Crabb, Colin. "Sting in the Tale for Bees." *New Scientist* (16 October 1997).

Cram, Laura. *Policy-Making in the European Union: Conceptual Lenses and the Integration Process.* New York: Routledge, 1997.

Crouch, Colin *Social Change in Western Europe.* Oxford and New York: Oxford University Press, 1999.

Dackweiler, Regina, and Reinhild Schäfer. "Bilanzen und Perspektiven der Frauenbewegungen. International oder gar nicht." *FJ NSB* 11, no. 1 (1998): 113–130.

Dalton, Russell. *The Green Rainbow: Environmental Groups in Western Europe.* New Haven, Conn.: Yale University Press, 1994.

———. *Citizen Politics in Western Democracies.* Chatham, N.J.: Chatham House, 1996.

Danese, Gaia. "Transnational Collective Action in Europe: The Case of Migrants in Italy and Spain." *Journal of Ethnic and Migration Studies* 24, no. 4 (1998): 715–733.

della Porta, Donatella, Hanspeter Kriesi, Dieter Rucht, eds. *Social Movements in a Globalizing World.* New York: St. Martin's, 1999.

Derville, Grégory. "Le combat singulier Greepeace-SIRPA. La compétition pour l'accès aux médias lors de la reprise des essais nucléaires français." *Revue française de science politique* 47, no. 5 (October 1997): 589–629.

de Vries, J., and W. Wackernagel. "Detection of NptII (Kanamycin Resistance) Genes in Genomes of Transgenic Plants by Marker-Rescue Transformation." *Molecular and General Genetics* 257 (1998): 606–613.

de Weerd, Marga, and Bert Klandermans. "Group Identification and Social Protest: Farmer's Protest in the Netherlands." *European Journal of Social Psychology* (1999).

Diani, Mario, and Paolo Donati. "Organisational Change in Western European Environmental Groups: A Framework for Analysis." *Environmental Politics* 8, no. 1 (1999): 13–34.

Dølvik, J. E. *Redrawing Boundaries of Solidarity: The ETUC and the Europeanisation of Trade Unions in the 1990s.* Oslo: ARENA and FAFO, 1997.

Donaldson, L., and R. May. "Health Implications of Genetically Modified Foods." Report commissioned by the UK National Department of Health, May 1999. <http://www.biotech-info.net/gmfoods_health_implications.pdf> (1 December 1999).

Dreyer, M., and B. Gill. "Germany: Continued 'Elite Precaution' alongside Continued Public Opposition." *Journal of Risk Research,* forthcoming.

Dyson, K. *Elusive Union: The Process of Economic and Monetary Union in Europe.* London: Longman, 1994.

Eckelkamp, C., M. Jäger, and B. Weber. "Antibiotic Resistance Genes in Transgenic Plants, in Particular Ampicillin Resistance in Bt-Maize." Report of the Ökoinstitut Freiburg, March 1998. <http://www.greenpeace.org/~geneng/reports/gmo/gmo001.htm> (1 December 1999).

Economist. "Genetically Modified Food: Food for Thought," *The Economist* (19 June 1999): 23–25.

———. "Who's Afraid of Genetically Modified foods?" Environics International Ltd.

"The Millennium Poll on Corporate Social Responsibility." Report commissioned by PriceWaterhouseCoopers, 19 June 1999. The Executive Briefing is available at www.pwcglobal.com (30 September 1999).

Eder, Klaus, Kai-Uwe Hellmann, and Hans Jörg Trenz. "Regieren in Europa jenseits öffentlicher Legitimation? Eine Untersuchung zur Rolle von Öffentlichkeit in Europa." In *Regierung in entgrenzten Räumen* (PVS-Sonderheft 29/1998), ed. Beate Kohler-Koch. Opladen: Westdeutscher Verlag, 1998, 321–344.

Egdell, Janet M., and Kenneth J. Thompson. "The Influence of UK NGOs on the Common Agricultural Policy." *Journal of Common Market Studies* 37 (March 1999): 121–131.

Eichengreen, B. "European Monetary Unification." *Journal of Economic Literature* 31 (September 1993).

ETUC. "For a More Effective ETUC." Brussels, 1990.

———. "Jobs and Solidarity at the Heart of Europe." Brussels, 1996a.

———. "Employment Manifesto." Brussels, 1996b.

———. "EMU: The Final Preparations." ETUC Memorandum, Brussels, October 1996c.

———. *Report of Activities (1995–1998).* 1999a. http://www.etuc.org

———. *General Trade Union Policy Resolution.* Adopted by the IXth Statutory Congress of the European Trade Union Confederation (Helsinki, 29/06–02/07/1999). 1999b. http://www.etuc.org

ETUI. *The Future of the European Union,* ed. European Trade Union Trade Union Institute. Brussels: ETUI, 1996.

———. *Multinationals Database: Inventory of Companies Affected by the EWC Directive.* Brussels: ETUI, 1998.

EU Commission. "European Social Policy: A Way Forward for the Union," COM (94) 333, Brussels, 27 July 1994.

———. 1995 Communication from the Commission and Proposal for a Council Decision on the Commission's Activities of Analysis, Research, Cooperation, and Action in the Field of Employment (Essen) COM (95) 250 final, Brussels, 13 June 1995.

———. 1997 Commission of the European Communities, Proposal for a Council Directive concerning the framework agreement on part-time work concluded by UNICE, CEEP, and the ETUC, Brussels, 23 July 1997, COM (97) 392 final.

EU DG-V. *1995 Social Europe,* February 1995.

Europe Information Service. "Austrians Say No to Genetically-Engineered Food." *European Report* (April 1997a).

———. "Biotechnology: Poll Reveals Increasing Concern among Europeans." *Agri-Industry Europe* (July 1997b).

Evangelista, Matthew. *Unarmed Forces: Transnational Relations and the Demise of the Soviet Threat.* Ithaca and London: Cornell University Press, 1999.

Fairbrass, Jenny, and Andrew Jordan. "National Barriers and European Opportunities: The Implementation of EU Biodiversity Policy in Great Britain." Paper presented to the ECPR Joint Sessions, Copenhagen, Denmark, 2000.

Fajertag, G., and P. Pochet, eds. *Social Pacts in Europe.* Brussels: European Trade Union Institute and Observatoire Social Européen, 1997.

Falkner, Gerda. "The Maastricht Protocol on Social Policy: Theory and Practice." *Journal of European Social Policy* 6, no.1 (1996): 1–16.

———. *EU Social Policy in the 1990s: Towards a Corporatist Policy Community.*

London and New York: Routledge, 1998.

Favell, Adrian. "The Europeanisation of Immigration Politics." *European Integration Online Papers* 2, no. 10 (1998a). <http://eiop.or.at/eiop/texte/1998–010a.htm>.

———. *Philosophies of Integration: Immigration and the Idea of Citizenship in France and Great Britain*. London: McMillan, 1998b.

———. "Introduction." The European Union: Immigration, Asylum, and Citizenship. Special issue of *Journal of Ethnic and Migration Studies* 24, no. 4 (1998c): 605–611.

Finnemore, Martha. "International Organizations as Teachers of Norms: The United Nations Educational, Scientific, and Cultural Organization and Science Policy." *International Organization* 47, no. 4 (1993): 565–597.

Fishman, Mark. *Manufacturing the News*. Austin: University of Texas Press, 1980.

Flam, Helena, ed. *States and Anti-Nuclear Oppositional Movements*. Edinburgh: Edinburgh University Press, 1994.

Fligstein, Neil, and Iona Mara-Drita. "How to Make a Market: Reflections on the Attempt to Create a Single Market in the European Union." *American Journal of Sociology* 102 (1996): 1–33.

Fligstein, Neil, and Ian McNichol. "The Institutional Terrain of the European Union." Harvard University Law School, Jean Monnet Working papers no. 2, 1997.

Food Issues Monitor 1999. Toronto, Canada: Environics International Ltd. 1999.

"Forum des migrants." *Statut*. Version adopted by the October 1995 General Assembly.

Fox, Jonathan."The World Bank Inspection Panel: Lessons from the First Five Years," Latin American and Latino Studies Program, University of California at Santa Cruz, 1999.

———. "Assessing Binational Civil Society Coalitions." Chicano/Latino Research Center Working Paper No. 26, University of California at Santa Cruz, 2000.

Francisco, Ronald. "Coercion and Protest: An Empirical Test in Two Democratic States." *American Journal of Political Science* 40, no. 4 (November 1996): 1179–204.

———. *The Politics of Regime Transitions. Boulder,* Colo.: Westview Press, 1999.

Franzosi, Robert. "The Press as a Source of Socio-Historical Data." *Historical Methods* 20 (1987): 5–16.

———. "From Words to Numbers: A Generalized and Linguistics-Based Coding Procedure for Collecting Textual Data." In *Sociological Methodology,* ed. Clifford Clogg. Oxford: Blackwell, 1989, 263–298.

Friends of the Earth Europe. "Revision of 90/220/EEC—Commission Rejects Most of Parliament's Amendments." *FoEE Biotech Mailout* 5, no. 3 (30 April 1999a): 2–3. <http://www.foeeurope.org/biotechnology/about.htm> (1 December 1999).

———. "Commission Starts Legal Action against France." *FoEE Biotech Mailout* 5, no. 5 (31 July 1999b): 7. <http://www.foeeurope.org/biotechnology/about.htm> (1 December 1999).

Gallup News Service. "What Biotech Food Issue?" 5 October 1999. <http://www.biotech-info.net/gallup_issue.html.> (1 December 1999).

Gamson, William A. "Political Discourse and Collective Action." In *From Structure to Action: Comparing Social Movements Across Cultures,* ed. Bert Klandermans, Hanspeter Kriesi, and Sidney Tarrow. Greenwich, Conn.: JAI Press, 1988, 220–244.

———. *The Strategy of Social Protest*. 2d ed. Homewood, Ill.: Dorsey, 1990.

———. *Talking Politics*. Cambridge: Cambridge University Press, 1992.

Gamson, William, and Gadi Wolfsfeld. "Movements and Media as Interacting Systems." *The Annals of American Academy of Politics and Social Sciences* 528 (July 1993): 114–125.

Gebhard, F., and K. Smalla. "Transformation of Acinetobacter sp. Strain BD413 by Transgenic Sugar Beet DNA." *Applied Environmental Microbiology* 64 (1998): 1550–1559.

Geddes, Andrew. "The Representation of 'Migrants' Interests in the European Union." *Journal of Ethnic and Migration Studies* 24, no. 4 (1998): 695–713.

Geertz, Clifford. *Local Knowledge*. Princeton: Princeton University Press, 1980.

Gerhards, Jürgen. Westeuropäische Integration und die Schwierigkeiten der Entstehung einer euopäischen Öffentlichkeit. *Zeitschrift für Soziologie* 22, no. 2 (1993): 96–110.

GfK. "Umfrage 'Zukunft Gentechnik ?!'" 1996. A summary of the opinion poll conducted by the GfK on behalf of Greenpeace is available at www.greenpeace.de/GP_DOK_3p/HINTERGR/C05HI10.HTM (1 December 1999).

Gitlin, Todd. *The Whole World Is Watching: Mass Media in the Making and Unmaking of the New Left*. Berkeley and Los Angeles: University of California Press, 1980.

Giugni, Marco G. "Was It Worth the Effort? The Outcomes and Consequences of Social Movements." *Annual Review of Sociology* 98 (1998): 371–393.

Glasgow Media Group. *Bad News*. London: Routledge, Kegan Paul, 1976.

Gledhill, M., and P. McGrath. "Call for a Spin Doctor." *New Scientist* (November 1997).

Global2000. Short telephone interview with Ulli Sima, gene technology expert of Global2000 (Austria) on 23 March 1999.

Gobin, Corine. "La Confédération européenne des syndicats et la négociation collective à l'échelle européenne." In *Quelle union sociale européenne?*, ed. Mario Teló and Corinne Gobin. Bruxelles: Editions de l'Université de Bruxelles, 1994, 243–271.

———. *L'Europe Syndicale*. Bruxelles: Presses de L'ULB, 1998.

Goetschy, J. "Le Dialogue Social Européen de Val Duchesse." *Travail et Emploi* 1(1991).

———. "The Construction of European Unionism: A Sociological View on ETUC." *Leisink* (1992).

Goetschy, J., and P. Pochet "The Treaty of Amsterdam: A New Approach to Employment and Social Affairs?" *Transfer* 3 (November 1997).

Goldstein, Joshua. "A Conflict-Cooperation Scale for WEIS Events Data." *Journal of Conflict Resolution* 36, no. 2 (1982): 369–385.

Goldstein, Judith, and Robert Keohane. *Ideas and Foreign Policy*. Ithaca, N.Y.: Cornell University Press, 1993.

Goldstone, Jack. "The Weakness of Organization: A New Look at Gamson's Strategy of Social Protest." *American Journal of Sociology* 85 (1980): 1017–1042.

Gottweis, Herbert. "Regulating Genetic Engineering in the European Union: A Post-Structuralist Perspective." In *The Transformation of Governance in the European Union,* ed. Beate Kohler-Koch and Rainer Eising. London and New York: Routledge, 1999, 61–82.

Grande, Edgar. "The State and Interest Groups in a Framework of Multi-Level Decision-Making: The Case of the European Union." *Journal of European Public Policy* 3, no. 3 (1996): 318–338.

Greenberg, S. "The British Test." Internal Monsanto report on biotechnology acceptance in Britain, 5 October 1998a, <http://www.greenpeaceusa.org/media/publications/ research_britaintext.html> (1 December 1999).

———. "The Maturing Crisis." Internal Monsanto report on biotechnology acceptance in Germany, 5 October 1998b, <http://www.greenpeaceusa.org/media/publications/ research_ germanytext.html> (1 December 1999).

Greenpeace. EinkaufsNetz campaign of Greenpeace Germany.<http://www. greenpeace.de/GP_DOK_3P/BRENNPUN/F9712.HTM> (1 December 1999).

Greenwood, Justin. *Representing Interests in the European Union*. Oxford and New York: Oxford University Press, 1997.

Greenwood, Justin, and Karston Ronit. "Interest Groups in the EC: Newly Emerging Dynamics and Forms." *West European Politics* 17, no. 1 (1994): 31–51.

Greenwood, Justin, Jurgen R. Grote, and Karsten Ronit, eds. *Organized Interests and the European Community*. London: Sage, 1992.

Guiraudon, Virginie. *Policy Change behind Gilded Doors: Explaining the Evolution of Aliens' Rights in Contemporary Western Europe*. Ph.D. dissertation. Cambridge: Harvard University Press, 1997.

———. "Citizenship Rights for Non-Citizens: France, Germany, and the Netherlands." In *Challenge to the Nation-State: Immigration and Citizenship in Western Europe and the United States,* ed. Christian Joppke. Oxford: Oxford University Press, 1998, 272–318.

———. "Weak Weapons of the Weak: Migrant Political Organizations in the European Union." *San Giacomo Charitable Foundation Working Paper 99–7,* Cornell University, Institute for European Studies, 1999.

Gundelach, Peter. "Grass-Roots Activity." In *The Impact of Values. Beliefs in Government, IV,* ed. Jan W. Van Deth and Elinor Scarbrough. Oxford and New York: Oxford University Press, 1995, 412–440.

Haas, Ernst. *The Uniting of Europe: Political, Economic and Social Forces*. Stanford, Calif.: Stanford University Press, 1958.

Habermas, Jurgen. "Citizenship and National Identity: Some Reflections on the Future of Europe." *Praxis International* 12 (1992): 1–19.

Haines, Herbert H. *Black Radicals and the Civil Rights Mainstream, 1954–1970*. Knoxville: University of Tennessee Press, 1988.

Hall, Stuart, Chas Critcher, Tony Jefferson, John Clarke, and Brian Roberts. *Policing the Crisis: Mugging, the State and Law and Order*. Basingstoke, U.K.: Macmillan, 1987.

Hall, M., et al. *European Works Councils: Planning for the Directive*. London: Eclipse Group Ltd. and Industrial Relations Research Unit, 1995.

Hall, Peter, ed. *The Political Power of Economic Ideas*. Cambridge: Cambridge University Press, 1989.

Hall, Stuart, Chas Critcher, Tony Jefferson, John Clarke, and Brian Roberts. *Policing the Crisis: Mugging, the State and Law and Order*. Basingstoke: Macmillan, 1987.

Halloran, James, Philipp Elliott, and Graham Murdock. *Demonstrations and Communication: A Case Study*. Harmondsworth: Penguin, 1970.

Hamouda, O. F. "Economic Integration: 'Gobble-ization' or Partnership? The Case of Southern Europe." *In Economic Integration Between Unequal Partners,* ed. Theodore Georgeakipoulos, Christos C. Paraskevopolus, and John Smithin. Broohfield, Vt.: Edward Elgar Publishing Company, 194, 186–200.

Harris, R. "Monsanto Says It's Sorry over GM Soya Introduction in EU." *Farmers*

Weekly, 27 February 1998.

Harrison, Martin. *TV News: Whose Bias? A Casebook of Analysis of Strikes, Television and Media Structures.* Hermitage: Policy Journals, 1985.

Helfferich, Barbara. "Frauenpolitische Arbeit im Integrationsprozess: Die Aktivitäten der Europäischen Frauenlobby im Kontext der Regierungskonferenz." *Femina politica Zeitschrift für feministische Politik-Wissenschaft* 2 (1998): 35–44.

Heritier, Adrienne. "Elements of Democratic Legitimation in Europe: An Alternative Perspective." *Journal of European Public Policy* 6 (1999): 269–282.

Hey, Christian, and Uwe Brendle. *Umweltverbände und EG. Strategien, politische Kulturen und Organisationsformen.* Opladen: Westdeutscher Verlag, 1994.

Hissting, A. Short e-mail interview with A. Hissting of the Arche GeNoah project, March 1999.

Hix, Simon. "The Study of the European Community: The Challenge to Comparative Politics." *West European Politics* 17, no. 1 (1994): 1–30.

———. "The Study of the European Union II: The 'New Governance' Agenda and Its Rival." *Journal of European Public Policy* 5, no. 1 (1998): 38–65.

———. The Political System of the European Union. New York: Palgrave, 1999.

Hix, Simon, and Jan Niessen. *Reconsidering European Migration Policies.* Brussels: CCME, 1996.

Hoffmann, Stanley. "Obstinate or Obsolete? The Fate of the Nation-State and the Case of Western Europe." *Daedalus* 85 (1966): 862–915.

Hoffman, T., C. Golz, and O. Schieder. "Foreign DNA Sequences Are Received by a Wildtype Strain of Aspergillus Niger after Co-Culture with Transgenic Higher Plants." *Current Genetics* 27 (1994): 70–76.

Höll, Otmar, ed. *Environmental Cooperation in Europe: The Political Dimension.* Boulder, Colo.: Westview, 1994.

Hooghe, Liesbet, and Gary Marks. "The Making of a Polity: The Struggle over European Integration." European University Institute Working Paper, no. 31, 1997.

Hoskyns, Catherine. "The European Women's Lobby." *Feminist Review* 38 (1991): 67–70.

———. *Integrating Gender: Women, Law and Politics in the European Union.* London: Verso, 1996.

Hug, Simon, and Dominique Wisler. "Correcting for Selection Bias in Social Movement Research." Working paper, 1998.

IFIC (International Food Information Council). "Americans Remain Positive on Food Biotechnology." October 1999. <www.biotech-info.net/IFIC_survey.html> (1 December 1999).

Imig, Doug, and Sidney Tarrow. "The Europeanization of Movements? Contentious Politics and the European Union, October 1983–March 1995." *Institute for European Studies Working Papers,* 96–93. Ithaca: Cornell University, 1996.

———. "From Strike to Eurostrike: The Europeanization of Social Movements and the Development of a Euro-Polity." Weatherhead Center for International Affairs, Harvard University Working Paper Series, Paper No. 97–10, 1997.

———. "The Europeanization of Movements? A New Approach to Transnational Contention." In *Social Movements in a Globalizing World,* ed. Donatella della Porta, Hanspeter Kriesi, and Dieter Rucht. London: Macmillan, 1999, 112–133.

———. "Political Contention in Europeanising Societies." *West European Politics* 23, no. 4 (Fall 2000): 73–93.

Ireland, Patrick. *The Policy Challenge of Ethnic Diversity: Immigrant Politics in*

France and Switzerland. Cambridge: Harvard University Press, 1994.

Jacobi, O., and P. Pochet, eds. *Union économique et monétaire et négociations collectives.* Brussels: Observatoire Social Européen, 1996.

Jacobson, David. *Rights across Borders: Immigration and the Decline of Citizenship.* Baltimore, Md.: Johns Hopkins University Press, 1996.

Jasanoff, Sheila. "Civilization and Madness: The Great BSE Scare of 1996." *Public Understanding of Science* 6 (1997): 221–232.

Joergensen, R. B., and B. Andersen. "Spontaneous Hybridization between Oilseed Rape (Brassica napus) and Weedy B. Campestris (Brassicaceae): A Risk of Growing Genetically Modified Oilseed Rape." *American Journal of Botany* 81, no. 12 (1994): 1620–1626.

Johnston, Hank, and Bert Klandermans. "The Cultural Analysis of Social Movements." In *Social Movements and Culture,* ed. Bert Klandermans and Hank Johnston. Minneapolis: University of Minnesota Press, 1995, 3–24.

Joppke, Christian. "Why Liberal States Accept Unwanted Migration." *World Politics* 50, no. 2 (1998): 266–293.

———. *Resilient Nation-States: Immigration in the United States, Germany, and Great Britain.* Oxford: Oxford University Press, 1999.

Jordan, Andrew, Roy Brouwer, and Emma Noble. "Innovative and Responsive? A Longitudinal Analysis of the Speed of EU Environmental Policy-Making," 1967–1997. *Journal of European Public Policy* 6, no. 3 (1999): 376–398.

Kastoryano, Riva. "Mobilisations des migrants en Europe: du national au transnational." *Revue Européenne des Migrations Internationales* 10, no. 1 (1994): 169–181.

———. *La France, l'Allemagne et leurs immigrés: négocier l'identité.* Paris: Armand Colin, 1996.

Katzenstein, Peter, ed. *Norms and National Security.* New York: Columbia University Press, 1996.

Keck, Margaret, and Kathryn Sikkink. *Activists beyond Borders: Activist Networks in International Politics.* Ithaca and London: Cornell University Press, 1998.

Keeler, John T. S. "Opening the Window for Reform: Mandates, Crises, and Extraordinary Policy-Making." *Comparative Political Studies* 25, no. 4 (1993): 433–486.

Kelly, Caroline, and Sarah Breinlinger. *The Social Psychology of Collective Action.* Basingstoke: Taylor and Francis, 1996.

Keohane, Robert O., and Stanley Hoffman, eds. *The New European Community: Decisionmaking and Institutional Change.* Boulder, Colo.: Westview Press, 1991.

Kepler, H. "Unterm Strich kommen keine Arbeitsplätze raus." *Die Tageszeitung* 5437 (21 January 1998).

Kettnaker, Vera. "The European Conflict over Genetically-Engineered Crops," 1995–1997. *San Giacomo Charitable Foundation Working Paper 99–7,* Cornell Institute for European Studies, 1999.

Kielbowicz, Richard, and Clifford Sherer. "The Role of the Press in the Dynamics of Social Movements." In *Research in Social Movements, Conflict and Change,* ed. Louis Kriesberg. Greenwich, Conn.: Jai Press, 1986, 71–96.

King, Gary, Robert O. Keohane, and Sidney Verba. *Designing Social Inquiry: Scientific Inference in Qualitative Research.* Princeton, N.J.: Princeton University Press, 1994.

Kitschelt, Herbert. "Political Opportunity Structures and Political Protest: Anti-Nuclear

Movements in Four Democracies." *British Journal of Political Science* 16, no. 1 (1986): 57–85.

Klandermans, Bert. *The Social Psychology of Protest.* Oxford: Blackwell, 1997.

Klandermans, Bert, Marga de Weerd, Maria Costa, and Jose-Manuel Sabucedo. "Injustice and Adversarial Frames in a Supranational Political Context: Farmers' Protest in the Netherlands and Spain." In *Social Movements in a Globalizing World,* ed. Donatella della Porta, Hanspeter Kriesi, and Dieter Rucht. New York: St. Martin's Press, 1999, 134–147.

Klotz, Audie. "Norms Reconstituting Interests: Global Racial Equality and U.S. Sanctions against South Africa." *International Organization* 49, no. 3 (1995): 451–478.

Kohler-Koch, Beate. "Changing Patterns of Interest Intermediation in the European Union." *Government and Opposition* 29 (1994): 166–180.

———. "The Evolution and Transformation of European Governance." In *The Transformation of Governance in the European Union,* ed. Beate Kohler-Koch and Rainer Eising, London and New York: Routledge, 1999, 14–35.

Kohler-Koch, Beate, and Rainer Eising, eds. *The Transformation of Governance in the European Union.* London and New York: Routledge, 1999.

Kolb, Felix. "Social Movements and European Integration. A Partial Theory of Movement Power in the European Union." (unpublished paper). Ithaca, N.Y.: Cornell University Press, 1999.

Koopmans, R. "Appendix: The Newspaper Data." In *New Social Movements in Western Europe,* ed. H. Kriesi, R. Koopmans, J. W. Duyvendak, and M. G. Giugni. Minneapolis: University of Minnesota Press, 1995, 253–273.

Koopmans, Ruud, and Paul Statham. "Challenging the Liberal Nation-State? Postnationalism, Multiculturalism, and the Collective Claims-Making of Migrants and Ethnic Minorities in Britain and Germany." Paper presented at the annual conference of the American Sociological Association in San Francisco, August 1998.

Koslowski, Rey. "European Union Migration Regimes, Established and Emergent." In *The Challenge to the Nation-State: Immigration and Citizenship in Western Europe and the United States,* ed. Christian Joppke. New York: Oxford University Press, 1998.

Kowaleski, David. "Global Debt Crises in Structural-Cyclical Perspective." In *Markets, Politics and Change in the Global Political Economy,* ed. W. P. Avery and D. P. Rapkin. Boulder, Colo.: Lynne Reiner, 1989.

Krasner, Steven. "Power Politics, Institutions, and Transnational Relations." In *Bringing Transnational Relations Back In: Non-State Actors, Domestic Structures, and International Institutions,* ed. Thomas Risse-Kappen. Cambridge and New York: Cambridge University Press, 1995, chapter 8.

Kriesi, Hanspeter, and Marco G. Giugni. "Ökologische Bewegungen im internationalen Vergleich: Zwischen Konflikt und Kooperation." In *Umweltsoziologie* (Special Issue no. 36 of *Kölner Zeitschrift für Soziologie und Sozialpsychologie*), ed. Andreas Diekmann and Carlo C. Jaeger. Opladen: Westdeutscher Verlag, 1997, 324–349.

Kriesi, Hanspeter, Ruud Koopmans, J. W. Duyvendak, and M. G. Giugni. *New Social Movements in Western Europe.* Minneapolis: University of Minnesota Press, 1995.

Lagneau, Eric. "Couvrir une campagne electorale: les journalistes de l'Agence France Presse et les elections legislatives des 25 mai et 1er juin 1997." Master's thesis, Institut d'Etudes Politiques de Paris, 1997.

Lagneau, Eric, and Pierre Lefébure. "The Spiral of Vilvoorde: Mediatization and Politicization of Protest." Paper presented at the 4th European Conference of Sociology, Amsterdam, August 18–21, 1999a.

———. "La spirale de Vilvoorde: Mediatisation et politisation de la protestation." *Cahiers du CEVIPOF* 22. Paris: L'Harmattan, 1999b.

Lahusen, Christian. "Joining the Cocktail-Circuits? Social Movement Organizations in Brussels." Paper presented at the 4th European Conference of Sociology: "Will Europe work?" Vreije Univeriteit Amsterdam, 18th–21st August 1999.

Lahusen, Christian, and Claudia Jauß. "Interessenvertretung in Mehrebenensystemen. Formen und Bedingungen einer europäischen Politik unter Bedingungen verbandlicher Partizipation." DFG-Endbericht MU 608/13-1. Otto-Friedrich-Universität Bamberg, 1999.

Lappé, M., and B. Bailey. *Against the Grain. Biotechnology and the Corporate Takeover of Your Food.* Monroe, Maine: Common Courage Press, 1998.

Lavenex, Sandra. *The Europeanization of Refugee Policies: Between Human Rights and Internal Security.* Ph.D. dissertation. Florence: European University Institute, 1999.

Lefébure, Pierre, and Eric Lagneau. "Les mobilisations protestataires comme interactions entre acteurs sociaux et journalists, in *Les effets d'information. Mobilisations, préférences, agendas,* ed. Jacques Gerstlé. Paris: L'Harmattan, forthcoming 2000.

———. "Protestation, médias et espace public européen." In *L'action collective en Europe,* ed. Richard Balme, Didier Chabanet, and Vincent Wright. Paris: Presses de Sciences-Po, forthcoming 2001.

Le Galès, Patrick, and Mark Thatcher. *Les réseaux de politique publique. Débats autour des policy networks.* Paris: L'Harmattan, 1995.

Leisink, P., ed. *The Challenges to Trade Unions in Europe: Innovation and Adaptation.* Cheltenham: Edward Elgar, 1995.

Lenschow, Andrea. "Transformation in European Environmental Governance." In *The Transformation of Governance in the European Union,* ed. Beate Kohler-Koch and Rainer Eising. London and New York: Routledge, 1999, 39–60.

Levidow, L. "Blocking Biotechnology as Pollution: Political Cultures in the UK Risk Controversy." Conference on "Alternative Futures and Popular Protest," MMU, 29–31 March 1999.

Levidow, L., S. Carr, and D. Wield. "Environmental Risk Disharmonies of European Biotechnology Regulation." <http://agbiotechnet.com/reviews/April99/Html/Levidow.htm> (1 December 1999).

Levitt, Peggy. "Transnationalizing Community Development: The Case of Migration between Boston and the Dominican Republic." *Nonprofit and Voluntary Sector Quarterly* 26, no. 4 (1997): 509–526.

Lezaun, Javier. "The GMO Controversy in Western Europe." Unpublished paper, Cornell University Department of Science and Technology Studies, 1999a.

Lezuan, Javier. "Transgenetic Contention: Uncertainty and Protest on Genetic Engineering in the UK." Unpublished paper, Cornell University Department of Science and Technology Studies, 1999b.

Liebert, Ulrike. "Gender Politics in the European Union: The Return of the Public." *European Societies* 1, no. 2. (1999): 191–232.

Liefferink, Duncan, Philip Lowe, and Arthur P. J. Mol, eds. *European Integration and Environmental Policy.* London and New York: Belhaven Press, 1993.

Liefferink, Duncan, and Mikael Skou Anderson, eds. *European Environmental Policy*. Manchester: Manchester University Press, 1997.

Lipsky, Michael. "Protest as a Political Resource." *American Political Science Review* 62 (1968): 1144–1158.

Long, Tony. "The European Lobby." In *British Environmental Policy and Europe,* ed. Philip Lowe and Stephen Ward. London: Routledge, 1998, 105–118.

Losey, J. E., L. S. Rayor, and M. E. Carter. "Transgenic Pollen Harms Monarch Larvae." *Nature* 399, no. 214 (May 1999).

Louloudis, Leonidas, and Napoleon Maraveyas. "Farmer and Agricultural Policy in Greece since the Accession to the European Union." *Sociologia Ruralis* 37, no. 2 (1997): 270–286.

MacKenzie, D. "Gut Reaction." *New Scientist* (30 January 1999). http://www.newscientist.com/ns/19990130/newsstory1.html> (1 December 1999).

Mak, Jennifer. "Dialogue and Deliberation as Informal Ways to Enhance Legitimacy in the EU?" Presented to the ECPR Joint Sessions, Copenhagen, Denmark, 2000.

Maraveyas, Napolean. "The Agricultural Strata in the European Union and the Common Agricultural Policy." In *The Impact of European Integration: Political, Sociological, and Economic Changes,* ed. George A. Kourvetaris and Andreas Moschonas. London: Praeger Publishers, 1996, 97–130.

Marks, Gary, Liesbet Hooghe, and Kermit Blank. "European Integration from the 1980s: State-Centric v. Multi-Level Governance." *Journal of Common Market Studies* 34 (1996): 342–377.

Marks, Gary, and Doug McAdam. "Social Movements and the Changing Structure of Political Opportunity in the European Union." *West European Politics* 19 (1996): 249–278.

———. "On the Relationship of Political Opportunities to the Form of Collective Action: The Case of the European Union." In *Social Movements in a Globalizing World,* ed. Donatella della Porta, Hanspeter Kriesi, and Dieter Rucht. New York: St. Martin's, 1999, 97–111.

Marks, Gary, François Nielsen, and Ray Leonard. "Competencies, Cracks, and Conflicts: Regional Mobilization in the European Union." *Comparative Political Studies* 29, no. 2 (1996): 164–192.

Marshall, T. H. *Class, Citizenship and Social Development*. New York: Doubleday, 1965.

Martin, A. "EMU and Wage Bargaining: The Americanization of the European Labor Market?" Brussels: ETUI/OSE Working Paper, 1999.

Martin, Andrew, and George Ross. *The Brave New World of European Labor: European Trade Unions At the Millennium*. New York: Berghahn Books, 1999.

Mazey, Sonia, and Jeremy Richardson. "Environmental Groups and the EC: Challenges and Opportunities." *Environmental Politics* (Special Issue) 1, no. 4 (1992): 109–129.

———. "Interest Groups and the 1996 Inter-Governmental Conference." *West European Politics* 20 (1996): 111–133.

———, eds. *Lobbying in the European Community*. Oxford: Oxford University Press, 1993.

McAdam, Doug. *Political Process and the Development of Black Insurgency*. Chicago: University of Chicago Press, 1982.

———. "Conceptual Origins, Current Problems, Future Directions." In *Comparative Perspectives on Social Movements: Political Opportunities, Mobilizing Structures, and Cultural Framings,* ed. Doug McAdam, John McCarthy, and Myer N. Zald. Cambridge and New York: Cambridge University Press, 1995, 23–40.

———. "On the International Origins of Domestic Political Opportunities." In *Social Movements and American Political Institutions,* ed. Anne N. Costain and Andrew McFarland. Lanham Md.: Rowman & Littlefield, 1998.

McAdam, Doug, Sidney Tarrow, and Charles Tilly. *Dynamics of Contention.* Cambridge and New York: Cambridge University Press, (in preparation).

McAdam, Doug, John McCarthy, and Mayer Zald. "Introduction: Opportunities, Mobilizing Structures and Framing Processes—Toward a Synthetic, Comparative Perspective on Social Movements." In *Comparative Perspectives on Social Movements: Political Opportunities, Mobilizing Structures and Cultural Framings,* ed. Doug McAdam, John McCarthy, and Mayer Zald. Cambridge: Cambridge University Press, 1996, 1–20.

McAdam, Doug, John McCarthy, and Mayer N. Zald, eds. *Comparative Perspectives on Social Movements: Political Opportunities, Mobilizing Structures, and Cultural Framings.* New York: Cambridge University Press, 1996.

McAdam, Doug, and William Sewell. "What is the Time?" *In Silence and Voice in the Study of Contentious Politics,* ed. Ronald Aminzade. Cambridge and New York: Cambridge University Press, forthcoming 2001.

McLaughlin, Andrew, and Grant Jordan. "The Rationality of Lobbying in Europe: Why Are Euro-Groups So Numerous and So Weak? Some Evidence from the Car Industry." In *Lobbying in the European Community,* ed. Sonia Mazey and Jeremy Richardson. Oxford: Oxford University, 1993, 122–161.

McNair, Brian. *The Sociology of Journalism.* London: Arnold, 1998.

Melucci, Alberto. *Challenging Codes. Collective Action in the Information Age.* Cambridge: Cambridge University Press, 1996.

Meyer, David, and Sidney Tarrow, eds. *The Movement Society: Contentious Politics for a New Century.* New York and Oxford: Rowman & Littlefield, 1998.

Mitsch, Frank J., and Jennifer S. Mitchell. "Ag Biotech: Thanks, but No Thanks?" Deutsche Bank Alex. Brown, 12 July 1999. <http://www.biotech-info.net/Deutsche.html>

Molotch, Harvey. "Media and Movements." In *The Dynamics of Social Movements,* ed. John McCarthy and Mayer Zald. Cambridge: Winthrop, 1979, 71–93.

Molotch, Harvey, and Marilyn Lester. "News as Purposive Behavior: On the Strategic Use of Routine Events, Accidents and Scandals." *American Sociological Review* 34, no. 1 (July 1974): 101–112.

Moore, Will H., and David R. Davis. "Ties That Bind? Domestic and International Conflict Behavior in Zaire." *Comparative Political Studies* 31 (1998): 45–71.

Moravcsik, Andrew. "Negotiating the Single European Act: National Interests and Conventional Statecraft in the European Community." *International Organization* 45 (Winter 1991): 651–688.

———. *The Choice for Europe: Social Purpose and State Power from Messina to Maastricht.* Ithaca and London: Cornell University Press, 1998.

Moravcsik, Andrew, and Kalypso Nicolaïdis. "Explaining the Treaty of Amsterdam: Interests, Influence, Institutions:" *Journal of Common Market Studies* 37, no. 1 (1999): 59–86.

Moreau, Marie-Ange. "A propos de l'affaire Renault." *Droit social* 5 (May 1997): 493–509.

Mueller, Carol McClurg. "International Press Coverage of Protests in East Germany." *American Sociological Review* 62, no. 5 (1997): 820–832.

Natural Law Party Canada. "Legal Action Filed against USA EPA over GE Crops." *GE News,* 18 September 1997. < http://www.natural-law.ca/genetic/NewsMay–Oct97/GENews9-18LSuit.html > (1 December 1999).

Nature. "US Attacks EU Gene-Food Labeling Move." *Nature* 387, no. 6636 (June 1997).

Neilson, J. W., K. L. Josephson, I. L. Pepper, R. B. Arnold, G. D. Digiovanni, and N. A. Sinclair. "Frequency of Horizontal Gene-Transfer of a Large Catabolic Plasmic (PJP4) in Soil." *Applied Environmental Microbiology* 60 (1994): 4053–4058.

Nordlee, J. A., S. L. Taylor, J. A. Townsend, L. A. Thomas, and R. K. Bush. "Identification of a Brazil-Nut Allergen in Transgenic Soybeans." *The New England Journal of Medicine* 334, no. 11 (1996): 688–692.

Ogelman, Nedim. "Identity, Organizations, and the Transnational Political Opportunity Structure of Turkish-Origin Inhabitants in Germany." Paper presented at the Eleventh Conference of Europeanists, Baltimore, Md., February 1998.

Olien, Clarice N., Phillip J. Tichenor, and George Donahue. "Media Coverage and Social Movements." In *Information Campaigns: Balancing Social values and Social Change,* ed. Charles T. Salmon. Newbury Park, Calif.: Sage, 1989, 139–163.

Pagnucco, Ron. "The Transnational Strategies for the Service and Justice in Latin America." In *Transnational Social Movements: Solidarity beyond the State,* ed. Jackie Smith, Charles Chatfield, and Ron Pagnucco. Syracuse, N.Y.: Syracuse University Press, 1977, 123–138.

Pedler, R. H., and M. Van Schendelen, eds. *Lobbying the European Union. Companies, Trade Associations and Issue Groups.* Aldershot: Dartmouth, 1994.

Peterson, John. "States, Societies and the European Union." *West European Politics* 20 (1997): 1–23.

Pierson, Paul. "The Path to European Integration. A Historical Institutionalist Analysis." *Comparative Political Studies* 29 (1996): 123–163.

Piven, Frances Fox, and Richard Cloward. *Poor People's Movements: Why They Succeed, How They Fail.* New York: Vintage Books, 1977.

Poldervaart, P. "Genmais: Image angeknabbert." *Die Tageszeitung* (2 December 1997): 2.

Portes, Alejandro. "Transnational Communities: Their Emergence and Significance in the Contemporary World System." In *Latin America in the World Economy,* ed. Roberto Patricio Korzeniewicz and William C. Smith. Westport, Conn.: Greenwood Press, 1998, chapter 8.

Princen, Thomas, and Matthias Finger. *Environmental NGOs in World Politics: Linking the Local and the Global.* London and New York: Routledge, 1994.

Radaelli, Claudio Maria. "The Public Policy of the European Union: Wither Politics of Expertise?" *Journal of European Public Policy* 6, no. 5 (December 1999): 757–774.

Reising, Uwe. "Taking European Integration to the Streets: Results from France and Belgium, 1980–1989." Paper presented to the Annual Meeting of the Midwest Political Science Association, 1997.

———. "Domestic and Supranational Political Opportunities: European Protest in Selected Countries 1980–1995." Paper presented to the Annual Meeting of the Midwest Political Science Association, Chicago, 1998.

———. "United in Opposition? A Cross-National Time-Series of European Protest in Three Selected Countries, 1980–1995." *Journal of Conflict-Resolution* 43, no. 3 (1999): 317–343.

Rhinard, Mark. "Actors and Institutionalization: The Role of Actor-Based Networks in Constructing the European Biotechnology Policy Domain." Presented to the ECPR Joint Sessions, Copenhagen, Denmark, 2000.

Rhodes, M. "Globalisation, Labour Markets and Welfare States: A Future of Competitive Corporatism?" In *The Future of European Welfare: A New Social Contract?*, ed. M. Rhodes and Y. Mény. London: Macmillan, 1997.

Riall, Lucy. *Sicily and the Unification of Italy: Liberal Policy and Local Power, 1859–1866*. Oxford and New York: Oxford University Press, 1998.

Richter, Daniel. "Renault Vilvoorde. Un cas d'école et une occasion manquée." *Les temps modernes* 597 (January 1998): 75–117.

Risse-Kappen, Thomas. "Ideas Do Not Float Freely: Transnational Coalitions, Domestic Structures, and the End of the Cold War." *International Organization* 48 (1994): 185–214.

———. "Exploring the Nature of the Beast: International Relations Theory and Comparative Policy Analysis Meet the European Union." *Journal of Common Market Studies* 34 (March 1996): 53–80.

———. "Transnational Actors, Networks, and Global Governance." Prepared for Walter Carlsnaes, Thomas Risse-Kappen, and Beth Simmons, eds. *Handbook of International Relations*. London: Sage, in preparation.

———, ed. *Bringing Transnational Relations Back in*. Cambridge and New York: Cambridge University Press, 1995.

Risse-Kappen, Thomas, Steve Ropp, and Kathryn Sikkink, eds. *The Power of Human Rights: International Norms and Domestic Change*. New York and London: Cambridge University Press, 1999.

Roederer, Christilla. "CAP Reforms and the Transformation of Domestic Politics: The Paradox of Farm Protest in France, 1983–1993." Paper presented to the Fourth European Conference of Sociology, Amsterdam, August 18–21, 1999.

Rogers, Joel, and Wolfgang Streeck. *Work Councils: Consultation, Representation, and Cooperation in Industrial Relations*. Chicago: University of Chicago Press. 1995.

Roose, Jochen. "Is the European Court of Justice a Political Opportunity for the German Environmental Movement?" Paper presented at the 4th European Conference of Sociology: "Will Europe work?" Vreije Univeriteit Amsterdam, 18th–21st August 1999.

Rootes, Christopher A. "Environmental Movements: From the Local to the Global." *Environmental Politics* 8, no. 11 (1999a): 1–12.

———. "The Transformation of Environmental Activism." *Innovation: the European Journal of Social Sciences* 12, no. 2 (1999b): 187–206.

———. "The Europeanisation of Environmentalism." In *L'action collective en Europe*, ed. Richard Balme, Didier Chabanet, and Vincent Wright. Paris: Presses de Science Politiques (forthcoming), 2001.

Roscho, Bernard. *Newsmaking*. Chicago: University of Chicago Press, 1975.

Rucht, Dieter. "Themes, Logics and Arenas of Social Movements: A Structural Approach." In *From Structure to Action: Comparing Social Movement Participation across Cultures,* ed. Bert Klandermans, Hanspeter Kriesi, and Sidney Tarrow. Greenwich, Conn.: JAI Press, 1988, 305–328.

———. "The Strategies and Action Repertoire of New Movements." In *Challenging the Political Order: New Social and Political Movements in Western Democracies,* ed. Russell J. Dalton and Manfred Kuechler. Cambridge: Polity Press, 1990, 156–175.

———. "'Think Globally, Act Locally'? Needs, Forms and Problems of Cross-National Environmental Groups." In *European Integration and Environmental Policy,* ed. J. Duncan Liefferink, Philip D. Lowe, and Arthur P. J. Mol. London and New York: Belhaven Press, 1993, 75–95.

———. Modernisierung und neue soziale Bewegungen. Deutschland. Frankreich und USA im Vergleich. Frankfurt: Campus, 1994.

———. "Limits to Mobilization: Environmental Policy for the European Union." In *Transnational Social Movements and Global Politics: Solidarity beyond the State,* ed. Jackie Smith, Charles Chatfield, and Ron Pagnucco. Syracuse, N.Y.: Syracuse University Press, 1997, 195–213.

———. "The EU as a Target of Mobilization: Is There a Europeanization of Conflict?" In *L'action collective en Europe,* ed. Richard Balme, Didier Chabanet, and Vincent Wright. Paris: Paris: Presses de Sciences-Po, forthcoming 2001.

———. "The EU as a Target of Political Mobilisation: Is There a Europeanisation of Conflict?" In *L'Europe des intérêts: lobbying, mobilisations et espace européen,* ed. Richard Balme, Didier Chabanet, and Vincent Wright. Paris: Presses de Science Politiques (forthcoming), 2000.

Rucht, Dieter, and Friedhelm Neidhardt. "Methodological Issues in Collecting Protest Event Data: Units of Analysis, Sources and Sampling, Coding Problems." In *Acts of Dissent: New Developments in the Study of Protest,* ed. Dieter Rucht, Ruud Koopmans, and Friedhelm Neidhardt. Berlin: Sigma, 1998, 65–89.

Rucht, Dieter, and Jochen Roose. "The German Environmental Movement at a Crossroads." *Environmental Politics* 8, no. 1 (1999): 59–80.

Rucht, Dieter, Ruud Koopmans, and Friedhelm Neidhardt, eds. *Acts of Dissent: The Study of Protest in Western Democracies.* Berlin: Sigma, 1998.

Ruzza, Carlo. "Inter-Organizational Negotiation in Political Decision-Making: EC Bureaucrats and the Environment." In *The Social Construction of Social Policy,* ed. Colin Samson and Nigel South. London: Macmillan, 1996, 210–223.

———. *Normal Protest: Social Movements and Institutional Activism.* Unpublished manuscript, 1999.

Salvati, Michele. "May 1968 and the Hot Autumn of 1969: The Responses of Two Ruling Classes." In *Organizing Interests in Western Europe,* ed. Suzanne Berger. Cambridge: Cambridge University, 1981, 331–366.

Sassen, Saskia. *Losing Control?* New York: Columbia University Press, 1996.

Saxena, Deepak, Saul Flores, and G. Stotzky. "Transgenic Plants: Insecticidal Toxin in Root Exudates from Bt Corn." *Nature* 402, no. 6761 (1999): 480.

Sbragia, Alberta M. "The European Union as Coxwain: Governance by Steering." Paper presented at the Seminar on Theories of Governance, Ross Priory, Gartocharn, Scotland, October 1997.

——, ed. *Euro-Politics: Institutions and Policymaking in the "New" European Community*. Washington, D.C.: Brookings Institution, 1992.

Scharpf, Fritz. "Community and Autonomy: Multilevel Policy-Making in the European Union." *Journal of European Public Policy* 1 (1994): 219–243.

———. *Games Real Actors Play: Actor-Centered Institutionalism in Policy Research*. Boulder, Colo.: Westview, 1997.

———. *Governing in Europe: Effective and Democratic?* Oxford: Oxford University Press, 1999.

Schattschneider, E. E. *The Semisovereign People: A Realist's View of Democracy in America*. New York: Holt, Reinhart and Winston, 1960.

Schlozman, Kay L. "What Accent the Heavenly Chorus? Political Equality and the American Pressure System." *Journal of Politics* 46 (1984): 1006–1032.

Schmidt, Vivien. "European Integration and Democracy: The Differences among Member States." *Journal of European Public Policy* 4 (1997): 128–145.

Schmitter, Philippe C. "Representation and the Future European Polity." Nuffield College Discussion Paper no. 23. Oxford: Centre for European Studies, 1993.

———. "Imagining the Future of the European Polity with the Help of New Concepts." In *Governance in the European Union*, ed. G. Marks, F. W. Scharpf, P. Schmitter, and W. Streeck. London: Sage 1996.

———. *How to Democratize the European Union and Why Bother?* Lanham, Md.: Rowman & Littlefield, 2000.

Schmitter, Philippe C., and Wolfgang Streeck. "Organized Interests and the Europe of 1992." In *Political Power and Social Change: The United States Faces a United Europe*, ed. Norman J. Ornstein and Mark Perlman. Washington: The AEI Press, 1991, 46–67.

Schubbert, R., C. Lettman, and W. Doerfler. "Ingested Foreign (Phage M13) DNA Survives Transiently in the Gastrointestinal Tract and Enters the Bloodstream of Mice." *Molecular and General Genetics* 242 (1994): 495–504.

Schulten, T. "Tarifpolitik unter den Bedingungen der Europäischen Währungsunionen—Überlegungen zum Aufbau eines Tarifpolitischen Mehr-Ebenen-Systems am Beispiel der westeuropäischen Metallindustrie." *WSI Mitteilungen* (July 1998): 482–493.

Secretariat of the European Commission. *An Open and Structured Dialogue Between the Commission and Special Interest Groups*. Brussels: Secretariat of the European Commission, 1992.

Sidenius, Niels Christian. "A Collective Action Problem? Danish Interest Associations and Euro Groups." In *Collective Action in the European Union*, ed. Justin Greenwood and Mark Aspinwall. London: Routledge, 1998, 81–107.

Sikkink, Kathryn. "Human Rights, Principled Issue-Networks, and Sovereignty in Latin America." *International Organization* 47, no. 3 (1993): 411–441.

Simmel, Georg. "Conflict." In *The Sociology of Georg Simmel*, ed. Kurt H. Wolff. New York: Free Press, 1955.

Simpson, A. *House of Commons Hansard Debates*, 22 March 1999, Columns 101,102. <www.parliament.the-stationery-office.co.uk/cgi-bin/tso_fx> (1 December 1999).

Smith, Jackie. "Globalization and Political Contention: Brokering Roles of Transnational Social Movement Organizations" Paper presented at the Annual Meeting of the American Sociological Association, August, 2000.

Smith, Jackie, Charles Chatfield, and Ron Pagnucco, eds. "Transnational Social Movement Organization in the Global Political Arena." *Voluntas* 5, no. 2 (1994): 121–154.

———, eds. *Transnational Social Movements and Global Politics: Solidarity beyond the State*. Syracuse, N.Y.: Syracuse University Press, 1997.

Snow, David A., E. Burke Rochford Jr., Steve K. Worden, and Robert D. Benford. "Frame Alignment Processes, Micro-Mobilization and Movement Participation." *American Sociological Review* 51 (1986): 464–481.

Snow, David, and Robert Benford. "Ideology, Frame Resonance and Participant Mobilization." In *From Structure to Action: Comparing Social Movements Across Cultures,* ed. Bert Klandermans, Hanspeter Kriesi, and Sidney Tarrow. Greenwich, Conn.: Jai, 1988, 197–217.

Soysal, Yasemin. *The Limits of Citizenship*. Chicago: University of Chicago Press, 1994.

Spar, D. L. "The Spotlight and the Bottomline. How Multinationals Export Human Rights." *Foreign Affairs* (March 1998): 7–18.

Spruyt, Hendrik. *The Sovereign State and Its Competitors: An Analysis of Systems Change*. Princeton, N.J.: Princeton University Press, 1994.

Starting Line Group. *Proposals for Legislative Measures to Combat Racism and the Promotion of Equal Opportunities*. Brussels: Migration Policy Group, 1998.

Stinchcombe, Arthur. "Review of *The Contentious French* by Charles Tilly." *American Journal of Sociology* 93 (1987): 1248.

Tarrow, Sidney. *Democracy and Disorder: Protest and Politics in Italy 1965–1975*. Oxford: Clarendon Press, 1989.

———. "Social Protest and Policy Reform: May 1968 and the Loi d'Orientation in France." *Comparative Political Studies* 25 (1993): 579–607.

———. "The Europeanisation of Conflict: Reflections from a Social Movement Perspective." *West European Politics* 18 (1995): 223–251.

———. "States and Opportunities: The Political Structuring of Social Movements." In *Comparative Perspectives on Social Movements: Political Opportunities, Mobilizing Structures, and Cultural Framings,* ed. Doug McAdam, John McCarthy, and Mayer N. Zald. Cambridge and New York: Cambridge University Press, 1996, 62-92.

———. "Fishnets, Internets and Catnets: Globalization and Transnational Collective Action." In *Challenging Authority: The Historical Study of Collective Action,* ed. Michael Hanagan, Leslie Page Moch, and Wayne te Brake. Minneapolis: University of Minnesota Press, 1998a, chapter 5.

———. *Power in Movement: Social Movements and Contentious Politics*. Cambridge and New York: Cambridge University Press, 1998b.

———. "Building a Composite Polity: Popular Contention in the European Union. Institute for European Studies." Working Paper 98.3. Cornell University, Ithaca, 1999a.

———. "Foreword." In *How Movements Matter?* ed. Marco Giugni, Doug McAdam, and Charles Tilly. Minneapolis: University of Minnesota Press, 1999b.

———. "Contentious Europeans: Is There a European Repertoire of Collective Action?" Paper presented at the Conference on Europeanized Politics, Nuffield College, Oxford, June 17–19, 1999c.

———. "Mad Cows and Social Activists" In *Disaffected Democracies: What's Troubling the Trilateral Countries,* ed. Susan Pharr and Robert Putnam. Princeton: Princeton University Press, 2000a.

———. "Political Exchange in Territorial Consolidations: The Revenge of the Periphery" Prepared for the Convener Group on Beyond Center-Periphery, University of California at Berkeley, December 2000b.

———. "Transnational Contention." Prepared for publication in the *Annual Review of Political Science*. Vol. 5, forthcoming 2001.

Tarrow, Sidney, and Melanie Acostavalle. "Transnational Politics: A Bibliographic Essay on Recent Research on Social Movements and Advocacy Groups," at Columbia University International Affairs Online (https:wwwc.cc.columbia.edu/sec/dlc/ciao.wpsfrm.html.), 1999.

Taylor, Charles Lewis, and Michael C. Hudson. *World Handbook of Political and Social Indicators*. 2d ed. New Haven: Yale University Press, 1972.

Taylor, Charles Lewis, and Davis A. Jodice. *World Handbook of Political and Social Indicators*. 3d ed., vol. 1. New Haven: Yale University Press, 1983.

Taylor, Verta, and Nancy E. Whittier. "Collective Identity in Social Movement Communities: Lesbian Feminist Mobilization." In *Frontiers of Social Movement Theory*, ed. Aldon Morris and Carol Mueller. New Haven: Yale University Press, 1992, 104–130.

Te Brake, Wayne. *Making History: Ordinary People in European Politics: 1500–1700*. Berkeley and Los Angeles: University of California Press, 1998.

Telo M., and Corinne Gobin, eds. *Quelle union sociale Européene?* Bruxelles: Editions de l'Université de Bruxelles, 1994.

Thomas, Daniel. *When Norms and Movements Matter: Helsinki, Human Rights, and Political Change in Eastern Europe, 1970–1990*. Ph.D. dissertation. Ithaca, N.Y.: Cornell University, 1995.

Tilly, Charles. *From Mobilization to Revolution*. Englewood Cliffs, N.J.: Prentice-Hall, 1978.

———. *The Contentious French*. Cambridge, Mass.: Harvard University Press, 1986.

———. "Speaking Your Mind Without Elections, Surveys, or Social Movements." *Public Opinion Quarterly* 47 (1993): 461–478.

———. *Popular Contention in Great Britain, 1758–1834*. Cambridge, Mass.: Harvard University Press, 1995a.

———. "Citizenship, Identity, and Social History." *International Review of Social History* 40, no. 3 (1995b): 1–17.

———. "How to Detect, Describe, and Explain Repertoires of Contention." Unpublished paper, New School for Social Research, Center for Studies of Social Change.

Tilly, Charles, ed. *The Formation of Western European Nation-States*. Princeton: Princeton University Press, 1975.

Tilly, Charles, Louise Tilly, and Richard Tilly. *The Rebellious Century; 1830–1930*. Cambridge, Mass.: Harvard University Press, 1975.

Tuchman, Gaye. *Making News: A Study in the Construction of Reality*. New York: Free Press, 1978.

Turner, Lowell. "The Europeanization of Labour: Structure Before Action." *European Journal of Industrial Relations* 2 (1996): 325–344.

Turner, Ralph H. "The Public Perception of Protest." *American Sociological Review* 34, no. 6 (1969): 815–831.

Van Schendelen, M. P. C. M. *National Public and Private EC Lobbying*. Aldershot: Dartmouth, 1993.

Van der Heijden, Hein-Anton, Ruud Koopmans, and Marco Giugni. "The West European Environmental Movement." *Research in Social Movements, Conflicts and Change,* Supplement 2 (1992): 1–40.

Vandamme, François. "La fermeture de l'usine Renault-Vilvoorde: conséquences politiques et sociales." *Revue du Marché commun et de l'Union européenne,* no. 411 (September 1997): 512–519.

Vidal, J. "Seed Contract 'Signals the End of Independent Farming.'" *The Guardian,* 19 December 1997, 4.

———. "US Chemical Firm Admits to PR Errors." *Manchester Guardian Weekly,* 19 April 1998.

Vidal, J., and M. Milner. "A $400bn Gamble with World's Food." *Manchester Guardian Weekly,* 21 December 1997, 1.

Visser, J., and B. Ebbinghaus. "Making the Most of Diversity? European Integration and the Transnational Organization of Labour." In *Organized Interests and the European Community,* ed. Justin Greenwood, Jürgen R. Grote, and Karsten Ronit. London: Sage, 1992.

Walker, Jack L. *Mobilizing Interest Groups in America: Patrons, Professions, and Social Movements.* Ann Arbor: University of Michigan, 1991.

Walton, John. "Debt, Protest, and the State in Latin America." In *Power and Popular Protest: Latin American Social Movements,* ed. Susan Eckstein. Berkeley and Los Angeles: University of California Press, 1989, 299–328.

Wapner, Paul. *Environmental Activism and World Civic Politics.* Albany: State University of New York Press, 1996.

———. "The Transnationalization of Environmental Activism: Searching for Governance in a Complex and Fragile World." Paper presented at the meeting of the American Political Science Association, Washington, D.C., 1997.

Ward, Stephen, and Philip Lowe. "National Environmental Groups and Europeanisation: A Survey of the British Environmental Lobby." *Environmental Politics* 7, no. 4 (1998): 155–165.

Warleigh, Alex. "Policy Entrepreneurs and Policy Coalitions: Exploring NGO Influence and Legitimacy in EU Environmental and Consumer Policies." Presented to the ECPR Joint Sessions, Copenhagen, Denmark, 2000.

Watts, S. "US Farmers Fear GM Crop Fallout." *BBC News,* 14 July 1999. http://news.bc.co.uk/hi/english/sci/tech/newsid_394000/394301.stm

Weale, Albert. "Environmental Regulation and Administrative Reform in Britain." In *Regulating Europe,* ed. Giandomenico Majone. London: Routledge, 1996: 106–130.

Webster, Ruth. "Environmental Collective Action: Stable Patterns of Cooperation and Issue Alliances at the European Level." In *Collective Action in the European Union,* ed. Justin Greenwood and Mark Aspinwall. London: Routledge, 1998, 176–195.

Wessels, Wolfgang. "An Even Closer Fusion? A Dynamic Marcopolitical View on Integration Processes." *Journal of Common Market Studies* 35 (1997): 267–299.

White, James W. *Ikki: Social Conflict and Political Protest in Early Modern Japan.* Ithaca and London: Cornell, 1995.

Wiesenthal, Helmut. "Akteurkompetenz im Organisationsdilemma. Grundprobleme strategisch ambitionierter Mitgliederverbände und zwei Techniken ihrer Überwindung." *Berliner Journal für Soziologie,* no. 1 (1993): 3–18.

Wolf, Klaus Dieter. "Defending State Autonomy: Intergovernmental Governance in the European Union." In *The Transformation of Governance in the European Union,* ed. Beate Kohler-Koch and Rainer Eising. London and New York: Routledge, 1999, 231–248.

Wolfsfeld, Gadi. "The Symbiosis of Press and Protest: An Exchange Analysis." *Journalism Quarterly,* no. 61 (1984): 550–556.

———. "Media, Protest and Political Violence: A Transactional Analysis." *Journalism Monographs* 127 (1991): 1–61.

Yashar, Deborah. "Citizenship Claims in Latin America: Parsing Out the Role of Globalization." Paper presented to the conference on "Citizenship Claims," Harvard University, October 1998.

Yearley, Steve. "Nature's Advocates: Putting Science to Work in Environmental Organizations," In *Misunderstood Misunderstandings: Social Identities and the Public Uptake of Science,* ed. Bryan Wynne, et al. Cambridge and New York: Cambridge University Press, 1996.

Yoon, C. K. "Reassessing Ecological Risks of Genetically Altered Plants." Special report, *New York Times,* 3 November 1999.

Young, Oren, ed. *Global Governance: Drawing Insights from the Environmental Experience.* Cambridge, Mass.: MIT Press, 1997.

Zanias, George P. "The Common Agricultural Policy in the Process of European Integration and Convergence." In *Economic Integration between Unequal Partners,* ed. Theodore Georgakopoulos, Christos C. Paraskevopoulos, and John Smithin. Brookfield, Vt.: Edward Alger, 1994: 110–121.

Index

Page references in italic type indicate information contained in tables and figures.

About the Contributors

Evelyn Bush is a Ph.D. candidate in sociology at Cornell University. Her research interests lie in the areas of social movements and organizations, with an emphasis on religion and contentious politics.

Marga de Weerd is a Ph.D. candidate in the department of social psychology at the Free University, Amsterdam, the Netherlands.

Virginie Guiraudon is a visiting fellow at the Center of International Studies of Princeton University and *Chargee de Recherche* at the CNRS. She holds a Ph.D. in government from Harvard University. She is the author of *Les politiques d'immigration en Europe* (Paris: L'Harmattan, 2000) and is completing an edited volume for Oxford University Press on *Dilemmas of Immigration Control in a Globalizing World.* She is the author of a number of articles and book chapters on various aspects of immigrant politics.

Barbara Helfferich is a member of the Cabinet of the European Commissioner for Employment and Social Affairs. Previously, she served as secretary general of the European Women's Lobby and was on the faculty of political science at the City University of New York. She holds a Ph.D. in political science from Columbia University and is the author of numerous publications on gender-related issues.

Doug Imig is associate professor of political science at the University of Memphis. He is the author of *Poverty and Power* (1996) and conducts research on social movements and the political representation of marginalized groups.

Vera Kettnaker is a Ph.D. candidate in computer science at Cornell University. She is interested in transnational activism and conducted this research as part of her minor in government.

Bert Klandermans is professor of applied social psychology at Free University, Amsterdam, the Netherlands. The emphasis of his work is on the social psychological consequences of social, economic, and political change. He has published extensively on the social psychological principles of participation in social movements and labor unions. In these areas he is one of the leading experts in the world. He is the editor of *Social Movements, Protest, and Contention,* a book series published by the University of Minnesota Press. His *The Social Psychology of Protest* was published in 1997.

Felix Kolb is a Ph.D. candidate in political science and sociology at Bremen University. He has published on the German antinuclear movement and civil disobedience, has performed training work for an environmental leadership education program, and since 1994 has served with the *Verdener Umweltwerkstatt* and as editor of a number of social movement newspapers.

Eric Lagneau is a Ph.D. candidate at the Institut d'Etudes Politiques (IEP) de Paris and a journalist at the Agence France Press (AFP). His research centers on newsmaking processes and how journalists shape political and social events. His publications include "Vilvoorde: médiatisation et politisation de la protestation. Un cas d'européanisation des mouvements sociaux" (special issue of *Les Cahiers du CEVIPOF,* January 1999), with Pierre Lefébure.

Pierre Lefébure is a Ph.D. candidate at the Institut d'Etudes Politiques (IEP) de Paris and associate young scholar at the Centre d'Etude de la Vie Politique Française (CEVIPOF). His research examines the influence of TV news and debates on assessments of democracy by citizens. His publications include "Vilvoorde: médiatisation et politisation de la protestation. Un cas d'européanisation des mouvements sociaux" (*Les Cahiers du CEVIPOF,* January 1999), with Eric Lagneau, and a reader on political issues in France to be published by Les Editions ouvrières in 2000.

Andrew Martin is a research associate at the Minda de Gunzburg Center for European Studies at Harvard University. In collaboration with George Ross, he has recently published *The Brave New World of European Labor: European Trade Unions at the Millennium.*

Mauro Rodriguez is a Ph.D. candidate in the department of social psychology at the University of Santiago de Compostela, Spain.

George Ross is Morris Hillquit professor in labor and social thought at Brandeis University, where he directs the Center for German and European Studies. He is also senior associate at the Minda de Gunzburg Center for European Studies at Harvard University and director of the European Union Center at Harvard University.

Dieter Rucht is professor of sociology at the University of Kent at Canterbury, England. His research interests include modernization processes in a comparative perspective, social change, social movements, and political protest. He is the author of numerous works, including, most recently, *Acts of Dissent,* co-edited with Ruud Koopmans and Friedhelm Neidhardt (1999); *Social Movements in a Globalizing World,* co-edited with Donatella della Porta and Hanspeter Kriesi (1999); and *Jugendkulturen, Politik und Protest,* co-edited with Roland Roth (2000).

José Manuel Sabucedo is a professor of social psychology at the University of Santiago de Compostela, Spain.

Pete Simi is a Ph.D. candidate in sociology at the University of Nevada, Las Vegas. His research interests include social movements, culture, and racial and ethnic relations, with an emphasis on right-wing fundamentalist movements.

Sidney Tarrow is Maxwell M. Upson professor of government at Cornell University, where he teaches West European politics and the sociology of social movements and contention. He is the author of *Peasant Communism in Southern* Italy (1967), *Democracy and Disorder* (1989), and *Power in Movement* (1994, 1998). He is currently collaborating with Doug McAdam and Charles Tilly on *Dynamics of Contention.*